LOVE NUMBERS

LOVE NUMBERS

A Numerological Guide to Compatibility

by
Sandra Kovacs Stein
and
Carol Ann Schuler

G. P. PUTNAM'S SONS
NEW YORK

Library of Congress Cataloging in Publication Data

Stein, Sandra Kovacs.
  Love numbers.

  1. Symbolism of numbers. 2. Love. I. Schuler,
Carol Ann, date   joint author. II. Title.
BF1623.P9S784 1980   133.3'354   80-17391
ISBN 0-399-12518-3

Printed in the United States of America

ACKNOWLEDGMENTS

Thanks to Elisabeth Jakab, our editor, for all the helpful suggestions and the prodding and the moral support . . .

We would like to dedicate this book to our teachers
Kevin Quinn Avery and Vera Scott Johnson,
who have each done so much to foster the spread of
numerology and the search for universal truth.

Contents

Introduction

Numerology is an ancient science that can give you a great deal of useful information about many areas of your life—including what is perhaps *the* most important area: love. Cause of the greatest joy and the greatest sorrow, love wields a power that no wise man has ever underestimated. Having someone to love who loves you in return makes the heart overflow with gladness. But the feeling that no one truly cares brings loneliness and despair. Infants deprived of loving human contact, although provided with proper food and other biological needs, have been known to pine away and even die for lack of this most basic need. Experiencing, sharing and expressing love make up the happiest moments of being human. Yet throughout history, the course of "true love" has seldom run smooth.

Maintaining a loving atmosphere (once the first magical sparks have died down) is not always easy and can require a good deal of effort. In order to keep the flame glowing, each person may have to make special efforts or compromises. Many potentially good relationships die because of a lack of understanding. When one or both of the parties involved doesn't understand what makes the other person tick, many an attempt to contribute to the relationship may be misinterpreted or go wrong. Take, for instance, the partner who is upset because her loved one persists in falling asleep at the ballet. "He *knows* how much it means to me," she cries. Well he does *go* with her doesn't he? "Greater love hath no man," he may think, "what's all this fuss over a little nap?" Or the husband who grumbles, "Why can't she ever remember to bring along the salt and pepper and mustard when we go on a picnic?" She may burst into tears at his lack of appreciation. After all, she *did* get up at four in the morning just to make those special sandwiches he likes so much . . . It is important to remember that smoothing the course of true love consists of being able to understand *why* your own true love acts the way he or she does, as well as why you act the way you do. Armed with this knowledge, the two of you can each give a little—and get a lot. That was why this book was written: to help you figure out just where your personality and that of your loved one(s) mesh and where they diverge, so that you can not only improve a faltering relationship, but make a good one even better.

We all tend to present our best image to the world. In the beginning of a relationship, faults and irritating habits tend to be masked or disguised. So, if your relationship is only just starting, what better time to call Numerology to your aid. Remember the old saying, "You never really know a person until you've lived with him?" Well, we can add to that, ". . . or have studied his numbers." Numerology can shed a great deal of light on how compatible you and that certain somebody you've just met are likely to be, and what types of adjustments may be neces- sary in order to achieve a harmonious relationship. It can help you recognize certain potential personality traits ahead of the game, so you can avoid unexpected disappointments later on. Numerology can also help put things in their proper perspective. When you think you are in love, it is very hard to be objective. Is it *really* love? Or might it be one of its seemingly infinite variations—infatuation, sexual attraction, or some kind of psychological game? Could it be that you are just overwhelmed by his or her looks or financial, social or career status? Or might you be captivated by the idea of setting up housekeeping together ("everyone else is doing it—it's time for me to make a commitment too . . .")? People fall in love with each other for all kinds of reasons and there is nothing wrong with any of them. But unless you understand what really draws the two of you together, there could be rough sailing ahead.

The numbers we will be analyzing in this book are the *motivation number*, the *inner-self number*, and the *expression number*.* Derived from the given name at birth, these three numbers provide a gold mine of personal information that can help you tune in to a person's true nature. However, you should keep in mind that background factors such as upbringing and education will also affect a person's makeup; two people with the same combination of numbers, brought up under very different circumstances will be different even though they may share the same basic desires and potential—a rich businessman's daughter and a child from the slums, for example.

Your *motivation number* describes what you want out of life. It gives the *real* reason behind everything you do. Your *expression number*, on the other hand, describes your talents and skills and is a good indicator of how you express yourself in your daily affairs. These are the numbers that have the most influence on compatibility. The *inner-self number*— which describes how you think of yourself (on a subconscious level, perhaps)—has more to do with the first impression you make on others

---

*For information on how to find your motivation, inner-self and expression numbers, see Chapter II: "What's In a Name—Setting up the Chart."

and the type of person you yourself are likely to be attracted to. You may feel you have a lot in common with someone whose *expression* number is the same as your *inner-self* number because many of the things he or she does correspond to the way you see yourself. (But this feeling is not necessarily mutual.) By the same token, people whose *motivation* number is the same as your *inner-self* number may feel irresistibly drawn to you—their first impression of you being that you are everything they have ever wanted. Whether or not this attraction will last, however, depends on how your other numbers combine.

When your motivation, inner-self or expression number matches any of your partner's numbers, there is bound to be some sort of tie between you—romantic or otherwise. For instance, we have found many lasting friendships between people who share the same motivation number. There is usually a strong emotional bond of harmony, sympathy and understanding between them, and they are able to cooperate with each other toward a common goal. Many good business partnerships have been formed between people who share the same expression number. They usually have common abilities and tend to pursue their interests in similar ways. But the ideal combination for love and romance is for one person's motivation number to be the same as the other person's expression number—the one expressing what the other desires.

At this point, you might say, "It's really true love and I don't care what our numbers say. I'm going to marry him!" Or, "Mary and I have been together for ten years now and sure it's rough sometimes, but we sure as hell aren't going to split up just because some numerologist says we're not compatible." Okay, slow down! Numerology is not fatalistic. You should keep firmly in mind that each number has both positive and negative characteristics associated with it—a strength that can be reversed into a weakness, a weakness that is a potential strength. You have the free will to use the number in either way. If it's really true love, your relationship can probably survive no matter what obstacles the numbers portray. But often a compromise must be made to insure lasting happiness, love and companionship. Numerology is just a way of helping you understand each other, so that you can better adapt to your partner's idiosyncracies. Its true value lies in explaining the differences in needs and personalities, thereby indicating what adjustments have to be made. Problems may arise, for example, when one partner wants to do everything together, from brushing teeth to folding sheets, while the other considers home a dumping ground for a briefcase and golf clubs. For a relationship to endure, efforts must be mutual. One-sided arbitrators can turn into bitter, cynical martyrs. Lackadaisical free spirits who don't understand why their partners "act crazy" should find out what's behind the animosity. Numerology can open up a whole avenue of communication. Slamming doors and nagging can be replaced by, "I have this "2" expression and you have that "3." What are we going to do about it?"* Sometimes it may be advisable to take separate vacations, hire domestic help so that both partners can be free to pursue careers, or have a certain hour of the evening when each person retreats to a different part of the house to be alone. Sometimes leading "separate lives" can enhance the one life you do share.

Mamie Eisenhower, when asked what the secret of her long marriage to Ike was, replied, "We have absolutely nothing in common." So make the most of your differences. You'll have all the more to talk about when you finally sit down together.

*For a description of "2" see chapter IV. For a description of "3" see chapter V.

I
Instant Information

To get a full picture of a person's character (and we will be going into this in detail in Chapter II) you need his or her full name as it appears on the birth certificate. However, if you've just met someone and this information is not immediately available to you, DON'T PANIC! There are ways of sizing up a person with much less. This chapter is meant to be used as a quick reference guide. With only a first name, a nickname, or a birthday, you can gain the following insight:

1. THE FIRST VOWEL of the person's first name (or nickname) tells something about his or her emotional reactions and how best he or she can be reached through the emotions.

    A   is creative, independent, and tends to accept advice only if it coincides with what he or she already believes. When operating negatively, he can be domineering, opinionated and critical. "A" can be appealed to through the mind, through original ideas and likes a direct approach—no beating around the bush. If you want to reach "A," come straight to the point.

    E   is restless, resourceful and outgoing. When operating negatively, he or she can be unreliable and overindulgent. "E" can be reached through the senses—if it feels good, looks good, or tastes good, "E" is all for it. Anything "new" or "different" holds appeal.

    I   is emotional, romantic and impractical. When operating negatively, he or she can be high-strung, oversensitive and have a tendency to brood. "I" can be reached through the emotions.

    O   is willful, self-contained, responsible and his or her first concern is for loved ones. When operating negatively, however, he or she can be opinionated, meddlesome, and full of unwanted advice. Try a traditional approach with "O," who prefers to stick to the "tried and true."

U   is social, expressive, emotional, intuitive, and enjoys chil-
     dren. When operating negatively, however, he can be
     selfish, moody, and untruthful. Praise, recognition and
     flattery are all ways to "U" 's heart.

Y*   is a good worker and teacher—perceptive, reflective, psy-
     chic. But he or she is always at a crossroads in life and has a
     tendency to vacillate. When operating negatively, this
     person can be secretive and sarcastic. Try an intellectual
     approach with "Y," who tends to pick his friends among
     intellectual equals.

2. THE FIRST LETTER of the person's first name (or nickname)
tells about the immediate mental reaction to things (even though he or
she may not necessarily *act* on this reaction). If the first letter happens
to be a vowel, there is a tendency for them to confuse their head with
their heart.

A   see FIRST VOWEL.

B   is shy, soft-spoken, and would rather follow than lead. He
     or she is unassertive and needs love, companionship,
     encouragement and appreciation. A negative "B" can be
     oversensitive and dependent.

C   is outgoing, creative, expressive, imaginative, and likes
     beautiful surroundings. A negative "C" can be jealous,
     gossipy and extravagant.

D   is practical, efficient, realistic, conservative, reliable, has
     strong willpower, enjoys routine, and tends to hold the
     emotions in check. He or she enjoys nature and gardening.
     A negative "D" can be stubborn, demanding and narrow-
     minded.

E   see FIRST VOWEL.

F   is friendly, hard-working, intuitive and responsible. This
     person wants harmony in his or her surroundings and
     likes doing things their own way. A negative "F" can be
     quite argumentative and a giver of unsolicited advice.

G   is intellectual, solitary, practical, hard-working and firm
     in his or her convictions. When operating negatively,
     however, he or she can be obstinate, secretive, oversensi-
     tive, and have a tendency to brood.

*Y is a vowel when it is the first letter of the name and is followed by a
consonant (as in Yves); when there is no other vowel in the syllable (as in Mary,
Phyllis, Yvonne); and when it is preceded by another vowel and sounded as one
(as in Fay, Harvey, Joy).

H is concerned with the accumulation of money and power. Efficient, ambitious and resilient, this person has good business ability and is open to new ideas and opinions. "H" also enjoys sports and being outdoors. When operating negatively, he or she can be autocratic, boastful, and a social climber.

I see FIRST VOWEL.

J is mental, responsible and direct. When operating negatively, however, this person can be selfish, headstrong, and have a tendency not to finish what he or she starts.

K is idealistic, intuitive, receptive and inspired. When operating negatively, however, he or she can be tense, nervous, high-strung and impractical.

L is expressive, creative, travel-oriented, and has good writing ability. He or she does not like to be told what to do, and when operating negatively can be critical and careless.

M is practical, strong-willed, 'earthy', and conservative. He or she may appear unfeeling through not knowing how to express their emotions. This person craves love but often appears to throw cold water on it by covering up true feelings, for example, with a joke. A negative 'M' can be rigid and self-restrictive.

N is restless, sociable, people-oriented, sensual, a lover of anything different or unusual, and has an active mind that never stops. When acting negatively, 'N' tends to repeat mistakes, overindulge in the sensual, and put self above others.

O see FIRST VOWEL.

P is self-sufficient, selective, and curious about the unknown. When acting negatively, however, he or she may be secretive, prone to false pride and ungrounded fears.

Q is intuitive, money conscious, inspired, and often involved with something offbeat. When acting negatively, however, this person can be erratic, use poor judgment, and neglect details.

R is active, emotional, understanding, inspired, humanitarian, and enjoys social prominence. A negative "R," however, can be bitter, self-pitying and self-centered.

S is emotional, creative, intuitive, and a user of both foresight and hindsight. When operating negatively, this person can be nervous, self-oriented, and possessive.

T is easily hurt but forgiving, and needs affection. Although full of inner tension, he or she appears slow-moving and calm, and makes a good teacher or mediator. A negative "T," however, can lack confidence and be a martyr for loved ones or a resentful doormat.

U   see FIRST VOWEL.

V   is able to cut through obstacles and do things on a large scale. This person is intuitive, needs to work with others, and expects immediate results. A negative "V" can be power-hungry, ruthless and unpredictable.

W   is social, adaptable, impressionable, impulsive, and free-dom-loving. A negative "W" can be self-destructive, over-indulgent and moody.

X   is emotional, self-sacrificing, and tends to put himself on the spot. When operating negatively, he or she can be jealous and prone to magnify their problems way out of proportion.

Y   see FIRST VOWEL.

Z   is domestically oriented, psychic, intuitive, interested in the occult, and is good at getting things done. A negative "Z," however, can be crafty and secretive.

3.   THE BIRTHDAY describes how the person functions best on a day-to-day basis. It tells what he or she is naturally fitted to do. Add the month and day together. Because in numerology we work with the numbers 1 through 9, 11 and 22, if the sum of the two numbers is larger than 9 (except for 11 and 22) add the digits together and get a new sum. Keep doing this until you get a sum of 1, 2, 3, 4, 5, 6, 7, 8, 9, 11, *or* 22. For example, November 9 is $11 + 9 = 20(2 + 0) = 2$. Or, January 10 is $1 + 10 = 11$ (remember 11 and 22 do not have to be reduced further). One final example: April 15 is $4 + 15 = 19(1 + 9) = 10 (1 + 0) = 1$.

1   is independent, creative, pioneering, ambitious and apt to take the initiative. A negative 1 can be selfish and stub-born.

2   is friendly, gentle, cooperative, shy, group-oriented, eager to please, and good with details. A negative "2" can be oversensitive, subservient, resentful, and petty.

3   is social, outgoing, talkative, versatile, creative, expressive, and has scattered interests. A negative "3" may be jealous, critical, vain, extravagant and gossipy.

4   is practical, realistic, hard-working and reliable. A negative "4" can be lazy, jealous, cruel and rigid.

5   is freedom-oriented, sensual, adaptable, adventuresome, opportunistic, and enjoys people, variety and change. A

negative "5" can be overindulgent, thoughtless and irresponsible.

6   is responsible, home-loving, parental, creative and service-oriented. A negative "6" may be dictatorial, meddlesome, suspicious, and expect too much from others.

7   is mental, introspective, selective and aristocratic—quality is more important than quantity. A negative "7" can be aloof, secretive, sarcastic and critical.

8   is materialistic, practical, ambitious, and has executive ability. This person is good at organizing but is not geared to dealing with petty details. He or she seeks recognition and prestige. A negative "8" may be harsh, intolerant, oppressive and unscrupulous.

9   is magnetic, romantic, compassionate, humanitarian, emotional, generous and understanding. A negative "9" may be fanatical, fickle, bitter or indiscreet.

11   is a visionary. Idealistic and sensitive, this person does not have a business mind. When operating negatively, he or she may be aimless, have trouble expressing themselves, and have difficulty functioning in the "real world."

22   is the practical idealist—the builder on a grand scale who has eyes on the stars and feet on the ground. Male or female, this person is more concerned about humanity than about himself or his family. A negative "22" can be ruthless, greedy, and use his power and magnetism for evil instead of good.

II
What's in a Name—
Setting Up the Chart

To do a numerology comparison between yourself and another person you need to have:

1. your full name *exactly* as it appears on your birth certificate. (If you have no birth certificate you should use the name you have always been known by.)
2. the full name of the person with whom you are comparing yourself. (We shall refer to this person as your partner.)

WHAT'S IN A NAME In any name you will be looking for three things: a *motivation number,* an *inner-self number* and an *expression number.*

Motivation Number: comes from the vowels in your name and plays a major role in the decisions you make and your reactions to people and situations. It is what you really want to be even though it is not necessarily what you will express or get out of life.

Inner-Self Number: comes from the consonants in the name. It tells how the inner person (the being within you) pictures that wonderful creature—*you* (sometimes without even realizing it). It is also the first impression you make on others before they actually get to know you.

Expression Number: comes from the combination of both consonants and vowels in the name. It describes how you interact with other people and how you go about getting what you want out of life. It is not necessarily what you *want* to do, but is what others see you do.

All these numbers are important. However, in a relationship, the *expression* number is perhaps the most important, as it is your way of interacting with others and therefore has the greatest influence on how they react to you. (Remember that your motivation number is hidden while your expression number is what you show.) The *expression* number colors the personality so strongly that an amazingly accurate picture of the person in question can be gotten from it. No one can completely hide his or her expression number—it comes through in one way or another. For example, if you are really observant, you will notice that

24

flirtatious, party-seeking "4" can't stand clutter and is very stubborn. Or that that outgoing, talkative "7" loves to curl up with a good book.

Next in importance is the *motivation* number, which explains why people sometimes act in ways that are hard to understand. When there is a conflict between your *motivation* and *expression* numbers—what you want out of life, and what you actually do—you may have a problem. Then it becomes harder for others to understand you because what they see is the outer *expression* and not the inner *motivation*. A case in point: Jean has a "6" expression. "6" is domestic, responsible, a concerned parent and charming host. She seems to have the perfect setup—an adoring husband, two beautiful children, a lovely home, lots of friends. WHY IS SHE SO MISERABLE??? Look at her *motivation*. It's a "5." An absolute necessity for the "5" in her is PERSONAL FREEDOM. That "5" *motivation* wants change and adventure. Being "boxed in" at home all day is definitely *not* "5"'s idea of a perfect setup. Responsibility, including domestic chores, can really get her down unless she has time to pursue her own interests as well—to get out into the world and explore, be it new places, new people, or new foods. If she and her husband understand this, there are many ways the conflict could be worked out—by her joining a club, taking a vacation, hiring a babysitter once a week so as to have time for herself. But in one way or another this conflict must be worked out or it *could* destroy an otherwise happy relationship.

The *inner-self* number can help you understand why your first impression of someone may be quite different from the way you see them later on. (Remember that the *inner-self* number may be what you first see, but the *expression* number is what ultimately prevails.) For example, you've just met someone who seems as sweet and as easygoing and as willing to please as her "2" *inner-self* number could possibly suggest. But before you have any dreams about her always being there to cater to your every whim and desire, take a look at her *expression* number. If it's a "1," she also has a mind of her own and likes doing things *her* way—at least part of the time. Furthermore, time to herself is important to her and she may become frustrated by demands for constant togetherness. Or, you have just been introduced to someone who appears to be the life of the party. True to his "5" *inner-self* number, he seems adventuresome, entertaining and outgoing—a free spirit at heart. But before you start thinking "I'll never be able to pin this one down," take a look at his *expression* number. If it too is a "5" you could be right! but if it is a "4," you can be assured that there is a domestic, security-oriented side to his nature as well.

SETTING UP THE CHART Start by entering your full name on line 2 of the sample chart worksheet on page 26. Then enter your partner's

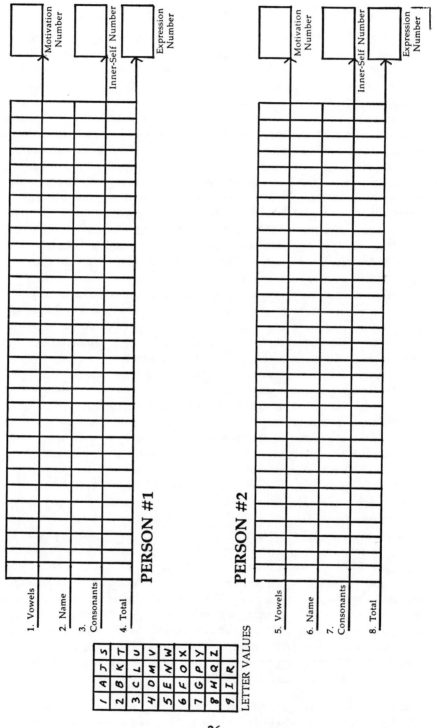

PERSON #1

1. Vowels

2. Name

3. Consonants

4. Total

Motivation Number

Inner-Self Number

Expression Number

PERSON #2

5. Vowels

6. Name

7. Consonants

8. Total

Motivation Number

Inner-Self Number

Expression Number

LETTER VALUES

1	A	J	S
2	B	K	T
3	C	L	U
4	D	M	V
5	E	N	W
6	F	O	X
7	G	P	Y
8	H	Q	Z
9	I	R	

26

name on line 6. The names must be entered exactly as they appear on the birth certificates—even if they are misspelled, incomplete, or recorded merely as "Baby Smith" or "Girl Jones." Do *not* add Jr., or II or III if it follows the name, nor any names added later on, for example, at confirmation.

The name recorded at birth describes your personality—what you came into this world with, who you are, what you really want and need, how you react, where your strengths and weaknesses lie. These things *cannot* be altered by a new name. You never lose what you were originally given. When you change your name you attract new vibrations to yourself, which usually show where you are placing the emphasis at this time of your life.* It can*not*, however, provide you with an ability or talent that you were not born with. For example, if you take on a name with strong artistic vibrations, it will not make you an artist unless there are artistic talents evident in your original name. What the new name *can* do is lead you into artistic associations, and create a market for your wares—all of which would be of great benefit if you happen to be an artist, but which would be of little value to you otherwise.

Since you are going to be working with numbers, the next step is to convert the letters of each name into numerical values using the following code:

1	2	3	4	5	6	7	8	9
A	B	C	D	E	F	G	H	I
J	K	L	M	N	O	P	Q	R
S	T	U	V	W	X	Y	Z	

To complete your sample chart, write the numerical value for each vowel in your name on line 1 (above your name). Write the numerical value for each vowel in your partner's name on line 5 (above his/her name). Then write the numerical value for each consonant in your name on line 3 (below your name), and for each consonant in your partner's name on line 7 (below his/her name). Using the code in the chart above, write the numerical value total for each letter in your name

---

*To set up an effective name change is a complicated process far beyond the scope of this book and should not be attempted by anyone who is not thoroughly familiar with what they are doing as it could cause more aggravation than benefit. It should be done by a professional numerologist. When a name change has been properly planned, it can act as an external aid to help promote the success and speed up the opportunities you have been promised at birth.

(both consonants and vowels) on line 4, and do the same for your partner on line 8.

As an example, we will use the names BETTY JOAN PERSKE (Lauren Bacall's given name) and HUMPHREY BOGART.

1. Vowels	5		7		6	1			5			5							
2. Name	B	E	T	T	Y	J	O	A	N	P	E	R	S	K	E			
3. Consonants	2		2	2		1			5	7		9	1	2				
4. Total	2	5	2	2	7	1	6	1	5	7	5	9	1	2	5			

PERSON #1

5. Vowels	3				5	7			6		1							
6. Name	H	U	M	P	H	R	E	Y	B	O	G	A	R	T				
7. Consonants	8		4	7	8	9			2		7		9	2				
8. Total	8	3	4	7	8	9	5	7	2	6	7	1	9	2				

PERSON #2

Motivation Number: To get your motivation number, add up all the numbers on line 1 (vowels) and write the sum in the box labeled "Motivation Number." Do the same for your partner on line 5. Any sum larger than 9 (except 11 and 22) must be reduced by adding the digits together. As we've noted earlier, this is because in numerology we work with the numbers 1 through 9, 11 and 22. If the sum of the digits is larger than 9 it must be reduced again. For example,

1978 (1+9+7+8) = 25 (2+5) = 7.

92 (9+2) = 11 (remember, 11 and 22 do not get reduced further).

BETTY JOAN PERSKE's motivation number is 11. HUMPHREY

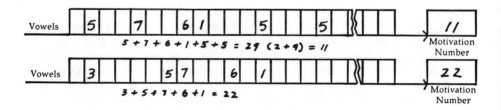

BOGART's motivation number is 22 (remember, 11 and 22 do not get reduced further).

Inner-Self Number: To get your inner-self number, add up all the numbers on line 3 (consonants). Write the reduced total in the box labeled "Inner-Self Number" at the end of line 3. Do the same for your partner on line 7.

BETTY JOAN PERSKE's inner-self number is 4. Her partner HUMPHREY BOGART's inner-self number is 11 (remember, 11 does not get reduced further):

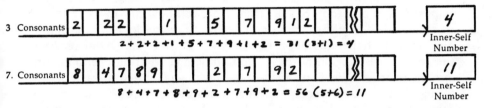

Expression Number: To get your expression number, add up all the numbers on line 4 (the total of both the consonants and the vowels in your name). Write the reduced total in the box labeled "Expression Number" at the end of line 4. Do the same for your partner on line 8.

BETTY JOAN PERSKE's expression number is 6. Her partner HUMPHREY BOGART's expression number is also 6.

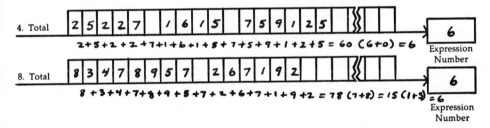

Now that you have calculated your motivation, inner-self and expression numbers, you are ready to look up what they mean in chapters III to XIII. Each chapter starts out with a general description of a number. You can apply this description to the motivation number to see what you really want in life, to the inner-self number to see what kind of first impression you make on others, and finally, to the expression number to see how you express yourself and interact with others.

Following the general description of each number is a section containing combinations of that expression number with all the different motivation numbers. Look up your own combination and that of your partner to see the way in which what you do is affected by what you really want. That is all there is to it! You are now ready to do your comparison.

As an example, let us compare BETTY JOAN PERSKE and HUMPHREY BOGART. Notice that they have the same expression number, "6," which indicates that they share similar talents and activities. Looking up "6," you will further notice that these may involve artistic pursuits (they both, of course, had acting careers), responsibility toward those close to them, interest in home and family, and entertaining others. You may also notice that Humphrey Bogart's inner-self number and Lauren Bacall's motivation are the same, indicating that her first impression of him (before she actually got to know him) was of someone who fulfilled all her wants and desires (possibly love at first sight). Now look at their motivation numbers—"11" and "22." After reading the general description of these two numbers you will notice that both are romantic and idealistic and are therefore well suited to each other, though "11" is more accommodating, wants love and companionship— someone to be at the center of its life, help put its ideas into practical form, and make important decisions for it, while "22" is practical and enjoys being the authority. And you can go on from there . . .

BEST COMBINATIONS FOR BUSINESS, ROMANCE, AND FRIENDSHIP

Person #1 Expression Number	Best Business Combinations Person #2 Expression Number	Best Romantic Combinations Person #2 Expression Number	Best Friendship Combinations Person #2 Expression Number	Best All-Around Combinations Person #2 Expression Number	Most Difficult Combinations Person #2 Expression Number
1	3, 5, 11, 22	3, 5, 11	3, 5, 9, 11	3, 5, 11	6
2	4, 6, 7, 8,	4, 6	2, 4, 6	4, 6	5
3	1, 5, 6, 9, 11	1, 5, 6	1, 3, 5, 6	1, 5, 6	4, 22
4	2, 4, 6, 8, 22	2, 6, 8	2, 4, 6, 7, 8	2, 4, 6, 8	3, 5, 9
5	1, 3, 7, 9	1, 3, 9	1, 3, 9	1, 3, 9	2, 4, 6, 11
6	2, 3, 4, 8, 9	2, 3, 4, 8, 9	2, 3, 4, 8, 9	2, 3, 4, 9	1, 5, 7
7	2, 5, 11	11	4, 7, 11	11	6, 8
8	4, 6, 22	4, 6, 22	4, 6, 22	4, 22	7
9	3, 5, 6, 8, 22	5, 6	1, 5, 6, 9, 11	5, 6	4
11	1, 3, 7, 22	1, 7, 9, 22	1, 7, 9, 11, 22	1, 7, 22	5
22	1, 4, 7, 8, 9, 11	8, 11, 22	8, 11, 22	8, 11, 22	3

31

III
Courage and Initiative: The Number 1

"1"s are inspired, daring, energetic—the leaders of the pack—and have a highly developed sense of integrity and responsibility. Not the type to beat around the bush, these individuals have a habit of coming right to the point, which may sometimes appear tactless. Male or female, they are strong, forceful people who enjoy making decisions for others and helping them with problems because it makes them feel useful and respected. But for all their outward appearance of independence and authority, "1"s are really very sensitive to the approval of others. Praise, encouragement and attention are necessary for their well-being. Criticism and disapproval give rise to anger and resentment.

"1"s do not like being ordered around or told what to do. They are not designed to be followers or to listen to advice (unless it happens to agree with their own ideas). More than any other number, they must learn from their own mistakes. Experience is their best teacher.

Naturally, "1"s find it hard to work under superiors. They do best when left alone to carry out their own ideas. Male or female, they like to initiate things—to promote, to explore, to originate. They have executive ability and can manage the organization of anything themselves. "1"s are self-starters, adding direction and purpose to the task at hand, but they are inclined to delegate finishing things to others.

Impulsive and impatient, "1"s want what they want *when* they want it which is usually NOW. Once their minds are set on something they will pursue it to the exclusion of all else and without consideration of the difficulties or obstacles that may stand in their path. When they don't get their way they can be petulant and moody, but victory over the seemingly impossible is one of their sweetest rewards.

"1"s are sexually aggressive and have an erotic imagination. In any relationship they need to be the dominant partner. They will be good mates provided they are married to someone warm and patient who is willing to defer to them, yet who is also strong enough to take charge when necessary. However, even when "1"s are totally committed to a relationship emotionally, they want some independence. "1"s need freedom to pursue their own interests, and if they feel tied down they will turn away or seek escape. They dislike being confined in any way—be it by routine or a demanding companion (they prefer to do the demanding themselves). "1"s rarely find satisfaction in domestic realms alone, and have a great need to excel in something—to be a winner in some area.

COMPATIBILITY GUIDE

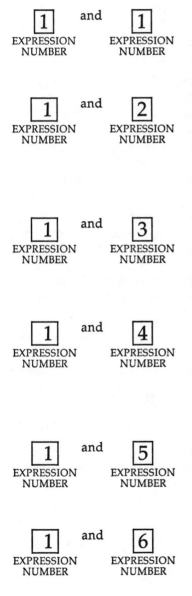

Strong initial attraction, which may turn to conflict over who takes the lead and makes the decisions. Lack of respect for each other's individuality may result in harsh words, jealousy or resentment.

Good business combination—"1" making the plans and directing the efforts, "2" handling the details. In a close personal relationship, "1" may feel smothered by "2"'s constant desire for togetherness; "2" may feel hurt by "1"'s need for independence.

Beneficial combination where "1" can add originality and initiative to "3"'s self-expression; "3" can both provide a channel for "1"'s ideas and use its own personality and charm to interest others in "1"'s projects.

Good business combination—"4" providing a practical foundation for "1"'s ideas. In a close personal relationship "1" may find "4" tedious, rigid, and hampering; "4" may find "1" brash and impractical and resent its need to dominate.

Exciting, adventurous combination full of energy and curiosity; "1" can give "5" purpose and direction (so long as it is not done dictatorially); "5" can broaden "1"'s horizons.

"6" is supportive of "1," adds harmony and practicality to its ideas, but in a close personal relationship can expect too much in return; "1" may feel smothered by "6" 's nurturing ways and resent "6" 's attempts to make it over to conform to its ideals; "6" may misunderstand "1" 's need for independence and feel hurt at its apparent selfishness.

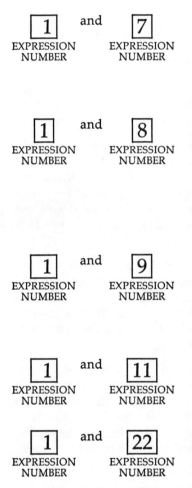

Good intellectual combination—"1" giving "7" incentive to take action, "7" perfecting "1" 's ideas. In a close personal relationship "7" may find "1" too active and exhausting, and may resent being ordered around.

Magnetic attraction, which may result in bitter clash of wills unless there is some give-and-take. Both are dominant, active, prestige-seeking personalities who admire each other's strength but want to do things their own way. Good business combination—"8" can organize "1" 's ideas.

Good creative combination—"1" exciting "9" 's curiosity and giving it direction, "9" encouraging "1" and adding universal scope to its ideas. Some conflict may arise between "1" 's interest in self and "9" 's humanitarian approach.

Good intellectual combination—"11" can inspire "1," and "1" can give "11" direction and purpose. Both are creative thinkers and can fire each other's ideas.

Good business combination—"22" can expand "1" 's horizons and put its ideas into practical form of the highest order.

Following are all possible combinations of a "1" expression number with the different motivation and inner-self numbers.

1
MOTIVATION
NUMBER

9
INNER-SELF
NUMBER

1
EXPRESSION
NUMBER

"The people who get on in this world are the people who get up and look for the circumstances they want, and if they can't find them, make them."

—Unknown

"1-1"s are true individualists. Although they may appear outgoing, they are just as happy doing things on their own. Active and full of energy, they are always on the go and if you want to share their company, you'll have to learn to keep up with them. Impatient, self-centered, impulsive and restless, "1-1"s seek to live life to its fullest, and your best bet for getting them to notice you is to become involved in something that interests them—whether it be photography, surfing or making the rounds of museums. Once you have captured their attention, compliment them, ask them for suggestions, make them feel important, and let them do the planning when you go out on a date. "1-1"s enjoy taking the lead. They do not like to listen to advice and are not prone to follow the crowd. Don't try to clip their wings or restrict them in any way. This combination is not geared to taking orders from anyone, including a spouse, and wants to be independent and in control.

Honest and outspoken "1-1"s are not always sensitive to the needs and feelings of a lover, but they enjoy a challenge and can be passionate and enthusiastic in the pursuit of love. Although they may be most attentive when you first start courting, don't count on them to pack a lunch for you every morning once you settle down. They'll be more concerned about finding a pair of pantyhose without runs or memorizing what they'll say at the 10 o'clock business meeting at work then worrying about whether you would prefer tuna salad or ham and cheese that day. And yet, in spite of this independent streak, "1-1"s are responsive to attention and praise and can be quite romantic at times—surprising you at the most unexpected moment with a sudden burst of affection. The best mate for this combination is someone who lets them have their own way (or at least lets them *think* they do).

At work, "1-1"s need challenge, variety and responsibility. A dull, routine job leads to frustration, whereas competition makes them thrive. They have an original approach to things and put their personal stamp on whatever they do. "1-1"s must either be their own boss or at least able to do things the way they want.

If you have a "1-1" child, keep in mind that his or her tremendous energy needs an outlet in some form of physical activity. "1-1"s are easily frustrated if driven or restrained, and since they are so willful, they do not like to be told what to do. Wise parents will use creative suggestion to make it appear that cleaning a room or raking the leaves could be fun and was "1-1"'s idea—not theirs. Anxious to tackle life, these children love to explore and find it hard to keep still. They need to be taught the importance of sharing and should be encouraged to shine in some area.

| 2 |
MOTIVATION
NUMBER

| 8 |
INNER-SELF
NUMBER

"Man travels faster alone, but loneliness intensifies hardships in a man's journey."

—*Unknown*

| 1 |
EXPRESSION
NUMBER

Your first impression of a "2-1" may be that he or she is strong, organized and controlled. But don't let that fool you! Beneath that facade of independence is a desire for someone to lean on. Not inclined to stay home, "2-1"s enjoy leading an active, interesting life, and though they may appear to be loners, they really prefer having someone to share their interests. In spite of their outward display of independence and individuality, they are attracted to marriage and family life. A good way to capture a "2-1"'s attention is to let them know you too are domestically inclined, and be there when they need you, but don't try to manipulate the relationship or boss them around. Let them take the initiative. Be patient with their moods; don't criticize or find fault with them—this combination is very sensitive and easily hurt and can become irritable and touchy at the drop of a hat. It would be better to concentrate on their good points and let them know how much you appreciate these.

Conflict between what they want and what they do may create a great deal of emotional turmoil for "2-1"s. Male or female, they want to love and be loved, to have peace, comfort, warmth and companionship. Yet their domineering ways may prevent this, causing frustration and insecurity when an established relationship breaks up. This combination seeks domestic, emotional and financial security, and may rush into the arms of a mate who seems to offer it. If, however, their more aggressive and ambitious side finds no outlet in the relationship, they will soon regret their haste.

Even at work there is conflict between a "2-1" 's constant search for security and his or her natural leadership abilities. They are good at gathering information and carrying out directions in a unique way. When giving orders they would want to make sure that all the details were properly taken care of, but would also want to be fair and try to be "nice guys." Appearances to the contrary, "2-1"s need reassurance that they are liked by their fellow employees and, in fact, may even settle for less than they are qualified for in order to feel they "belong"—only to regret it later on when their more aggressive creative urges surface.

"2-1" children resemble the cowardly lion—bossy and insensitive on the outside, but inwardly craving love and affection. Like their adult counterparts, they need lots of reassurance and appreciation. Love and friendship are very important to them, yet they have trouble getting what they want, owing to a tendency to be selfish and inconsiderate of other people's feelings. They do not always know how to be cooperative and tactful even though they would like to be. Sensitive and easily hurt, they do not realize when they themselves are the cause of a broken friendship. These children can derive great benefit from an active pet (such as a dog), who can be an undemanding, understanding companion and accompany them on their outings. They also like to collect things, and parents may be quite surprised at some of the unexpected "treasures" they find in their "2-1" 's pockets on laundry day.

3

MOTIVATION
NUMBER

7

INNER-SELF
NUMBER

1

EXPRESSION
NUMBER

"The enthusiastic to those who are not, are always something of a trial."

—*Alban Goodier*

Although you are more apt to meet a "3-1" at an adult-education class than in a bar, don't be too quick in labeling him or her a bookworm. "3-1"s may at first seem aloof and somewhat hard to approach, but this first impression can be quite deceiving. Once you get to know them, they are fun-loving, loquacious and full of enthusiasm. In fact, you will need an abundance of energy and vitality to keep up with them—and keep up with them you must if you want to catch their eye. Male or female, "3-1"s love to be admired for their looks and talents, and flattery is the key to their heart. Versatile, talented, and opinionated, they are happiest in the company of someone attractive and entertaining who is receptive to their constant flow of ideas and who won't try to dominate them.

"3-1"s thrive on love and affection, but a happy domestic situation is not enough for them because they get bored easily with daily routine. If they do find themselves tied down with home and family, they should be encouraged to keep busy at something creative—whether it be joining an art class or directing plays at the drama club.

Although friendly and outgoing, this combination can be selective in their choice of friends and would rather do things alone than socialize with people they don't like. "3-1"s can be charming hosts and throw wonderful parties, but they are quickly turned off by obnoxious behavior or anyone who exhibits poor taste. They could easily have a fit if their mate unexpectedly brought someone undesirable home for dinner.

Selectivity carries over into the "3-1"'s work situation. Attractive surroundings are important to them and they would not be happy in a cramped, stodgy office atmosphere. Furthermore, they prefer colorful, artistic or people-oriented work, which provides some form of creative expression. Even though they might work independently or in a small department, some social contacts are important. "3-1"s shine in a spotlight whether it be literal or figurative.

"3-1" children want to be social, popular and admired, but may repel those close to them by being critical, demanding and prone to temper tantrums when things go wrong. Don't open *their* door without knocking! They can be quite talkative and may exaggerate the truth to get attention. Wanting so much to be noticed, they thrive on praise and words of appreciation.

Like their adult counterparts, "3-1" children are high-strung and full of nervous energy, which needs some sort of creative outlet. They should be encouraged to develop an expressive talent of some sort—music, art or drama, for example.

MOTIVATION
NUMBER

6

INNER-SELF
NUMBER

1

EXPRESSION
NUMBER

"Where there is a will, there is a way."
—*George Crabbe*

"4-1"s enjoy sports and the great outdoors. You would be more likely to meet one on a tennis court or while out jogging than at the library or a museum. Strike up a conversation by asking for advice on how to do that terrific backhand or about which brand of sneakers provides the most support, but don't try to pressure them into a relationship. Give them the opportunity to take the lead and let them feel it was their idea to do so. One way of getting a "4-1"'s attention is to develop a genuine interest in their business or family. Male or female, they are usually close to their kin, and if you want to win this combination over it wouldn't hurt to win their mother over as well.

Hard-working and dedicated, "4-1"s are drawn to the world of business. They want to be respectable and financially solid. However, they also want a secure relationship with a faithful, home-loving, practical mate. They have earthy natures and enjoy the comforts of home, good food, and country living. In fact, one of the things to remember when courting them is that it is more important to plan to be *together* than it is to plan something exciting or expensive. Not happy with an "I never know when he's going to call" setup, "4-1"s need someone they can depend on. The comforting feeling of knowing that they always have a date on Saturday night, for example, is all-important to them.

Of all the "1"s, "4-1"s can be the most rigid and inflexible—opinionated, demanding, jealous and stubborn. Yet they can be faithful, loyal, and good providers too. It is not uncommon for them to take the carpool of kids to school on their way to work, for instance, or pick them up from a Brownie meeting on the way home. "4-1"s want love and love deeply themselves, but tend to bottle up their feelings so that those close may think they are being taken for granted. But keep in mind that even though this combination doesn't always know how to show affection and may unconsciously repel emotional attentions, the well-being of their loved ones *is* of the utmost importance to them.

At work "4-1"s are determined and persevering. They have great stamina and are not afraid to get their hands dirty. Willing to start at the bottom and work their way up, they are the builders—be it of a business or a building.

"4-1" children, like their adult counterparts, can be bossy and stubborn in spite of a great need for love and affection. They like doing things their own way, and although they may be willing to carry out responsibilities, they will usually end up doing so in a unique or individualistic manner.

MOTIVATION
NUMBER

INNER-SELF
NUMBER

EXPRESSION
NUMBER

"The life of a man is worth very little if he has not the courage to be himself."

—Unknown

"5-1"s have an irresistible urge to explore the world. They have a need to feel free and unbound—to lead exciting, eventful, action-packed lives. Not ones to sit on the sidelines and cheer, they by far prefer participating to being a spectator. You are more apt to meet a "5-1" cross-country skiing or practicing jumps at the ice arena than sitting in front of the fire at the lodge.

While they enjoy being surrounded by people, having an on-going relationship is not so important to this combination as is having the freedom to do what they want when they so please. If a partner happens to enjoy the same kinds of adventures, he or she is welcome to come along for the ride. But if there is any commitment involved a "5-1" will think twice. It takes more than a passing fancy to pin this one down! When they do become involved with someone, it is usually with a person they find interesting and stimulating and who is able to keep up with them both physically and mentally. But even if you fit the bill and have managed to capture the attention of a "5-1," don't count on his or her reliability. Sitting by the phone will likely be a waste of time—their calls tend to be sporadic and on the spur of the moment. Remember they do things when the spirit moves them rather than in any predictable fashion. You may have to do the pursuing yourself and in a way that doesn't make your "5-1" feel trapped. Always have a good excuse handy such as hard-to-get tickets to opening night of a Broadway show, or unusual dinner guests. And never let a "5-1" take you for granted!

This combination is easily bored and, preferring a challenge, is apt to lose interest in someone they know too well.

"5-1"s are quick to grasp opportunities that come their way. They can have so much going at the same time it is a rare patch of grass that has time to grow under their feet. They have trouble settling down and being faithful to one person and may unwittingly hurt those close to them through thoughtless words or actions. Their minds are in such a constant whirl, they cannot always be counted on to follow through with their commitments. And even though they may easily forget their promises to you or keep you waiting for them on a date, one of the surest ways to turn them off is to make a big issue out of it. Better to be understanding and accept them the way they are. Look at the positive side of the picture—freedom to do your own thing too! They are less apt to be jealous or possessive and demanding of your time than most of the other combinations in this book.

At work as in their daily lives, "5-1"s dislike routine and detail. They can efficiently handle more than one thing at a time and tend to remold the job to suit themselves. They look for ingenious solutions to problems and are good at getting their own way. Not geared to being stuck in an office Monday through Friday from nine to five, they work best when allowed to set their own schedule and pace.

Like their adult counterparts, "5-1" children are full of curiosity and always asking "Why?" They love speed, excitement, thrills, and many of the things other kids might find scary—jumping from the highest diving board, exploring dark caves, or riding the biggest roller coaster in the park. Always ready to take a dare, these little rebels are likely to be the ones who run away from home to see the sights, who stow away on board a ship, or who get caught up in the wrong company. Adventure beckons overwhelmingly!

If you have a "5-1" child, be firm but don't try to still his or her expression. When discipline is needed, appeal to him through something new or different. Having a surprise reward when a task is finished, for instance, could prevent pokiness or procrastination.

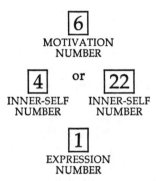

6
MOTIVATION
NUMBER

4   or   22
INNER-SELF   INNER-SELF
NUMBER   NUMBER

1
EXPRESSION
NUMBER

"I share no man's opinions; I have my own."
                                   —Turgenev

You are more likely to meet a "6-1" outdoors at a neighbor's barbecue or through a friend than at a library or a museum. It's not that they shy away from these places, but they prefer a formal introduction. Your first impression of this friendly, forthright combination will probably be how steady, reliable and practical they seem. You may think you've found someone who will always be there when you need them. Yes, they can be, but don't try to rush them into anything. Even though they are geared toward having one steady relationship with someone they can eventually settle down with, it takes more than a one-night stand to convince them to make a commitment. "6-1"s have minds of their own and they do things if and when *they* please. And if their inner-self number is a "22," they may be even harder to please since their expectations of themselves and others will be even higher.

Once a commitment has been made, "6-1"s may have a double standard about many things. For example, they would be hurt, frustrated and suspicious if their "heartthrob" wanted to spend a weekend or evening alone. Yet if they themselves went out with friends one night, they would not see any cause for their loved one to mind. This combination wants someone loyal and homeloving who will pamper them and take care of them and make them feel emotionally secure—someone who will make them breakfast every morning, see that their clothes are freshly pressed, and rub their aching muscles after a hard day at work. Wanting a happy, harmonious home, "6-1"s are also willing to be helpful and shoulder their share of responsibilities—whether it be mowing the lawn, doing the grocery-shopping, or helping around the house. But, they can also be domestic tyrants—trying to instill their own ideals and principles and expecting the rest of the family to do all the adjusting to *their* way of thinking. "6-1"s need easygoing mates who can make them feel important while discreetly pointing out that there are two sides to every viewpoint.

Though demanding at home, this combination can be most charming in social situations, leading many an admiring member of the opposite sex to tell a "6-1" 's spouse how lucky they are to be married to him or her. The "lucky spouse" may respond with a smile but silently think, "Yeah, *you* don't have to *live* with him/her!"

At work, "6-1"s prefer jobs that give them authority and responsibility while at the same time allowing them to be of service to others. They love to give advice, and if they can help people and get paid for it besides, so much the better. If they do happen to have a business-oriented job, they may devote one evening a week to being a scout leader or sports coach just to have the feeling of satisfaction that comes from doing a service (and being able to tell someone what the right way of doing something is).

"6-1"s work well with the establishment, and can handle routine work efficiently in their own individualistic way. Honor and respect are important, and they would never stoop to anything shady even if it meant extra money for themselves. "6-1"s can sacrifice much to fight for a principle. Loyal and dependable, they may choose to remain in a position where they feel close to their associates and needed for their talents, rather than accept a promotion that means a transfer to an alien company.

As for the children of this combination, they are the most obedient and willing to take on responsibilities of all the "1"s. They are the ones most likely to stay after school to help the teacher, or to help mother take care of the younger ones. Willing babysitters, they thrive on being left in charge. It gives them a chance to tell others what to do and to feel important by gaining acceptance and recognition from the adults who count.

"6-1" children want to be popular and accepted, but may sometimes turn their friends off by meddling in their affairs, by being nosy, or by being tattletales. When possible they should be encouraged to play outdoors, where they can vent their frustrations in physical activity.

7
MOTIVATION
NUMBER

3
INNER-SELF
NUMBER

"I never said, 'I want to be alone.' I only said, 'I want to be left alone.' There is all the difference."
—Greta Garbo

1
EXPRESSION
NUMBER

You are more apt to meet "7-1" at the opera than in an office situation. Selective in their choice of friends, they are impressed by refinement, wisdom, or some other unique distinction. They prefer the company of people who are mentally stimulating and they tend to gravitate toward those with intellects similar to their own. The best way to gain their attention is to keep dates light (as far as the love interest goes), and be conversant on a variety of subjects from books on the best-seller list to music to the latest shows. Try to find out what topics are of interest to them and learn to discuss those too. They don't like a partner to be demanding or possessive. Although they may appear to be social or flirtatious, they want just so much from a relationship and if pressure is applied to get close, they may decide to fly the coop.

Appearances to the contrary, "7-1"s can be very sensitive and easily hurt. They rarely show emotion and their cool exterior often belies the anxiety and depression to which they are prone. Since they are secretive about their true feelings it may be difficult to get them to talk about what's bothering them—especially if they feel you are prying. They are easily turned off by anyone they think is giving them the third degree. If rings have already been exchanged and/or you've combined separate households into one, "7-1"s must be allowed to have their privacy. If they come home late, don't badger them with an annoyed "Where were you?" Your reward for allowing them space will be freedom to pursue your own interests and a grateful, appreciative mate.

"7-1"s have analytical minds and are happiest in some highly techni- cal or literary field where they can be an authority and be consulted by others. Even though they have leadership ability, they prefer working alone. Perfectionists themselves, they tend to do whatever they do well and can be demanding, critical bosses—not overly concerned about what others think of them. They do not especially enjoy hard physical labor nor getting their hands dirty unless the job has a certain amount of prestige attached to it.

Like their adult counterparts, "7-1" children can be self-centered, critical and prone to ungrounded fears. They have trouble showing their true emotions and may often feel inadequate, inhibited and shy. Parents of a "7-1" child should keep in mind that even though this combination may repel affectionate overtures by appearing cool and aloof, he or she needs a great deal of love and reassurance.

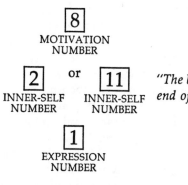

8
MOTIVATION
NUMBER

2   or   11
INNER-SELF   INNER-SELF
NUMBER   NUMBER

1
EXPRESSION
NUMBER

"The best place to find a helping hand is at the end of your own arm."
—Sam Levenson's Father

You are more apt to meet an "8-1" at work or at an adult-education class than at a singles' dance or bar. At first you may think they are quiet and retiring, but don't make the mistake of underestimating them. Behind that shy, reserved facade is a headstrong, aggressive person, well able to stand on his or her own two feet. "8-1"s warm up to people who recognize their good qualities and encourage their ambitions, and once you get to know them well, they can be quite charming and responsive. One way to win them over is to always be there when they need you and to offer them moral support. But don't try to dominate them or impose your opinions on them. This combination has a rebellious streak that may cause them to impulsively go against your wishes just for spite if they feel you are trying to push them around.

Not prone to fooling around, "8-1"s want togetherness in a relationship and independence in everything else. They are generous with loved ones and loyal, and expect the same in return. Comfort is important and having the necessities for living the good life are taken for granted. Male or female, they are willing to help expand the bank account. Money-making comes easily and they are full of ideas they can make pay off.

Whether it be a business or a household, self-sufficient "8-1"s can run it with the efficiency of a six-person staff. They have great physical and mental stamina and a deep-seated need to prove themselves over and over again. If they have an "11" inner-self number they are more easily disappointed and prone to depression when they fail to achieve their goals. They are also more likely to need a creative outlet such as painting, photography, or playing the piano. "8-1"s may get so involved with the pressures of work that they unwittingly neglect their partners' needs. All an understanding spouse need do, however, is point out (tactfully of course) that he or she needs "8-1"'s attention. Since "8-1"s do not like being ignored or taken for granted themselves, they won't consciously take advantage of their mate. What keeps this combination going is their partner's love, affection and emotional support. "8-1"s are great suckers for a big hug and a kiss.

At work, "8-1"s aspire to positions of power, influence and prestige. They prefer to work independently and to choose their own hours. They expect credit for what they produce as well as financial reward. Organized and efficient, they have foresight and executive ability and are best suited to administrative roles. However, they may appear gentle and compromising and therefore could be misjudged by superiors who give them fewer responsibilities than they are qualified for.

"8-1"s are good at handling large problems, but can agonize at great lengths over trivialities. Details are not their forte. However, they thrive on work that is challenging or competitive. Working under stress gives them incentive and they come through with flying colors when in situations of pressure. They have little patience with those who waste time and prefer to do a task themselves rather than take a chance on someone else botching it up or being too slow.

Like their adult counterparts, "8-1" children want to excel in some area and have a competitive spirit. Furthermore, they hate to lose—whether it be a game or an election for class president. They are easily upset if they feel they have been slighted or have not been included in some desirable activity. They can be very impatient and impulsive and "later" or "tomorrow" are not acceptable words in their vocabularies.

Since "8-1" children are always ready to prove themselves, the best way to get them to do something is to put it in the form of a challenge they can't resist.

9
MOTIVATION
NUMBER

1
INNER-SELF
NUMBER

"So little done—so much to do."
                    —Cecil John Rhodes

1
EXPRESSION
NUMBER

Magnetic and charismatic, "9-1"s are incurable romantics who dislike personal restriction and who search for variety in love. Independent and aggressive, they often have a "love 'em and leave 'em" reputation; however, if you have just lost your heart to one, don't despair—they can be loyal once they have found their true mate, at which point their desire to love everyone becomes more theory than practice.

Ambitious and talented, "9-1"s have an enthusiastic zest for life and not nearly the outlet for all their interests. Their main frustration in life is likely to be that a twenty-four-hour day just isn't long enough to do all the things they would like to do, and they can never seem to accomplish as much as they would like to. Drawn to universal concepts—what people have in common as opposed to their differences—they look for something they can identify with in everyone, and can become interested in seemingly-opposite types. This combination loves travel, sports, being wined and dined, and the great outdoors. You could just as easily meet a "9-1" at the beach or at the health club as in a museum or at a concert in the park. You will need a lot of energy to keep up with this one. Also be prepared to take a seat in the shade. If you want to gain a "9-1" 's affection, the best course to follow is to be agreeable to their plans and to willingly go along with them on their adventures. The surest way to antagonize them is to openly oppose them or to try to push them around.

Open, sincere and affectionate, "9-1"s expect everyone to accept them as they are. They don't put on any airs and you usually know exactly where you stand with them. Sexually aggressive, they have erotic imaginations and tend to be the dominant partner in a relationship. While desiring to be tolerant, they can show themselves to be just the opposite if their authority is challenged. Reluctant to admit being wrong, this is the combination of a leader who does not take orders from others easily. A little romance, an appeal to their sentimental side, and making them think they are number one may get you your way, but in arguments, be prepared to do the giving-in at least 75 percent of the time.

"9-1"s are happiest working in some professional or humanitarian capacity. They enjoy serving the public in some way, and are often attracted to politics. However, they can become so discouraged by all the bureaucracy and not-so-benevolent side of government, that they may not stay in that field long. Creative, forceful and sometimes nonconformists, they are happy so long as they can be the authority, do things their own unique way, and have the final say. Highly intuitive, their first impression of a situation or person is usually right.

Like their adult counterparts, "9-1" children are charming, warmhearted and prone to take the side of the underdog. Even at an early age they look for a cause to champion. Strong-willed and stubborn, they dislike personal restriction and will more readily obey a creative suggestion than an order. They can be impatient and careless with details.

"9-1" children are often class or group leaders and have many underlings to carry out their errands. They can be quite bossy and dictatorial and need to feel in charge of something. Despite this outward appearance of bravado, however, they are very sensitive emotionally and their feelings are easily hurt. They have varied interests and are always in love with something. Of all the "1"s, they are most likely to develop a crush on someone.

MOTIVATION
NUMBER

| 8 |
INNER-SELF
NUMBER

"Something to do; Someone to love; Something to hope for."

—*Unknown*

| 1 |
EXPRESSION
NUMBER

"11-1"s are complex personalities. On the one hand they are idealistic daydreamers; on the other they are materialistic and covetous of the finer things in life. You are more likely to meet one at a lecture on UFOs or portfolio management or through a friend than in a disco or a bar. But then, they have a tendency to fluctuate so the reverse could be equally true. This fluctuation exists even in courtship where you may never know what to expect next. Dates may vary from going out to a romantic dinner one night to staying home to polish silver and organize closets the next. "11-1"s can convince you that the latter is fun, and with them it probably will be.

Your first impression of an "11-1" may be that he or she is reserved, aloof and indifferent to the opinions of others, but nothing could be further from the truth. Highly sensitive and easily disillusioned, "11-1"s are apt to reflect the moods and tensions of those close to them. They tend to gravitate toward people who share similar interests and though they may have many acquaintances, close and loyal friends are few. They are responsive to any show of love and kindness, and emotional security is the key to their heart.

"11-1"s need warm, practical mates who share their high ideals and understand their moods. They want to be consulted in all major decisions and have a knack for making their love see a situation their way. Prone to emotional conflict between being possessive and independent, optimistic and disillusioned, outgoing and reserved, they often act one way once and completely different another time. "11-1," for instance, is the man who is not bothered at all when his lover goes to bed in rollers on Monday night, but on Wednesday he has a fit. Or, the woman who tolerates a boring neighbor on Saturday afternoon, but on Sunday asks him in no uncertain terms to come back a more convenient time. "11-1"'s partners may accuse them of living in the clouds and being self-centered and insensitive to the needs of others. This only bewilders them since they are unaware of such actions and certainly don't want to hurt anyone on purpose. In fact they *want* to please—they *want* a steady meaningful relationship, it's just that sometimes they have difficulty expressing all that.

At work, "11-1"s are idealistic visionaries who want recognition for their ideas. They are upset when others disagree with them or take credit for their thoughts. They want to inspire others with their creativity and win them over to conform to their ideals.

Also read the description for "2-1," which starts on page 36. "11" is such a high vibration that it is impossible to operate on it all the time. Children act like its lower octave—"2"—most of the time, and adults operate on the "2" at least part of the time.

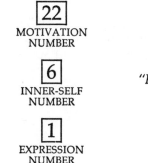

22
MOTIVATION
NUMBER

6
INNER-SELF
NUMBER

1
EXPRESSION
NUMBER

"Fortune favors the audacious."

—*Unknown*

You are most likely to meet a "22-1" at work or through a friend. And, if you have your eye on one, be patient! Slow to warm up and show their true feelings, they are inclined to long courtships. This combination admires intelligence and stability, but wants to be catered to as well. The best way to capture their attention is to be intellectually stimulating and to share their goals. So use your waiting time to do some research and become conversant on whatever interests them. Get them to talk about their work and aspirations and let them know how admirable you feel they are. Let them feel respected and important and be willing to take a back seat to their plans.

"22-1"s tend to be high-strung, temperamental, demanding, and ten steps ahead of everyone else. They want to master every situation and find new, enlightened, practical ways of doing things. Their interests and concerns are universal and boundless and they want to have a wide circle of friends from a variety of different nations and backgrounds, if possible. They have tolerant, humanitarian ideas, but can be uncompromising in close relationships due to a strong need to assert themselves, which may result in their unwittingly overlooking the feelings and opinions of loved ones.

Although charming and persuasive, "22-1"s can also be quite impatient with those who are slower than they, and are prone to sudden outbursts of temper. They may, for instance, be counted on to open doors for you and buy you a birthday present without being reminded, but if you have trouble balancing the checkbook, they are likely to fly off the handle and call you a stupid idiot.

"22-1"s expect domestic perfection and breathing space at home. However, they do not want to be alone (although it may sometimes seem that way). They need an understanding, family-oriented, productive mate who is there when needed and who is willing to respect "22-1"s independent streak as well. It may sound like a tall order, but this combination would find it difficult to stay with a spouse who is not on the same wave length or who does not measure up to his or her standards.

Also read the description for "4-1," which starts on page 39. "22" is such a high vibration that it is impossible to operate on it all the time. Children act like its lower octave—"4"—most of the time, and adults operate on the "4" at least part of the time.

IV
Sensitivity and Cooperation: The Number 2

"2"s are patient, kind, forgiving people who want to feel needed and appreciated. Although shy and reluctant to take the limelight, they gain popularity by being tactful, diplomatic, and good listeners. They are able to see all angles of a situation at the same time, and will do almost anything to keep the peace and avoid taking sides. This may make them appear vacillating, "wishy-washy," even untruthful, and they may be criticized for not having minds of their own.

"2"s are very sensitive to other peoples' feelings and will go out of their way to make those close to them happy. In fact, so great is their desire to please and their fear of being misunderstood or criticized, that they are easily taken advantage of. They may frequently find themselves doing something they don't really want to be doing—stuck in an unwanted job or love affair, for example—just because they are afraid of upsetting another person.

"2"s seek love, marriage, companionship, sympathy, understanding, and emotional support. Ruled by their hearts, they feel deeply, and have warm, giving, caring, domestic natures. They can be most unhappy when alone or unloved. Gentle, subservient and cooperative, "2"s are content to play a background role. They prefer having someone else make decisions for them, and are willing to let other people have their way. They are sexually passive and reluctant to make the first move, but are quick to respond and easily swayed through their emotions. Neither flirtatious nor promiscuous, they are loyal, faithful spouses and expect the same in return. They are happiest with a solid, dependable mate they can look up to and respect.

"2"s enjoy sharing and live for their friends and loved ones—often placing the welfare and happiness of others above their own. Yet they can also be petty and unreasonable in their expectations, taking it for granted that others "know" what they want and will automatically place the same value on things that they do. Although they do not express their true feelings nor discuss their needs, "2"s are easily upset and prone to emotional lows when those close do not respond the way they would like them to. For example, they place great importance on the small and sentimental—"2"s never forget a birthday or anniversary

51

and are deeply hurt and disappointed when a friend forgets theirs.

"2"s also tend to build up resentment at the things that upset them rather than to discuss their displeasure. For instance, punctual people themselves, they do not like to be kept waiting. Yet they may not mention it to the offending party for fear of hurting him or her. If they feel they are being taken advantage of they will bottle up their angry feelings, then later vent their frustration in some seemingly unrelated way which the person toward whom it is directed may find unexpected and hard to understand. While keeping the real cause of their discontent to themselves, "2"s may become argumentative, "nit-picking," hard to reason with, or even quick-tempered—exploding at some apparent trifle.

"2"s enjoy the rhythm of music and poetry and are usually good dancers. They are also nostalgic and enjoy collecting and being surrounded by the things they love—people, pets, plants or knickknacks. "2"s hate to throw anything out—even old wrapping paper or bits of string. They believe in saving everything for a rainy day. "You never know when it may come in handy" is likely to be their motto. Anytime you need something and despair of finding it elsewhere, try asking a "2"—he or she probably has one stashed away somewhere!

COMPATIBILITY GUIDE

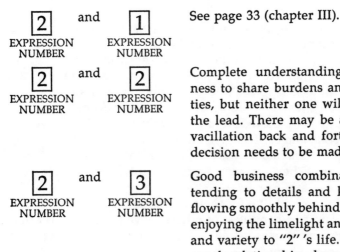

2 EXPRESSION NUMBER	and	**1** EXPRESSION NUMBER

See page 33 (chapter III).

2 EXPRESSION NUMBER	and	**2** EXPRESSION NUMBER

Complete understanding and willingness to share burdens and responsibilities, but neither one will want to take the lead. There may be a great deal of vacillation back and forth whenever a decision needs to be made.

2 EXPRESSION NUMBER	and	**3** EXPRESSION NUMBER

Good business combination—"2" attending to details and keeping things flowing smoothly behind the scenes; "3" enjoying the limelight and adding spark and variety to "2"'s life. In a close personal relationship, however, "2" may feel jealous and resentful of "3"'s flirtations; "3" may get bored with "2", finding him too simple and passive.

2 and	**4**	Good business, friendship or marriage combination—"2" helping and encouraging "4." "4" might unintentionally take advantage of "2" 's good nature giving rise to hurt feelings, but mostly there is respect for each other's talents and ideas, and a common bond of understanding and sympathy between them.
EXPRESSION NUMBER	EXPRESSION NUMBER	

2 and	**5**	Poor combination—"2" 's slow, passive nature conflicting with "5" 's hyperactive, changeable one. "2" may find "5" confusing, hard to cope with, misleading, and never there when he needs him. "5" may find "2" tiring, possessive and irritating.
EXPRESSION NUMBER	EXPRESSION NUMBER	

2 and	**6**	Magnetic attraction between two peace-loving, easygoing, family oriented numbers. Good combination for business or marriage—"2" cooperating with "6" and helping execute its plans; "6" providing "2" with sympathy, guidance and advice.
EXPRESSION NUMBER	EXPRESSION NUMBER	

2 and	**7**	Good business or psychic combination—"7" adding vision to the project, "2" lending moral support and carrying out the details. In a close personal relationship, however, "7" may find "2" distracting and oversensitive. "2" may feel hurt by "7" 's reserve and need for privacy.
EXPRESSION NUMBER	EXPRESSION NUMBER	

2 and	**8**	Good business, friendship or marriage combination—"2" following "8" 's lead and taking care of the details. In a close personal relationship "8" may find "2" petty or boring but will always appreciate its loyalty, cooperation and support.
EXPRESSION NUMBER	EXPRESSION NUMBER	

2 and	**9**	Good business combination—"2" adding practicality and efficiency to "9" 's creativity and imagination. In a close
EXPRESSION NUMBER	EXPRESSION NUMBER	

personal relationship, however, there may be conflict between "2"'s desires for togetherness and "9"'s broader outlook. "9" may feel limited by "2"; "2" may resent "9"'s outside interests.

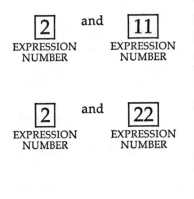

| 2 | and | 11 |
| EXPRESSION NUMBER | | EXPRESSION NUMBER |

Peaceful, harmonious combination—"2" lending moral support to "11" and adding practicality and efficiency to its visions; "11" uplifting "2" and broadening its horizons.

| 2 | and | 22 |
| EXPRESSION NUMBER | | EXPRESSION NUMBER |

Good business combination—"2" taking care of all the details and being a faithful, trustworthy assistant to "22." In a close personal relationship, however, "22" may belittle "2" for being petty and slow. "2" may find "22" demanding and feel confused and hurt at its impatience and unpredictability.

Following are all possible combinations of a "2" expression number with the different motivation and inner-self numbers.

| 1 |
| MOTIVATION NUMBER |

| 1 |
| INNER-SELF NUMBER |

". . . a hive of contradictions—between his word and his deed, his will and his work, his life and his principles."

—*Henrik Ibsen*

| 2 |
| EXPRESSION NUMBER |

When you first meet a "1-2"—whether it be at work, at a convention, or through a friend—your first impression is likely to be that he or she is outgoing, self-confident and enterprising. And in truth, "1-2"s *are* inwardly ambitious and enthusiastic, but once you get to know them better, they may come across as being cautious and vacillating. While this discrepancy may prove confusing to you, keep in mind that it is not only confusing, but frustrating to them as well. They may, for instance, seem willing to have their partner decide what to do on a date, yet build up resentment when not asked at least for a preference. Even when they have comfortably settled down with someone, "1-2"s win more battles in fantasy than in reality. They may, for instance, rant and rave and swear to their friends that the next time their partner comes home late from a poker game, he or she won't find them there—they will have gone to spend the night at mother's. Yet when that "next time" arrives, they just give him or her an annoyed "it's about *time* you got back!" and leave it at that.

A great deal of "1-2"s time and effort is spent in trying to resolve the conflict of expressing dependence when what they really want is independence. They would like to have the final say, but usually end up being the one who gives in. When they do make a decision, they may fret about not having done the right thing and mentally weigh all the alternatives. The key to this combination's heart is to be understanding and supportive. Notice and praise their accomplishments. Encourage them to assert themselves and be the dominant personality at least part of the time. But don't act totally dependent on them or expect constant togetherness. "2-1"s appreciate warmth and devotion, but not to the point of being smothered by it. In fact, they admire strength and intelligence and can be turned off by someone who seems to cling to them, or who sits adoringly at their feet without ever making any of the decisions or asserting him or herself.

At work as in their private lives, "1-2"s are trustworthy and reliable. They enjoy being involved with people and projects that emphasize change and improvement. Good at constructive compromise, they can appease opposing sides and settle disagreements on the job. Even though they may act cautious and uncertain, they see themselves as leaders and find it hard to accept subordinate roles. When passed by, they have a tendency to console themselves by saying, "I could have done just as well or better if only I'd had the chance."

Like their adult counterparts, "1-2" children want to be leaders and may feel confused and frustrated when their actions don't live up to their dreams. They may fantasize about being heroic celebrities— Superman or the Bionic Woman, for example—and feelings of being put down or rejected can lead to outbursts of temper at the most unexpected times.

"1-2" children enjoy puzzles and games that allow them to be doing something on their own while in the company of others. They also like outdoor activities such as running and climbing trees, and usually have at least one pal they can count on to join them on their outings.

2
MOTIVATION
NUMBER

9
INNER-SELF
NUMBER

"All who joy would win must share it—happiness was born a twin."

—*Byron*

2
EXPRESSION
NUMBER

"2-2"s want someone to lean on and do not enjoy being alone. However, they are unlikely to make the first move toward forming a relationship. Impressionable and easily led, they are drawn to people who seem strong and dependable. They want a steady partner whom they can rely on, who will make the decisions, and who is also considerate. For instance, although they are apt to respond with an "anything you like" or an "I don't care," "2-2"s do appreciate being asked what they would like to do or where they would like to go. They themselves make attentive and self-sacrificing lovers who can be somewhat smothering in their need for constant togetherness. So great is their need to be liked and their fear of hurting the other person's feelings, they may also seem wishy-washy and unable to make up their minds.

Sensitive to non-verbal communication, they intuitively pick up what others feel. Sharing is their keynote—preferably within a permanent give-and-take relationship. They place great importance on thoughtfulness and attention to little things, and are easy to reach through their emotions. "2-2" is the woman who starts to cry when a lover remembers her birthday with flowers, and likewise bursts into tears of disappointment when he forgets their anniversary. He is also the proud father who displays in his office a homemade valentine that says, "I love you, Daddy."

Gentle and considerate, "2-2"s are usually well liked. Rather than risk hurting the other person's feelings, they may be self-sacrificing and refrain from asserting themselves. They need warm, understanding, firm mates who are sensitive to their moods and shyness. When they find such a person they are often inclined to let their every move revolve around him or her and are the combination most willing to give up a career to stay home and keep house. But although home-oriented, content with basic comforts, peaceful surroundings and, of course, a loving relationship, they should be encouraged to have friends, join clubs, and participate in community activities. Otherwise they can become clinging vines or whining nags. Whether it be singing in the church choir, taking an exercise class or joining a bowling league, outside interests help alleviate pressure on their mates for constant togetherness and support.

At work as in their private lives, "2-2"'s have no desire to be leaders. Cooperative and subservient, they prefer background roles and tend to shy away from positions of authority. Their instinctive inclination is to wait for someone else to tell them what to do. They are not good at making decisions and may vacillate between alternate solutions. Tactful and patient, they have a good sense of rhythm and timing and are good at details. However, they can get lost in minutiae and need to be reminded from time to time of the overall picture or the long-term goal.

"2-2" children, just as their adult counterparts, can be sensitive, finicky, dependent and shy. They are the ones most likely to hide behind "Mama" 's apron strings when a stranger approaches. They are the youngsters who don't want to be left with a babysitter or leave Mommy to go to school for the first time. Obedient, quiet and well-mannered, they may appear to be model children. In fact, so great is their desire to please that they are not always truthful, and have a tendency to tell people what they think they want to hear. Affectionate and willing to share, companionship is very important to them and they often have an imaginary playmate.

"2-2" children (and adults too) enjoy collecting things—bottle caps, pretty rocks, berets, crumpled pieces of colored paper, stale potato chips—all kinds of things. If one precious object were to get thrown out, a flood of tears would most certainly result. But if they know someone else could make better use of it they would be more willing to part with it. Try initiating a compromise. For example, "You can keep the bubblegum wrappers if you give the potato chips to the hungry birds."

Child or adult, "2-2"'s need constant reassurance that they are loved. Without praise and encouragement they may withdraw for fear of being hurt. They seek direction and are the combination most prone to ask, "What should I do now?"

| 3 |
MOTIVATION
NUMBER

| 8 |
INNER-SELF
NUMBER

"The greatest pleasure of life is love."
—*Sir W. Temple*

| 2 |
EXPRESSION
NUMBER

"3-2"s do not like being by themselves and you are more likely to meet one at a social event or in an elevator then jogging alone in the park. Since this combination wants someone beautiful upon whom to shower their affection, looks may well be what first catches their eye. But besides being good-looking, they would like their partner to provide novelty and excitement without being overbearing or domineering.

"3-2"s love to be in the limelight, and crave attention. Flattery and kind words are definitely ways to their heart. They may be accused by some of being shallow and superficial, but once they outgrow the infatuation stage they can be loyal devoted companions. "3-2"s will bend over backward to please their partner as long as they feel loved and appreciated, but they will resent being taken advantage of or taken for granted. They enjoy being wined and dined, and signs of affection—be they kisses, sweet nothings whispered in their ear, or baubles—are essential to their well-being.

Entertaining and vivacious, "3-2"s can be charming hosts, and whether it be a party of two or fifty, they have a knack for making those they serve feel special. Furthermore, this combination has a youthful outlook and rarely looks his or her years. They enjoy children and can be wonderful parents.

Creative and expressive, "3-2"s don't really want to be bothered with details, but usually end up dealing with them in one way or another anyway. Although they would like to make a good salary at work, they often find themselves having to choose between a job they love that pays poorly and an establishment office job that pays well but which they may not find satisfying. Sometimes they solve this conflict by keeping the office job and taking art classes, joining a drama club, or doing volunteer work at night. Whatever his or her chosen field, however, a "3-2" is a people person. They need reinforcement that they are doing a good job and other ears off which to bounce their ideas.

In the same way as their adult equivalents, "3-2" children are popular, friendly and talkative. Social activities are the highlight of their existence and more than any other "2" these children would likely consider it cruel and inhuman punishment to be sent to their room on a sunny afternoon. Joiners of groups, they like parties and always want to look their best. As they get older, having someone special to date is important to them and they may spend a great deal of time on the phone. They may not show much concern for the future and could be indifferent when talk turns to college or a future career. They need to be taught the importance of responsibility and should be counseled about the real world.

4
MOTIVATION
NUMBER

7
INNER-SELF
NUMBER

2
EXPRESSION
NUMBER

"To feel that one has a place in life solves half the problem of contentment."
—*George E. Woodberry*

Selective in their choice of friends, "4-2"s prefer to stick to those of their own background and status. Although they may appear tolerant and friendly to all, they usually have many hidden prejudices. You are more likely to meet this combination at a class reunion or a family get-together than at a way-out beach resort. And once you have caught their eye, expect a conventional courtship. They will call faithfully and most dependably, and if they suddenly don't, you can be sure something is wrong. "4-2"s have a tendency to build up resentment rather than discuss what's bothering them. The silent treatment is often their first retaliation when their feelings are hurt. And guilty or not, don't expect them to be the first to apologize. "4-2"s have a stubborn streak and may harbor smoldering resentments for a long time. They expect you to *know* what's bothering them without having to ask. It is important to establish communication in such instances and lovingly make it clear that you are not a mind reader.

This combination wants a place to go home to at night and they don't want it to be empty. They seek warm, practical down-to-earth mates who are there when needed. However, they often have double standards about things and they themselves may not always be faithful to one person. Nevertheless, they are security conscious and will rarely let outside influences interfere with the one relationship which gives them a sense of belonging.

"4-2"s are not always easy to live with. Neat and orderly, they want tidy surroundings and are conservative in taste. They expect their mates to know what they want without being told and can be quite finicky about small things such as leaving the cap off the toothpaste, or clothes that aren't hung up right away. Any threat to their emotional or material security may result in an unexpected burst of temper toward some seeming trifle. They benefit from a patient mate with a sense of humor who can tactfully encourage them to widen their horizons and try new things.

Hard-working and dependable, "4-2"s recognize the importance of work and do not have delusions of grandeur. Neither do they mind starting at the bottom. They may be slow-moving but they're thorough, good at details, and they give stability to any group effort. If overtime is required, they will be there to pitch in.

"4-2" children are usually obedient, responsible and unassuming, but they can also be bossy, stubborn, and fussy about small things. They may, for instance, clean their room when Mother tells them Aunt Marge is coming to visit, but refuse to wear the outfit this aunt gave them for Christmas because they don't like its big stripes. Like their adult counterparts, these children are selective in their choice of friends and can be cliquish and clannish and not above spreading rumors. They should be encouraged to join groups such as the Scouts or 4-H that can help expand their horizons by introducing them to many children and teaching them a sense of camaraderie as well as skills or crafts.

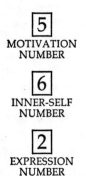

5
MOTIVATION
NUMBER

6
INNER-SELF
NUMBER

2
EXPRESSION
NUMBER

"Man lives by habit indeed, but what he lives for is thrills and excitement."
— William James

If you want to meet a "5-2," try someplace where people gather to have a good time. They love beach parties, picnics, fairs, ski trips, cruises, or even just dropping over at a friend's house for a beer. What this combination is looking for is someone fun-loving but stable and understanding who can add variety to their life and who won't take them for granted.

When "5-2"s' interest has been sparked, they may shower you with attention, but don't be surprised if just when you think you have them, they start looking in other directions. Appearances to the contrary, they are not all that easy to pin down. Kind, affectionate and self-sacrificing, they are nevertheless, wanderers at heart. They don't want as much responsibility in a relationship as they may indicate, but neither do they want to hurt anyone's feelings. When they start calling up to say they have to cancel your date because they'll be working late at the office or they have to take Mother to the doctor, chances are they're trying to wangle out of the evening without being brave enough to tell you right out.

"5-2"s are restless, indecisive and may appear to procrastinate and vacillate because of all the interesting alternatives that come to mind. However, once they decide to settle down with someone they can be loyal and dependable due to their active and prodding consciences. They may, for example, feel burdened by child rearing if they had no domestic help or cooperation from a spouse. Yet any shirking of responsibility to pursue the freedom so naturally sought after would cause pangs of guilt and worry. They enjoy the sensual aspects of life and are strongly attracted to the opposite sex, but they would feel guilty and afraid of being discovered if they cheated on their spouse. When they do give in to temptation, fear of the consequences could lead them, for instance, to ask their ex-girl or boyfriend to return their love letters at the end of an affair.

At work, as in their private lives, "5-2"s prefer variety, and flexible hours when possible. Adaptable, friendly and perceptive, they are good at finding ingenious solutions to problems and enjoy working with other people. Troubleshooting or mediating are right up their alley. Or, their love of travel could lead them into making a career out of that. They can be excellent tour guides, making sure each trip is memorable and each person has a good time. They also make good salesmen as long as they don't have to get involved in "dog-eat-dog," cutthroat competition. Their sensitivity and basically passive, easygoing nature would not be comfortable in an unfriendly atmosphere.

"5-2"s juvenile counterparts are drawn to that which is exciting and different, and their curiosity often leads them astray. They might play hooky from school to go to the circus, or pour black ink out the window to see what it looks like trickling down a white wall, and are bewildered when the adults in their environment don't share their amusement. Their mischievous acts are not done out of maliciousness but only out of curiosity, and it is difficult for them to understand punishment. If you are the parent of a "5-2" child, make sure to always explain *why* their transgression—damaging property, for example—is not acceptable behavior.

"5-2" children tend to be absentminded and disorderly. They need to be encouraged to develop some pattern of self-discipline and routine, such as being held responsible for making their beds or picking up their clothes. For a job well done little rewards (like having some friends over or taking a trip to the park) would have better results than constant nagging, which they may just "tune out."

6
MOTIVATION
NUMBER

5
INNER-SELF
NUMBER

2
EXPRESSION
NUMBER

"I place the needs of others above my own . . ."
—*Anonymous*

Loyal, self-sacrificing, "6-2" could be the debonaire, intriguing stranger you meet in the hospital when visiting a friend, or who strikes up a conversation with you while standing in line at the post office waiting to buy stamps. You may not take them seriously when they say they'll call, but sure enough they do. This combination is much more dependable and reliable than a first impression might suggest.

Idealistic and romantic, "6-2"s are looking for the perfect love with whom to settle down and raise a family. They want a harmonious give-and-take relationship with someone warm, understanding, attentive and communicative. If you want to strike a sympathetic chord with them, wine them and dine them and gear the conversation to love, marriage and children. Show an interest in their relatives and home, and keep in mind that a "6-2" is usually close to his or her mother, so you may have to take her on as well.

"6-2"s want stability in their relationships. Emotional comfort and security are important to their well-being and they are easily upset by partners who frequently change their minds about things, who fail to keep promises, or who are critical, impatient or argumentative; they have high expectations of those close, and can be disappointed when they don't live up to them. Even when married, they may not always voice their wants, yet they expect their mates to do things their way and to step in and give them a hand without being asked. They can get resentful when a spouse does not adjust to their routines, and without mentioning what is really bothering them, may pick a fight about something totally unrelated. When a "6-2" complains about the burnt toast, for example, he or she may really be venting frustration at the car being parked in the wrong place *again*. If you happen to be the mate of a "6-2," you would do well to always find out what's at the bottom of an argument.

"6-2"s make good parents and charming hosts. Domestically inclined, they enjoy cooking and believe in keeping the larder well stocked. They are also interested in school activities, local politics, and community projects. Finding it difficult to say "no," they have a tendency to bite off more than they can chew—serving on many committees, chauffeuring the children back and forth, and entertaining friends.

At work as in their private lives, "6-2"s enjoy giving advice and being parental. If they can make that part of their profession—as a bartender who lends a compassionate ear to his customers' hard luck tales, for example—so much the better. They also enjoy jobs that make use of their domestic talents. Many chefs, for instance, have this combination, as do caterers, dietitians, and cooks in school cafeterias. No matter what they do, they are happiest when they feel they are providing a service for others.

"6-2" children, like their adult counterparts, are sensitive and anxious to please. Being popular is very important to them, and if the gang thinks it's a good idea to have a tug-of-war, "6-2" is unlikely to risk being thought of as "uncool" by voicing another opinion. These children enjoy doing small errands that result in words of praise from appreciative parents, and can be a big help looking after younger brothers or sisters. They show early domestic inclinations and are especially eager to be around when Mother or Father is cooking. Scraping the bowl with an anxious little finger as the cake goes into the oven can well be the highlight of their day. Family outings go over big and "6-2" children will count the days until a trip to the circus, amusement park or animal farm.

7
MOTIVATION
NUMBER

4   or   22
INNER-SELF   INNER-SELF
NUMBER   NUMBER

2
EXPRESSION
NUMBER

"Happiness lies in the absorption in some vocation which satisfies the soul."
—*Sir William Osler*

You are more apt to meet a "7-2" at work, at the bridge club, or through a friend than at a disco or in a bar. This combination prefers the intimacy of a small group to the hustle and bustle of a crowd. They may at first seem reserved, aloof and hard to approach, but once you get to know them they can be friendly and outgoing.

Selective in their choice of friends, "7-2"s tend to gravitate toward those who are on the same intellectual wavelength as they are. Intelligence is important to them and they would never remain with someone whose only asset was good looks. Qualities such as academic achievement and mental victory appeal to this combination, especially those with a "22" inner-self number, and they will seek the company of people who are refined or distinguished in some way. "7-2"s find trivial chatter annoying and look down on coffee klatches, soap operas, or Sunday afternoon football games on TV as activities which are meaningless and boring. What turns them on is mental stimulation of some kind—chess, theater, a lecture or a guided tour through a museum, for example. If you want to capture their attention, gear the conversation toward a subject that you know interests them. Keep abreast of the latest books, movies, plays; and steer away from anything that smacks of prying into their private lives. Personal questions about their love life or about how much money they make can quickly turn this combination off.

"7-2"s want strong relationships that provide emotional security as well as sufficient freedom to pursue outside interests. Although they will show undying devotion to the one they love, they need privacy and some time alone each day. The key to their heart is to be warm and understanding and sensitive to their moods. A mate who knows when to initiate communication to break down barriers of gloom and misunderstanding and when to be silent is greatly appreciated.

"7-2"s like to have order around them but they don't like to throw anything out. They can do laundry every Monday, remember to take pills on time, and balance the checkbook. When it comes to drawers and closets, however, they have a problem. No matter how well they organize, there never seems to be enough room for all the stuff they accumulate. Their mate needs patience to explain that when the string-ball gets to be a certain size, there is no need to save any more; that old suit in the closet which hasn't been worn for eight years will probably never be in style again and should be given to charity; the magazines from 1968 are only collecting dust; and so on.

At work "7-2"s have no great desire to be boss. They prefer working behind the scenes with others with whom they have some mental rapport. Intuitive and observant, they combine insight with factual know-how. They have technical minds and are good at analysis and breaking things down into their component parts. They can work with details, but may have a tendency to get bogged down in them and lose sight of the overall picture.

"7-2"s, if treated fairly, quickly build up a sense of loyalty to their employers and will work tirelessly when their efforts are needed— giving up a weekend without expecting to get paid, for example, to help with the office move. Since they are not aggressive and make little effort to sell themselves, they rarely make as much money as their more outspoken peers. Pride often gets in the way and they may have the attitude that their work speaks for itself and they should automatically be rewarded with salary increases and promotions. It's almost as if it is beneath them to ask for a raise.

Like their adult counterparts, "7-2" children can be cautious and taciturn—appearing shy, withdrawn and reluctant to talk about what's on their minds. However, there is a lot of mental activity going on beneath the surface. They want to be included in everything and one of the biggest causes for tears is feeling rejected. If Mother's response is less than appreciative when her "7-2" child—wanting to delight her with a bouquet of flowers—surprises her with a fist-full of tomato blossoms plucked from her vegetable patch, he or she is bound to feel crushed and devastated. Sensitive and often misunderstood, these children need a great deal of love, understanding and reassurance to build up their fragile egos.

8
MOTIVATION
NUMBER

3
INNER-SELF
NUMBER

"For where your treasure is, there will your heart be also."

—*Matthew 6:21*

2
EXPRESSION
NUMBER

Active and energetic, "8-2"s usually enjoy sports and being outdoors. You have a better chance of meeting one at work, on a tennis court or at a barbecue than in a museum or a bar. They may appear friendly and outgoing to all, but they are very appearance conscious and inclined to judge a person by what they own and by their station in life. Although they themselves do not actively seek the limelight, they do have an inner desire to be noticed, and when, for instance, they put five dollars in the collection plate, they want everyone to know it's a five-dollar not a one-dollar bill. Praise and admiration are music to their ears, and they seek the company of attractive, efficient people who can be a credit to them and build up their egos.

"8-2"s want to be in control of their relationships but they do compromise for the one they love. Good-looking or not, they have a certain charm that attracts members of the opposite sex. They don't mind footing the bills or giving emotional support so long as they don't feel taken for granted or used. They have a good sense of humor and are slow to anger, but are prone to blue moods or explosions of temper if someone disappoints them. They may feel frustrated when they fail to assert themselves, and a wise partner will be astute enough to recognize that an argument over a triviality may mean something more important is bothering them, but they're keeping it bottled up inside.

At work as in their private lives, "8-2"s are ambitious and want authority. Their "go along with the crowd" expression, however, does not always convey the drive of their motivation. Owing to this conflict between what they want and what they do, they may not communicate the good ideas they have even though they're unhappy with their work situation. "8-2," for example, is the boss who stays overtime to redo a poor report rather than bring its unsatisfactory aspects to the attention of the employee who wrote it or ask him or her to stay late to fix it.

"8-2"s are happiest in a position of some authority and control working with people they like. They want recognition and expect to be paid for what they accomplish, but here again, they may not speak up for their rights. More likely they would encourage someone else to intercede on their behalf. Their pleasant personalities along with their good reasoning ability make them qualified for jobs requiring tact and diplomacy, and they are good at smoothing things over between irate customer and store, for example, or between two workers who both want the same week's vacation but who can't be away at the same time.

"8-2" children are manipulative and imaginative. They will, for instance, make sure the dog is under the table whenever Mother serves liver for dinner, or find a strip of old film along a road and decide to make their own home movie. They will devleop their natural talents and find excuses to avoid doing things at which they might fail. If, for example, they're good at sports but not so hot at the piano, they will insist that the gang is waiting for them at the baseball diamond when Aunt Harriet wants a little recital.

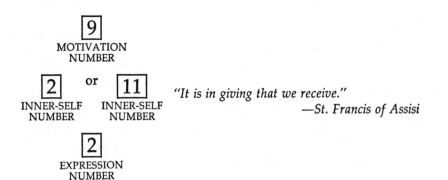

| 9 |
| MOTIVATION NUMBER |

2   or   11
INNER-SELF NUMBER   INNER-SELF NUMBER

2
EXPRESSION NUMBER

"It is in giving that we receive."
—*St. Francis of Assisi*

A peace rally, a dance class, a poetry reading, are all likely places to meet "9-2"s. Although they may appear shy and retiring, they have an inner drive for romance and variety of experience. Broad-minded and humanitarian, they enjoy a multitude of friends from different backgrounds and walks of life, but their dream is for a very special someone with whom to settle down. They enjoy being wined and dined in cozy atmospheres—candlelight, soft music, words of love—but they are very sensitive to criticism and are easily hurt and turned off by a partner who lies or fails to keep a promise to them. Generous, compassionate and affectionate, they instinctively seek peace and sharing in a relationship and would be most unhappy in the company of someone who showed signs of prejudice, bigotry, or on a more personal level was possessive or rigid. A live and let live atmosphere is essential to their well-being.

Ideals are more important to "9-2"s (especially if they have an "11" inner-self number) than the practicality of stark reality. Sympathetic, understanding, and above all, sentimental, they respond to everything emotionally and have a desire to reach out and help those less fortunate than themselves. Suckers for a sob story, they can become bewildered and disappointed when others do not share their attitudes. The most giving of all the "2"s, they can be extravagant with their partner's resources as well as their own, and their partner may have a difficult time explaining his or her aggravation at "9-2"s having given away all their canned goods to the neighborhood "Save the Starving Children Fund," leaving their own cupboard bare.

At work as in their private lives, "9-2"s are happiest doing something humanitarian or serving a cause that would benefit others. Healing or teaching would be much more appealing to members of this combination than the daily routine of an office job. Although they like being part of an exciting atmosphere, they don't mind staying in the background. They can, for instance, find satisfaction as a campaign worker who does the grueling tasks—addressing envelopes, putting up posters, calling people to vote for a candidate they believe in—without expecting glory themselves. Or, they can be of great help working backstage in a theater, taking care of costumes, performing in the chorus or in the orchestra. Their natural sense of rhythm gives them a talent for dancing, and whether it's a profession or a hobby, they usually find a place for it somewhere in their lives.

"9-2" children are imaginative and idealistic. Music and art will most likely be preferred to math or science, and when they get older they may show a talent for poetry. "9-2"s love to daydream and pretend that the castles they make in the sand are real, that the fairy who replaced the tooth under their pillow with a dime was beautiful, and that their teddy bear really did talk. They are often the last child in their class to stop believing in Santa Claus.

11
MOTIVATION
NUMBER

9
INNER-SELF
NUMBER

2
EXPRESSION
NUMBER

"Much of life's joy is lost because we look too far away for the things that bring us happiness."
— *Unknown*

An animal-care center, an adult-education class, a camera club, or a volunteer group are all likely places for meeting an "11-2." Sensitive and compassionate, they are repelled by unnecessary suffering, cruelty or injustice. Even little things can move them to tears and they should always have a handkerchief along when watching a sad movie. Idealistic in love as well as in everything else, they are easily hurt when those close don't live up to their expectations. They set such high standards that most likely their image of an ideal mate is to be found only in their own fantasy, and they are often accused by others of being impractical and living in the clouds.

Loyal, devoted, and trusting themselves, "11-2"s seek someone warm, affectionate and understanding who shares their ideals and who is their intellectual equal. In fact, mental rapport and emotional compatibility are more important to them than physical attraction. Naturally giving, "11-2"s have trouble asserting themselves and may verbally agree to another way of doing something in order to keep the peace. A wise partner will be aware of this propensity and watch for signs of secret resentment at having given in. Good communication is a must in order to straighten out problems as they occur. Otherwise, moodiness on "11-2"'s part may put a damper on the relationship.

At work as in their private lives, "11-2"s are happiest communicating their high ideals to others. Good at details, they nevertheless need to feel that what they do is important. If the job has a lot of busy work, such as typing or filing, they may look for a second vocation to fill their desire to accomplish something worthwhile. Natural arbitrators, they work well in situations demanding tact and diplomacy but prefer having someone else make the final decisions. They would also enjoy careers involving some form of artistic expression, such as music or poetry.

If you have an "11-2" child, keep in mind that he or she is apt to be highly impressionable and easily moved to tears. Love, understanding, patience and acceptance are all-important to his or her well-being.

Also read the description for "2-2," which starts on page 56. "11" is such a high vibration that it is impossible to operate on it all the time. Children act like its lower octave—"2"—most of the time, and adults operate on the "2" at least part of the time.

MOTIVATION
NUMBER

| 7 |

INNER-SELF
NUMBER

"Lose no time; be always employed in something useful . . ."

—*Benjamin Franklin*

| 2 |

EXPRESSION
NUMBER

Whether you meet "22-2"s at a political club, on the diving team, or at work, you will probably be struck by their strong sense of purpose. Although they may at first seem aloof and hard to approach, they can be charming, generous and compassionate once you get to know them. There is, however, a dual side to their nature, and on occasion they can be demanding, critical and seemingly indifferent to your needs as well. This comes from an ongoing conflict between their self-sacrificing outward expression and their inner motivation, which would prefer to have the last say in matters. "22-2"s may resent their soft side and when they fail to assert themselves they can become irritable and prone to unpredictable outbursts of temper.

Practical idealists in love as well as in everything else, "22-2"s are looking for a permanent relationship with someone who is as inspired, efficient, hard-working and productive as they are. Intrigued by different customs and ways of life, this combination could fall in love with a pen pal in a foreign country or be attracted to someone with a background completely different from their own. But however they may meet, earthiness as well as intellectual stimulation are the keys to "22-2" 's heart. Physically attractive and dumb doesn't cut it. Intelligent and cold doesn't cut it either. Sincere, smart, and sexy is what has the best chance for getting this combination to tie the knot.

"22-2"s are not content to work in mediocre positions. They crave efficiency at the highest level and although they don't have to be the boss, they at least want a powerful position in the group. Imaginative and good at visualizing ways of putting ideas into practice, they add stability to group efforts and make good second in commands. They need a cause to be devoted to—whether it be the peace movement, spreading technical knowledge to the Third World countries, or saving the whooping crane from extinction. Scrubbing floors or washing dishes is not their idea of creating for the future or making the world a better place.

Also read the description for "4-2," which starts on page 59. "22" is such a high vibration that it is impossible to operate on it all the time. Children act like its lower octave—"4"—most of the time, and adults operate on the "4" at least part of the time.

V
Sociability and Self-Expression:
The Number 3

"3"s are social beings who seek love, admiration and friendship. Outgoing, charming and gregarious, they have the gift of gab and rarely are at a loss for words—even when they have nothing to say. Frank and outspoken, they have an opinion or reaction to everything, and since they can talk a little about any topic, they may appear to know more than they actually do. "3"s are persuasive and good at selling their ideas to others, and can talk their way in and out of anything. They may even exaggerate or stretch the truth to make something *sound* better.

"3"s love being in the limelight. Natural performers, they like to entertain, and thrive on praise and flattery. Although appearing optimistic, enthusiastic and happy-go-lucky, however, they do not always have a good self-image. They may worry excessively about their appearance and make mountains out of molehills where looks are concerned. Fearing rejection, they are always worried about what is said about them and think others see their faults rather than their virtues. "3"s are easily influenced by their environment and need constant reassurance that they are attractive and desirable. When this is not forthcoming they are prone to spells of the blues.

Flirtatious and often fickle or even promiscuous, "3"s are sexually aggressive and may allow sensual desires to control common sense. Craving attention and romance, they live for today and find it hard to settle down with one person. However, in spite of their "here today, gone tomorrow" reputation, they can be adoring and forgiving mates when they have a spouse who gives them the attention and affection they desire. Once someone has captured their interest, "3"s will go all out to impress him or her. Their greatest happiness is in loving and being loved.

Living with a "3" can be like pitching tent in Grand Central Station. Charming hosts or hostesses, they love to be surrounded by their friends, and there is bound to be a constant flow of people eager to accept their hospitality. But when they are not being the life of the party, they can exhibit negative traits that make life difficult for their spouse. When "3"s feel unhappy or neglected they can be vain, extravagant, moody, petulant, jealous or temperamental. They need tolerant, demonstrative, easy-going mates who can give them emotional support and pampering.

"3"s enjoy the lighter side of life and function best when relatively free from serious responsibilities or material cares. Fun-loving, impetuous and lighthearted, they love children and enjoy handling them. They also have a flair for fashion, decorating, entertaining and languages. So great is their versatility that they are prone to scatter their energies—flitting from one thing to another without finishing what they start. Their tendency to skim the surface and overlook details may make them appear superficial and scatterbrained, and their restlessness and impatience makes them ill-suited for a job that requires strict routine. Unless they find a focus for their energies, they could end up frittering away their potential. "3"s need an outlet for their talents and a means of expressing their creativity. They need to be seen and heard!

COMPATIBILITY GUIDE

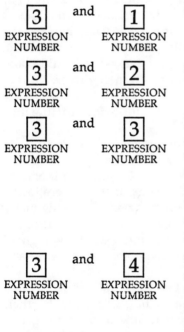

| 3 and 1 | See page 33 (chapter III). |
| EXPRESSION NUMBER | EXPRESSION NUMBER |

| 3 and 2 | See page 52 (chapter IV). |
| EXPRESSION NUMBER | EXPRESSION NUMBER |

| 3 and 3 | Expressive, fun-loving, social combination—good for friendship or creative endeavors. In a close personal relationship, however, there may be conflict as to who shoulders the responsibilities, who gets the limelight, and double standards may lead to jealousy and moodiness. |
| EXPRESSION NUMBER | EXPRESSION NUMBER |

| 3 and 4 | Conflicting interests make this a difficult combination. In a business situation, "4" could benefit from "3"'s creative ideas, but "3" may find "4" too demanding and difficult. In a close personal relationship, "3" may find "4" dull, inhibiting and confusing; "4" may find "3" frivolous, shallow and extravagant. |
| EXPRESSION NUMBER | EXPRESSION NUMBER |

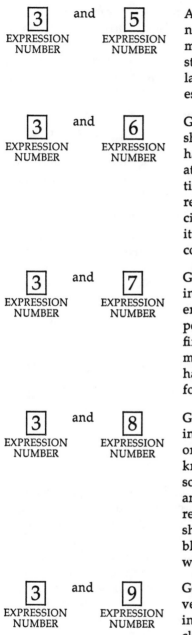

3 and **5** EXPRESSION NUMBER EXPRESSION NUMBER	Active, creative, pleasure-loving combination—good for business, friendship or marriage. There may be some lack of stability or purpose, but both enjoy similar activities and share common interests.

3 and **5**
EXPRESSION NUMBER   EXPRESSION NUMBER

Active, creative, pleasure-loving combination—good for business, friendship or marriage. There may be some lack of stability or purpose, but both enjoy similar activities and share common interests.

3 and **6**
EXPRESSION NUMBER   EXPRESSION NUMBER

Good combination for business, friendship or marriage—"6" allowing "3" to have the limelight; "3" enjoying "6"'s attentions and care. Both are social, artistic, and talented. "3" provides the relationship with color, charm and vivaciousness; "6" shoulders the responsibilities and adds harmony, stability and common sense.

3 and **7**
EXPRESSION NUMBER   EXPRESSION NUMBER

Good creative combination—"7" providing the details and "3" finding the proper means of expressing them. In a close personal relationship, however, "7" may find "3" frivolous and distracting. "3" may find "7" cold and uncaring and have trouble understanding "7"'s need for privacy.

3 and **8**
EXPRESSION NUMBER   EXPRESSION NUMBER

Good business combination—"3" adding charm, talent and color to "8"'s organizational talents and financial know-how. "8" can profit from "3"'s social contacts and enjoys pampering and showing "3" off. In a close personal relationship, however, "8" may find "3" shallow, extravagant, and undependable. "3" may find "8" too "stuffy" and wrapped up in work.

3 and **9**
EXPRESSION NUMBER   EXPRESSION NUMBER

Good creative combination—"3" adding versatility and self-expression to "9"'s inspiration and universal appeal. In a close personal relationship, however, "9" may find "3" shallow and frivolous. "3" may be jealous of "9"'s outside interests.

[3] and [11]
EXPRESSION   EXPRESSION
NUMBER   NUMBER

Good creative combination—"11" broadening "3"'s horizons; "3" interesting others in "11"'s ideas and finding appealing ways of expressing them. Both enjoy similar activities, and share common interests and talents.

[3] and [22]
EXPRESSION   EXPRESSION
NUMBER   NUMBER

Good business combination—"3" adding color, charm and creativity to "22"'s practical know-how. In a close personal relationship, however, "22" may belittle "3," finding it shallow and frivolous. "3" may find "22"'s expectations unpredictable and confusing.

Following are all possible combinations of a "3" expression number with the different motivation and inner-self numbers.

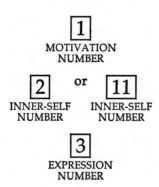

[1]
MOTIVATION
NUMBER

[2] or [11]
INNER-SELF   INNER-SELF
NUMBER   NUMBER

[3]
EXPRESSION
NUMBER

"At first she seemed quiet and demure, but now we are not quite so sure."

—*Unknown*

"1-3"s have a spirit of independence and adventure that often pays off when there are plenty of unattached people around. In fact, you are quite likely to meet this combination in a public place. Unafraid of going to parties by themselves, they are not about to lose out on a good time just because they don't have a companion to go with. A friendly smile and a facility with words helps them through those first-time meetings that many others find awkward. They are usually popular and attractive to the opposite sex, and can easily be the stranger who asks someone to pass the garlic salt at the pizza stand on Wednesday, and ends up having a date with him or her on Friday.

Charming but self-centered, personable but with a mind of their own, "1-3"s have an independent streak which makes them reluctant to commit themselves, and they can be just as happy playing the field as settling down with one person. They are attracted to partners who are articulate, who are able to put up with their willful ways, and who enjoy discussing and debating as much as they do. Impatient with people who are slower than they are, "1-3"s are nevertheless agreeable to compromise if an argument is well stated. The key to their heart is to praise and encourage their creative expression (especially if they have an "11" inner-self number), to allow them freedom to pursue their interests, and to let them have the limelight in social situations.

"1-3"s are impulsive and have a tendency to be extravagant when it comes to spending money on themselves. Their love for keeping up with the latest fashion may send them to fine boutiques where they can find one-of-a-kind items. (They would be quite upset if they arrived at a party and saw someone else wearing the same outfit.) Lectures from a more tight-fisted mate will most likely go in one ear and out the other. Subtle tactics such as, "Why don't you wait for a sale?" or, "The children need to have their teeth straightened," will be more effective than, "You don't need another pair of shoes."

At work "1-3"s can do well in any individualistic form of self-expression—writing, speaking or the arts. Their conversational ability makes them well suited for saleswork so long as they can give the pitches their own way. They have creative imaginations and the ability to inspire others but new ideas may come so fast that they don't always follow through with their projects or finish what they start. Trend-setters who are not content to stay in one place for very long, "1-3"s are happiest in professions that provide both independence and variety—a lawyer, for instance, who meets an assortment of clients, gets to travel for his or her research, and has frequent meetings out of the office; or a designer who creates a "new look" for the next season and promotes his or her fashions all over the country.

In the same way, "1-3" children need creative outlets for their pent-up energy. Their thoughts fly fast and they tend to be impulsive, willful and impatient. They may also have a nonconformist streak leading them to hang out with friends down the street a ways instead of with the gang from their own block. Or they may be insistent that certain things be done *now* or be fussy about what they wear.

"1-3" children do well in school so long as the subject maintains their interest, and parents may be bewildered to find four A's and an F on their report card. (Guess which subject "1-3" found boring.) Charming and ingenious, they are not above using both to their advantage. "1-3," for instance, is the student who not knowing the answer to that 50-point question on the surprise test at school puts his verbal skills to use and writes down the answer to *another* similar question he *is* prepared for. A teacher who is fond of him anyway may fall for it and give him full or at least partial credit for his efforts. Child or adult, "1-3"s' ability to talk themselves in and out of situations will be an asset throughout their entire lives.

2
MOTIVATION
NUMBER

1
INNER-SELF
NUMBER

3
EXPRESSION
NUMBER

"Too much of a good thing can be wonderful."
—*Mae West*

As a rule, "2-3"s like to be introduced to love prospects through friends. However, those informal chance meetings can and often do occur. If, for instance, while in the laundry room they catch the eye of someone who seems intriguing and friendly, they are not adverse to striking up a conversation on the merits of his detergent versus hers.

"2-3"s may appear outgoing and extroverted, but are really sensitive on the inside. Although they have a tendency to be flirtatious, they don't mean anything by it and would be aghast if their partner chastised them for it. Being very impressionable, they may have trouble separating their own feelings from the moods of those around them, and they often lack self-confidence. When "2-3"s feel inadequate, they are given to moodiness, depression, temper, or even withdrawal from the very company they crave.

"2-3"s are looking for special permanent relationships, and are attracted to affectionate, fun-loving, understanding partners who can give them reassurance and a strong shoulder to lean on. Sentimental at heart, they appreciate a mate who remembers birthdays and other special occasions. They enjoy being pampered and indulged, and kisses or evenings out are eagerly accepted at any time. If you really want to please a "2-3," take him or her dancing. Courtship should be romantic, and don't let the mushy stuff die out when you settle down—"2-3"s want it to last forever.

Of all the "3"s, "2-3"s are the best at listening to what others have to say—including little ones. They enjoy children and being parents. But like other domestic responsibilities, "2-3"s expect raising kids to be a joint effort, and they expect their mates to help out.

At work, "2-3"s are reliable and eager to please. They are willing to attend to routine jobs and details. They have enough creative imagination to invent clever ways of completing assignments—using shortcuts, for example, or referring to existing reports, or asking just the right person for information. But lack of confidence may prevent them from living up to their full potential unless they receive moral support and encouragement from others. "2-3"s need people around who make them feel needed and appreciated.

"2-3"s' friendliness and willingness to listen makes them the ones most likely to find out all the office gossip. Word may soon get around that "if you want to know about so-and-so's latest affair, just ask '2-3.' " They are, however, extremely sensitive about what is said about themselves, and may leave in a huff if a comment in the lunchroom was the least bit insulting or they interpreted it as such.

"2-3" children can be obedient and cooperative and can help care for younger brothers and sisters, seeing to it they are properly dressed and fed. However, parents should be aware that these children also need a lot of time to spend with their friends. Popularity is important to them and they need constant reassurance that they are liked. Being forced to stay home alone in their room would be considered the cruelest of punishments.

$\boxed{3}$
MOTIVATION
NUMBER

$\boxed{9}$
INNER-SELF
NUMBER

$\boxed{3}$
EXPRESSION
NUMBER

"Then he will talk—good gods! how he will talk!"
                                              —Nathaniel Lee

"3-3"s flirt with everyone. Sooner or later someone is bound to respond, and the more enthusiastically, the better. Entertaining and vivacious, they enjoy being surrounded by friends and can be quite the social butterflies. A wise mate soon learns to accept the fact that coquetries are as much a part of this combination's normal behavior as eating breakfast. The key to their heart is to let them feel they are the apple of your eye. They love being admired, pampered and the center of attention.

These colorful personalities place great importance on looks and can be quite vain. They enjoy ornamentation, jewelry and flamboyant clothes and may sometimes wear outrageous hairdos or too much make-up. Other attention-getting devices might be gossiping, exaggerating the truth or overacting. They crave attention and may truly believe that bad as it is to have something derogatory said about you, it is even worse not to have anything said at all. When they fail to gain the limelight, they can be moody, petulant and jealous.

"3-3"s talk a lot but may not be very good listeners. It is difficult to get a word in edgewise when conversing with them. They may say things they don't mean and hurt others without realizing it. However, their natural charm often compensates for their verbosity and their optimism and enthusiasm can be catching. They are good at cheering up a mate who is down in the dumps and can usually find a silver lining in any dark cloud.

"3-3"s live for the moment and are not prone to give much thought to the future. Being thrifty is not one of their strong points, and a mate who is saving pennies to send the kids to college may have a fit when "3-3" goes on a shopping spree. They enjoy children, but don't have time to be bothered with responsibilities. What "3-3"s need is a stable, fun-loving partner who is not too much of a stickler and who won't faint if he or she walks into the house and the place looks like a tornado just passed through. Domestic help could be an alternative solution to divorce.

At work, "3-3"s are not known for punctuality and may have trouble in a nine to five job where following strict routine is important. They seek pleasant surroundings and freedom of expression. Not too strong on practicality, they have good imaginations and an opinion or reaction to everything. They are interested in fashion and can contribute trend-setting ideas concerning what people wear and how they smell. Their facility with words makes them good critics or salesmen. Their love of an audience often draws them into the entertainment field—whether it be acting, singing, playing an instrument or dancing. And they are also well suited for working with children. They enjoy playing games with them or making dull lessons come alive, and they can be most comforting when administering first aid to a skinned knee, or fixing a broken doll.

Because "3-3" children need to be seen and heard, their mothers may sometimes wish they had a zipper on their mouths. They chatter incessantly and may even exaggerate the truth to get attention. Restless and fidgety, they find it impossible to sit still for long. They are very social and from their teens or even before, the telephone may seem like an attachment to their ears. "3-3"s want to join everything, but their interests tend to be short-lived. They need encouragement to stick to things and see projects through to their conclusion.

4
MOTIVATION
NUMBER

8
INNER-SELF
NUMBER

3
EXPRESSION
NUMBER

"True to his words, his works, his friends."
—*Unknown*

"4-3"s are solid and homeloving. Single or married, their socializing tends to center around the place where they live, and having people congregate in their home is one of their greatest satisfactions. They will automatically invite a friend's visiting cousin or old college roommate who happens to be in town to join the regulars who frequent their haunt. (What a perfect opportunity for chemistry-testing—and on home territory yet!) If you want to win this one over, expect to fold his or her family and friends into your life as well. Being critical of any one of them will surely turn him or her off. And be prepared to do a lot of entertaining should you decide to tie the knot. Tradition is important to "4-3"s and they take pride in having a tableful of expectant guests at their extravagant Christmas, Passover or Thanksgiving dinners.

Although they may appear flirtatious and unlikely to marry or settle down, "4-3"'s secret desire is for a strong, stable relationship with one person. Feeling secure and loved is essential to their well-being, and in spite of their happy-go-lucky appearance, they can be possessive and jealous. They expect to get their way, and will try to dominate a relationship if their partner allows it.

At work, as in their private lives, "4-3"s want structure, security and recognition for their efforts. Organized, responsible, and practical, they are unlikely to choose a creative or artistic career. Predictability and a regular paycheck are important. However, they are likely to incorporate beauty and decoration into their work in other ways. They may, for example, be an importer-exporter who deals in pretty jewelry boxes and elegant silk shirts; or a carpenter who carves ornate doors and delicate chairs; or an office manager who decorates the office with plants and flowers. And no matter what their chosen field, they are likely to be well spoken and smartly dressed.

"4-3" children can be quite stubborn about what they wear and what activities they simply *must* join. They want to be important in any group or team they belong to, and although they are usually social and friendly, they can also be selfish and reluctant to share when they don't get their way.

Like their adult counterparts, "4-3" children have a facility with words—whether it be public-speaking, writing or mastering a foreign language. They also enjoy crafts such as woodworking or sewing, and can patiently work for hours on a project that interests them, such as a decorative birdhouse for the garden or an embroidered pillowcase.

5
MOTIVATION
NUMBER

7
INNER-SELF
NUMBER

"Distracted from distraction by distraction."
                                        —Unknown

3
EXPRESSION
NUMBER

Until they find their one true love, "5-3"s may be fickle and flit from affair to affair. Easily bored, they have a lot of nervous energy and want to be on the go all the time. Their sense of adventure makes them seek out active, fun-loving people who offer opportunities to visit new places and try new things and they are not opposed to having blind dates, or even to answering an intriguing add in a singles' newspaper column. But in order for them to further the relationship, their partner must be physically appealing as well as interesting. Though a "5-3" may announce to friends that looks aren't important, they would wait a long time before finding him or her involved with someone unattractive. If you have captured this one's eye and would like to keep the flame going, make sure you have something novel to add to the relationship just often enough to keep it from getting stale. Don't put all your cards on the table—a little guessing and something new to discover about you will keep their attention where you want it. And don't, above all, show any signs of being jealous or possessive as this will surely turn them off. If they don't call as often as you might like them to, just keep in mind that it does not necessarily mean they have lost interest. They could just be busy with something else.

"5-3"s can be swayed by flattery and presents. They love to be admired for their looks as well as their brains and they enjoy jewelry, fine clothes, perfumes—things that are sensual and romantic. Optimistic at heart, they prefer looking at the light side of life rather than dwelling on anything depressing or heavy. Since they don't always take things seriously, they may unintentionally distort facts, say things they don't really mean, or betray a confidence—making them appear insensitive to other people's feelings. Yet they would not intentionally hurt someone and would be shocked to hear that they had.

Impulsive and quick to express their emotions, "5-3"s can get carried away by their overactive imaginations. Although generous and usually open-minded, their spit-fire temper can as easily express jealousy and possessiveness. They enjoy children but don't like to feel tied down by responsibilities. They are also artistically inclined, have good taste, and like beautiful surroundings, but may have difficulty finding time to make their home look as neat and organized as they would like it to be. "5-3"s are happiest with easygoing mates who do not get upset by an occasional handkerchief dropped on the floor, or a pile of unread magazines stacked high on the coffee table.

At work as in their private lives, "5-3"s thrive on variety and change. Attractive surroundings are important and they want to decorate their little corner to suit their tastes. They work well with other people, make friends easily, and have a talent for finding ingenious solutions to things. Good at promotion and asking the right questions, they do well in fields such as market research, public relations, or census-taking. Or, combining their love of travel with their sociability, they can be excellent tour guides. "5-3"s also find working with children satisfying— especially if they are bright and creative and constantly coming up with the darndest things.

"5-3" children are easy to keep content so long as there is *something* to do. They have a flair for drama and love role-playing. Ingenious at inventing fun pastimes they might play house in the living room by turning over chairs and topping them with a sheet; or ride their tricycle "cross country" assigning each area of the yard to a different state; or they may just enjoy helping Mother in the kitchen. Whatever their present activity, however, they are unlikely to continue doing it for very long. Their attention span is short and they need encouragement to follow through on projects they start.

"5-3" children are not afraid to try new things, and if Father puts mustard on his eggs, they will too. Anxious to imitate adults in speech as well, this combination is likely to pick up words and expressions that bewilder parents and make them think twice before saying certain things in front of him or her.

6
MOTIVATION
NUMBER

6
INNER-SELF
NUMBER

3
EXPRESSION
NUMBER

"What I loathe is not being taken seriously."
—*Rona Jaffe*

"6-3"s may appear restless or flirtatious, but family and close relationships are the most important concerns in their life. They seek domestic harmony and enjoy children. Once you get to know them well you will find they are much more dependable than you at first suspected. You can be as assured they'll be there to escort you to your company picnic or your friend's wedding, as you can count on them to take their shirts to Mother's on laundry day. Charming and outgoing, they enjoy parties and social events and like being the center of attention. They can be quite vain about their own appearance, and, feeling that their partner is a reflection on them, do not like to keep company with someone who is sloppy or unkempt. Drawn to members of the opposite sex who are open, interesting and good-looking as well, they are turned off by behavior that seems gross or vulgar in any way. Eventually "6-3"s want to settle down to a home and family, so if you have captured their interest and would like to fan the flames, let them know you too are domestically inclined and willing to dedicate yourself to their needs.

Friendly and communicative, "6-3"s are intent on explaining or teaching things to whoever cares to listen. They want to be involved with others and may be active in community affairs. (Keep in mind that being involved in them yourself is a good way to meet one.) "6-3" can well be the chairman of the volunteer committee to paint the firehouse, who ends up dating the person who organized the bake sale which supplied the money to buy the paint. Romantic and idealistic, they fall in love easily, but may expect too much of a relationship. Although they themselves dislike being criticized or told what to do, they can be quick to find fault and to give unwanted advice. They may mean well, but recipients of their theories about the correct way to behave may not appreciate their opinions.

"6-3"s want their home to look nice, and whether it be cozy or elaborately decorated, they want everything to be "just so" when company arrives. Perfect hosts and hostesses, they enjoy entertaining but may be upset by unexpected guests if they feel anything is out of order when they appear. Parental toward spouse as well as children, they may frequently be heard to admonish, "Don't forget to put on your gloves," or, "Don't go out without your hat."

At work, "6-3"s do best on a one-to-one basis, whether it be teaching voice lessons, showing someone how to make bread, or interviewing a celebrity on a talk show. They like to combine creative expression with responsibility and service to others and are the most likely "3" to end up teaching. Communication skills are among their talents and they love to give advice. Money is not the prime motivating force behind their career aims. They are more likely to be found in a job because they want to be there than in one that they hate but is high paying. "6-3"s do not have the temperament for banking or accounting or high pressure executive management. They have little patience with company politics and red tape, and are uncomfortable with cutthroat business competition.

In the same way, "6-3" children are talented and artistic. They enjoy creative activities such as drawing, making dolls' clothes or scenery for the school play, decorating the auditorium for the sock hop, acting or singing. They expect, and usually get, a lot of attention. Charming and talkative, they can put on a good act to get what they want. They are the children who tell Mother how pretty she looks because they know it will put her into a more agreeable mood when they ask for some cookies later on. They can also be meddlesome and nosy wanting to know everybody's business. "6-3"s can be the walking gazettes of their class with an opinion on everything. When other children ask them for advice (and even when they don't) "6-3"s always know what is right for them.

7
MOTIVATION
NUMBER

5
INNER-SELF
NUMBER

3
EXPRESSION
NUMBER

"How is it that I always behave quite differently from what I should in other people's company?"
—Anne Frank

Although they may appear talkative and social, "7-3"s are selective about who they associate with and shy away from average, mediocre people. They look for some kind of unique distinction and may collect quite a miscellaneous bag of friends. A likely place to find this combination is in a group that specializes in some art—the Folklore Society, for instance, or the camera club, or an opera group. They are especially attracted to people who have a talent they themselves wish they had but don't. They want a partner they can admire for his or her looks and manners as well as for some ability or skill. Don't be too intimate on your first date—appearances to the contrary, "7-3"s need time to warm up to someone and they don't like to feel rushed. Anything gross or in bad taste will surely turn them off.

Once you have captured "7-3" 's interest, expect them to get in touch with you regularly and soon. If they are erratic or make frequent excuses for getting out of dates, chances are they are trying to give you an indirect message rather than come right out and tell you they don't want to see you anymore. If you have a steady relationship going with a "7-3," expect him or her to be faithful to you even though they may still appear to enjoy the attentions of the opposite sex. You would be wise to realize that their flirtations are nothing to lose sleep about and leave it at that.

"7-3"s have a conflict between what they want and what they do. They want to spend time alone to follow intellectual pursuits but at the same time they have a strong need for self-expression—be it through writing, storytelling, nagging or conversing. They may sometimes resent the situations they get themselves into—for instance, impulsively agreeing to go to a party, then later regretting it and wishing they were home with a good book instead. Yet they can be moody and miserable if there is no one special to talk to.

Once the knot has been tied, a spouse may be surprised to find out how much privacy "7-3"s need. Social and charming with others, at home they may lock themselves in the den for hours reading, or if no other room is available for complete privacy, they may indulge in forty-five-minute showers or two-hour baths just to savor the moments of solitude. And that's not all that may come as a surprise! Although "7-3"s can be loyal and devoted, their mate may be taken aback by their unanticipated bursts of criticism or impatience. Good at hiding their true feelings, "7-3"s may seem charming and content on the outside, but feel restless and depressed on the inside. There is usually something more profound behind petty arguments than what meets the eye, and establishing good channels of communication is very important for the well-being of the relationship.

"7-3"s are avid pursuers of knowledge but may find it difficult to specialize in one field owing to their many and varied interests. Their tendency to scatter their energy can be frustrating to them since they would like to excel in some area, and they are often discontent at not being able to live up to the goals they set for themselves.

At work, "7-3"s are good at synthesizing or analyzing—putting parts together to form a whole, or picking things apart to find out what makes them tick. They are also good at writing or criticizing. Efficient office workers, they can do well in bookkeeping, data-processing, or middle management. Often "7-3"s have a facility for languages, but being such perfectionists they may hesitate to use them professionally unless they are fluent.

Sometimes outgoing, sometimes reserved, "7-3" children may be hard to understand. They can be happy-go-lucky one moment and full of tears the next. Those close may be perplexed as to why they are so reluctant to share their feelings or talk about what's on their minds. Although their actions may deny it, these children need privacy and are often quite frustrated when parents or siblings butt into their business.

"7-3" children, just like their grown-up counterparts, gravitate toward intelligent people who are "different" in some way. Others may ridicule the class brain for being funny-looking, but "7-3" likes his or her personality, admires his or her unique science project, and hopes to have him or her for a friend. They would like to do well in school, but may have a tendency to get lost in their own fantasies when studying a subject that doesn't interest them. However, they can be hard workers, reliable and true to their word, and with strong motivation, some self-discipline, and the right contacts, these little people can excel.

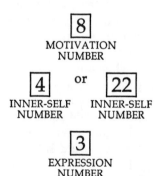

8
MOTIVATION
NUMBER

4   or   22
INNER-SELF   INNER-SELF
NUMBER   NUMBER

"When I say something, I mean it."
—Unknown

3
EXPRESSION
NUMBER

"8-3"s may appear considerate and charming but they can also be critical and demanding (especially if their inner-self number is a 22). You may, for instance, be a bit taken aback when after a carefree, nonchalant date, they make a crack about the hair you left in their bathroom sink when you went in to freshen up. Although they can be eloquent and adept at using persuasion and flattery to manipulate and control others, they are not necessarily tactful with a partner who has fallen out of favor. Wanting to be in control of their affairs and to have the last word, they prefer being the one to break up a floundering relationship themselves rather than the other way around. They are more likely to bluntly state, "Things just don't seem to be working out between us and I think it would be better if we stopped seeing each other for a while," than to resort to more devious means in order to spare a partner's feelings.

"8-3"s can be loyal, devoted lovers, but when it comes to picking a mate, love alone is not enough. Always aware of the effect they create, they want someone who can enhance their station in life. They admire people who are powerful, influential and efficient. Both appearance and prestige are important, and they will seek a partner who is stable, dependable, and a credit to them. Since they consider their mate a reflection of themselves, they expect him or her to look and act digni- fied when they go out together and to avoid extremes of dress or behavior.

Of all the "3"s, "8-3"s are the most organized. They run an efficient household and are adept at arranging everything from the kids' lunches to the carpool. They take pride in having a beautiful home, and will pay special attention to getting fine furniture, attractive drapes and colorful wall decorations—financial conditions permitting. Their home is their castle and they enjoy entertaining friends with elaborate dinner parties. (If there are guests present who can help them climb the social ladder, so much the better.) They may not always show the affection they feel, and loved ones may at times think they are being taken for granted and tire of being dictated to. But "8-3"s can be warm and responsive to a patient, understanding, appreciative mate who provides emotional sup- port and encourages their ambitions.

At work, "8-3"s can be efficient and far-sighted. They are unlikely to be tripped up by details because they're good at delegating to others what they don't want to do themselves. They have creative talents, but may not always develop them since they are more interested in security. They would prefer to have an establishment job that gives them a paycheck every week than an art studio where they would have to depend on irregular sales for making a living. If they can combine something creative with a steady profession, fine. Otherwise, it will probably never get past the hobby stage.

"8-3" children like to feel important and can be quite bossy. Just like "8-3" adults, they hate to lose an argument and can become petulant and moody when they don't get their way. Their egos, although big, are also sensitive. They want to be successful in everything they try and a parent or teacher who criticizes their mistakes without praising their achievements may cause them to lapse into moods of depression. On the other hand, if they're spoiled and always allowed to have their own way, they can be quite obnoxious.

At times "8-3"s have good intentions of being orderly and getting their work done only to have their minds wander on to something else. They may, for instance, be in the middle of making their beds or picking up their toys, when suddenly, distracted by their dog's barking, they run out to play with him. If a parent questions their still-untidy room, "8-3" might be genuinely surprised that he or she never finished it.

Once a little discipline is learned, "8-3"s usually do well in school. They also enjoy being class leaders, and good at organizing and chairing committees, they will probably be active in school politics, newspaper or yearbook staff.

|9|

MOTIVATION
NUMBER

|3|

INNER-SELF
NUMBER

"I am most fond of talking and thinking, that is to say, talking first and thinking afterward."
—*Osbert Sitwell*

|3|

EXPRESSION
NUMBER

Fun-loving "9-3"s can be found any place where people congregate to have a good time—parties, roller rinks , discos, or even at a friend's. They can talk incessantly, and a relationship with someone who is not a good listener is bound to start off on the wrong foot. They enjoy interesting friends from different backgrounds, and are attracted to people who are exuberant, adventuresome, witty and broad-minded. They don't like to feel stifled or restricted in any way, and anyone rigid, bigoted, possessive or humorless will surely turn them off. Very clothes conscious, they always want to look their best, and would prefer that their partner be attractive as well.

Kindhearted and generous, "9-3"s can also be flighty, emotional and dramatic. Their theatrics, however, may be more show than substance. They just plain love to be in the limelight and are prone to moodiness and fits of temper when they're not. Single or married, outside interests are important to them, and they are not likely to sit home by the fireplace every night. They have extravagant natures, love spending money, and enjoy traveling, being wined and dined, and romantic courtships. Flattery, admiration, and being showered with attention are the keys to their heart, and if you want to keep the flame glowing, don't be critical or expect them to cater to your every whim. "9-3"s don't like having faults pointed out to them and they want to have center stage themselves.

Although they may be fickle and have a hard time fixing their emotions on just one person, "9-3"s can be quite jealous and possessive when the shoe is on the other foot. They hate to admit to a mistake, and are good at turning things around and putting the challenger on the defensive. They will talk their way out of a situation rather than admit they are wrong.

At work as in their private lives, "9-3"s may lack discipline and have trouble settling down. Their restless, talkative natures can create problems in situations where silence or long periods of utmost concentration are expected. Flexible hours and an exciting atmosphere are preferable to the drudgery of a dull routine job, and they are happiest when they can put their persuasive and dramatic talents to use—onstage, on the telephone, or out in the field.

Creative and imaginative, "9-3"s are good at seeing the overall picture but have a tendency to overlook the details. Clever at making things sound good, they are easily tripped up by some little thing they didn't consider. They may, for instance, brag about their firm's net profit having doubled since last year, but neglect to mention anything about the biggest competitor going out of business.

"9-3" children are restless and impulsive, with a tendency to start many different projects, then lose interest in them. Imaginative and expressive, they have so much to say it may spill over into writing or keeping a diary. They need help channeling their energies constructively and should be encouraged to develop their creative talents through art, music or drama.

Even at an early age, "9-3" children are fashion-conscious and fussy about their appearance. They may, for instance, experiment with make-up at home long before they are allowed to wear it in public, or insist on styling their hair with a blower before going off to school in the morning. However, "9-3"s are also careless about taking good care of their possessions. They are the youngsters who inadvertently step on a favorite toy or piece of jewelry, or who always manage to misplace building blocks, puzzle pieces, and clothes.

11

MOTIVATION
NUMBER

1

INNER-SELF
NUMBER

3

EXPRESSION
NUMBER

"Appearances often are deceiving."

—Aesop

"11-3"s have lofty ideals, and although they may seem friendly to all, they prefer the company of people who share their views on life. You are more likely to meet this combination at a church, or at a group-encounter meeting, or in line at the Small World exhibit at Disneyland, than at a singles' dance or in a bar. They are unlikely to make the first overture themselves, but are quick to respond if they find the other person interesting.

Sensitive and impressionable, "11-3"s tend to be influenced by the moods of those close to them. However, they may camouflage their emotional vulnerability by appearing social and entertaining. It can sometimes be very hard to know just where you stand with them because they have so much trouble saying "no." They want to be liked and are reluctant to refuse anyone a favor outright. They are more likely to say "yes" and then later make an elaborate but convincing excuse to get out of it.

Charming and romantic, "11-3"s can be quite flirtatious, but are easily hurt and prone to jealousy when the shoe is on the other foot. They have a tendency to be unrealistic and to make extravagant demands—emotionally as well as financially. Needing to feel loved and appreciated, they are happiest with a warm, dependable, attentive mate who can offer reassurance and encouragement when necessary, and who does not mind being parental at times. Loath to making decisions on their own, "11-3"s are apt to call their spouse out of an important business meeting to report that the kitchen sink has developed a leak, or to awaken them out of a sound sleep to ask what to do for their stubbed toe.

Little things are important to "11-3"s. Talented and imaginative, they enjoy putting a personal touch on whatever they do—a fancy bow on a present, for instance, or an "I love you" message on a valentine cake. They have a special way with children (their own or others') and can often be found telling them stories, comforting them, or helping them with projects.

"11-3"s are inspired and creative. They like recognition for their ideas and at work, as in their private lives, they prefer doing something they feel is artistic or of some benefit to others. They have a flair for decorating, which can extend anywhere from doing a whole house to organizing closets, and they often start something creative as a hobby (quilting or making jewelry, for example), only to have it turn into a business later on.

Also read the description for "2-3," which starts on page 76. "11" is such a high vibration that it is impossible to operate on it all the time. Children act like its lower octave—"2"—most of the time, and adults operate on the "2" at least part of the time.

22
MOTIVATION
NUMBER

8
INNER-SELF
NUMBER

3
EXPRESSION
NUMBER

"I would rather write a perfect system of ethics than practice an everyday one."
—*Dr. Patton*

"22-3"s have a restless nature and a need to express themselves freely. Having a satisfying career is as important to them as a happy homelife, and you are more likely to meet this combination at work or through a friend.

Although charming and outgoing, "22-3"s have trouble accepting people for what they are and can be critical and demanding with those close. Unrealistic in their expectations, they are prone to seek the impossible in a partner—someone who is not only gorgeous and rich, but powerful, brilliant, generous, well spoken, and a fantastic lover to boot. Needless to say, they are easily disappointed. When they do meet someone who captures their attention, they may give him or her a whirlwind courtship but will resent any attempts to pin them down. "22-3"s want to be in control of their relationships and make all the decisions themselves. The key to their heart is to be admiring, appreciative, and to let them have center stage.

Appearances to the contrary, "22-3"s can be faithful and devoted once they meet someone who fulfills their needs. Although they may appear flirtatious, they prefer emotional security and their earthy, romantic natures will prevent them from straying far from the loving arms of a loyal, attentive mate. Lively, open conversations are important to them and they enjoy a friendly battle of wits every now and then to keep them on their toes. And even after they've settled down, a candlelit dinner or an occasional small gift for no special reason wouldn't hurt either.

At work, "22-3"s are not satisfied with an ordinary job. They want to reach multitudes of people and would like power and efficiency at the highest possible level. Their expectations are high, but they have a tendency to get sidetracked. Frustration results when they disappoint themselves and they may take it out on those close by being moody and temperamental. "22-3"s often pursue music, art or theater as careers, and if they do not sing, act or play an instrument themselves, they may write about others who do, or become involved in the business end of putting on a concert or theater production.

Also read the description for "4-3" which starts on page 79. "22" is such a high vibration that it is impossible to operate on it all the time. Children act like its lower octave—"4"—most of the time, and adults operate on the "4" at least part of the time.

VI
Practicality and Perseverance: The Number 4

"4"s are practical, hard-working and dependable, and can be counted on to see a job through to the bitter end. They are also serious and exacting, and their desire to be in control of what they are doing may make them appear stubborn, "slow" or rigid. Needing some sense of security and permanence, they are set in their ways and can be confused by sudden changes or demands. They do not like to be rushed into things, yet they themselves can be impatient and intolerant. Determined and efficient, they love order and precision and are extremely reliable. Demanding of themselves, they expect others to have the same sense of self-discipline they do, and are not above belittling or criticizing those who fail to live up to their expectations. They themselves, however, are extremely sensitive to criticism. Finding it as difficult to accept error in themselves as to tolerate it in others, they are easily put on the defensive.

"4"s usually have nimble hands. They enjoy nature and find satisfaction building things, dealing with real estate, buying and selling. Down to earth, they are usually fair in their relationships, but may sometimes be blunt, outspoken or even cruel. Earthy and homeloving, "4"s are most comfortable among friends who are their equals both culturally and educationally. When choosing a partner, they seek someone whose background is similar to their own and who is acceptable to their family. Loyal and faithful, they take good care of those close to them. "4"s never turn their back on family or friends and will help them out of any problems—no matter how great. On the other hand, they are intolerant of what they perceive to be dishonesty or deceit in others, and may build up resentment, harbor grudges, or even seek revenge if they feel that they or a loved one has been wronged.

"4"s want to be liked and respected. They feel deeply, and although love is important to their well-being, they have trouble responding. They find it difficult to express themselves and their tendency to conceal their true feelings makes them clumsy about handling touchy situations. They may repel signs of affection directed toward them by unwittingly throwing cold water on them—perhaps making a joke, or seeming to ignore a gesture (when in reality they just don't know how to respond appropriately).

"4" s' domestic life can be rigid and restricted. They have strong opinions on what is right and what is wrong and are prone to set down rules of conduct by which they expect everyone to abide. They may be jealous, possessive, critical and demanding, but despite their tough outward appearance, they are basically insecure. They are prone to develop bad self-images, which may result in bitterness or depression. Being contradicted undermines their self-confidence and can make them defensive, argumentative or even ill-tempered. They appear to be stern parents, impatient with foolishness, but underneath it all they are proud of their children (especially when they do well or are a credit to them).

"4"s are happiest with warm, dependable, practical mates who conform to their ideals while gently introducing some color and variety into their lives. Neatness is an added plus since "4" 's cannot stand clutter or chaotic surroundings. Slow and deliberate, they need time to mull things over. Fixed in their likes and dislikes, they are not too big on experimenting with anything unfamiliar. Patience and a sense of humor on the part of an understanding partner can do wonders toward getting them to try something new . . . and they may even end up enjoying it. When "4"s feel loved and needed, those they care for will usually get their way.

COMPATIBILITY GUIDE

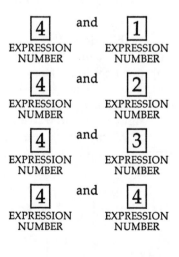

4 and 1		See page 33 (chapter III).
EXPRESSION NUMBER	EXPRESSION NUMBER	
4 and 2		See page 53 (chapter IV).
EXPRESSION NUMBER	EXPRESSION NUMBER	
4 and 3		See page 72 (chapter V).
EXPRESSION NUMBER	EXPRESSION NUMBER	
4 and 4		Hard-working combination—good for business, friendship or marriage. They may get stuck in a rut, but each will be loyal and responsible to the other and they will satisfy each other's need for security.
EXPRESSION NUMBER	EXPRESSION NUMBER	

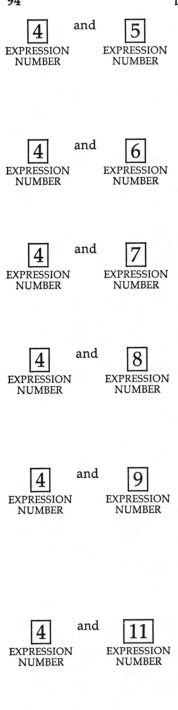

Poor combination creating constant clash and conflict. In a close personal relationship, "4" may find "5" flighty, undependable and irritating; "5" may find "4" rigid, boring, and possessive, and resent "4"'s attempts to curtail "5"'s freedom.

Good combination for business, marriage or friendship—"4" providing stability; "6" doing the nurturing. Both are homeloving, conservative, responsible, and have much to gain from the association.

Good creative combination combining "4"'s concern for perfected method on the physical plane with "7"'s on the mental. "4" can put "7"'s ideas into practice. "7" appreciates "4"'s practicality.

Good friendship, marriage or business combination with great potential for material success—"4" providing practicality and discipline; "8" adding good judgment and executive ability. Both have common interests and enjoy similar activities.

Good business combination—"9" providing inspiration; "4" being the stabilizer and giving practical foundation to "9"'s artistic and humanitarian goals. In a close personal relationship, however, "9" may find "4" rigid, cold, and restricting. "4" may find "9" impractical, emotional and extravagant and be jealous of its outside interests.

Good business combination—"11" broadening "4"'s horizons; "4" adding stability and practicality to "11"'s ideas. In a close personal relationship, however, "4" may find "11" too much of a dreamer. "11" may find "4" dull and restricting.

4	and	22
EXPRESSION NUMBER		EXPRESSION NUMBER

Good business combination—"22" adding scope, "4" backing it up. "22" appreciates "4"'s practicality and diligence but may find it restricting and limited in a close personal relationship.

Following are all possible combinations of a "4" expression number with the different motivation and inner-self numbers.

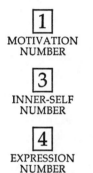

1
MOTIVATION NUMBER

3
INNER-SELF NUMBER

"Last night I thought over a thousand plans, but this morning I went my old way."

—*Chinese proverb*

4
EXPRESSION NUMBER

"1-4"s may seem social and outgoing and willing to strike up a friendship with the customer who comes into their restaurant for breakfast every Sunday, or the stranger who helps them up from an embarrassing flop on the ice-skating rink, but this first impression can be deceiving. There is conflict between what they want and what they do, and appearances to the contrary, they may be full of inner turmoil. In spite of a desire to be daring and adventuresome, something seems to hold them back even when a relationship seems tempting. Don't be surprised if despite their friendliness and willingness to engage in long conversations on the phone, it takes a long time before they are comfortable enough to go out on a date. Some outlet such as tennis, jogging, or playing an instrument could do wonders in relieving some of their tension before it vents itself in a sudden and unexpected outburst of temper.

"1-4"s respond to patience and understanding, and do not like to feel pressured or rushed into anything. They themselves, however, can be rigid and demanding in their expectations of others. They do not take "no" for an answer, and once they have their heart set on someone or something, they will pursue it relentlessly without letting anyone or anything stand in their way. They like to feel respected and admired, and never want to be wrong. If caught in an error, it is not uncommon for this combination to try to make excuses or put the blame on someone else. Although they may not be aware of it, "1-4"s can be intolerant, possessive and jealous in their love relationships. They expect absolute loyalty, but may not always reciprocate. Not that they would actually be unfaithful, but they need freedom to pursue outside interests and will resist any attempt to restrict their pioneering, independent spirit.

At work, ambitious, hard-working "1-4"s prefer being their own boss. They do not appreciate being ordered around or told what to do, although they themselves may be exacting and demanding of those who work for them. They can be well organized, disciplined, and willing to put in long hours if they believe in the cause. However, they would rebel if they thought the work petty, unnecessary, or someone else's job.

"1-4"s are happiest in some area where they can plan or organize and at the same time be creative. However, since they can do dull routine jobs so well, they may easily get stuck in one unless they speak up and pursue something else.

"1-4" children are independent and willful. They may amaze parents when they work so hard in one area but are so difficult to discipline in others. These are the children who practice the piano for three hours a day, for instance, so they can win the audition and receive acclaim from their teachers and peers, but who forget to pick up their toys and make up excuses for why they shouldn't have to walk the dog. They want recognition for some talent or achievement and will work hard to get it, but will avoid putting energy into something they consider boring or mundane. However, they will respond to the logic that toil has its rewards. For example, hoeing, weeding and watering a garden will produce beautiful flowers or vegetables; studying diligently can result in a good report card; and helping Grandma and Grandpa with marketing or housework can make you feel good because you did something nice for someone and your efforts are so greatly appreciated.

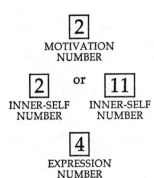

| 2 |
| MOTIVATION NUMBER |

| 2 | or | 11 |
| INNER-SELF NUMBER | | INNER-SELF NUMBER |

"I wish there was windows to my soul, so that you could see some of my feelings."
                                                        —Artemus Ward

| 4 |
| EXPRESSION NUMBER |

"2-4"s prefer meeting people in places where they feel secure and comfortable—at work, at an adult-education class, or through friends, for example—rather than at parties or dances where they must be more outgoing and perhaps risk rejection. They are unlikely to agree to a blind date without much coaxing, or respond to a wink from the driver of the car next to theirs while stopped for a red light. "2-4"s are more inclined to date someone who has been around on a regular basis for a while, and who they have had a chance to get to know beforehand.

Gentle and peace-loving, "2-4"s may seem calm, stable and confident, but don't let appearances fool you! Although they may have endearing personalities and seem to instinctively know how to deal with people, especially if their inner-self number is an "11," they are deeply sensitive and often sorely lacking in confidence as well. Wanting to be loved and appreciated, they go to great lengths to please and can lapse into periods of depression over little things. A minor slight, for instance, can be interpreted as a rejection and give rise to feelings of inferiority and inadequacy. Hurt feelings and frustrations may be festering behind their charm, unless a partner is wise enough to realize that what may seem petty or insignificant to him or her may be very important to "2-4"s.

Not too good at expressing their true emotions, "2-4"s appreciate someone who is warm, patient, supportive and understanding. They seek love, reassurance and the security of a place to call home. They want a strong shoulder to lean on and a partner who is willing to make the important decisions. In return, "2-4"s can be loyal, helpful and willing to compromise. They are inclined to make many sacrifices to keep domestic peace.

Methodical, precise and systematic, "2-4"s have common sense and the ability to build firm foundations in whatever area is dear to them— be it marriage, friendship or business. They are good at coming up with practical solutions to problems and they function well in routine or detail-oriented jobs. Loyal and reliable, they are not ones to job hop at the drop of a hat. If they like the people they work with and their position gives them a sense of accomplishment, it would take more than a few dollars to convince them to switch companies.

"2-4"s are very security conscious and tend to be drawn more to conservative, establishment-oriented fields than the creative avant-garde areas where competition is more cutthroat and the atmosphere is fast-paced and changing all the time. Self-discipline is one of their strongest assets and they work well on a team. They have no desire to be boss, but expect to be a valued participant in the overall structure.

"2-4" children, like their adult counterparts, can absorb knowledge almost effortlessly, and once something is learned, they do not forget it. The same holds true in their personal life. "2-4"s remember things other family members have long-forgotten. Real or imagined wrongs may be carried around and allowed to fester beneath the surface for years.

"2-4" children like building things that involve small pieces—a five-thousand-piece puzzle, for instance, rather than a one-hundred-piece one, or a house made of tiny Lego building bricks rather than one made of large building blocks. Lovers of nature, they enjoy digging for worms, planting seeds, or catching the biggest bullfrog in the stream. Bits of rope or broken wire that they might be able to use on a future project just can't be passed by. Collectable items such as matchbox cars, pencil stubs, rocks, or leaves are also appealing, and parents may be quite surprised at the things they find in their "2-4" 's possession.

3
MOTIVATION
NUMBER

1
INNER-SELF
NUMBER

"Enthusiasm finds the opportunities, and energy makes the most of them."
— *Anonymous*

4
EXPRESSION
NUMBER

Restless and curious, "3-4"s want to know and be included in everything that's going on. You are more likely to meet them at a convention or a party than walking alone in the park. With an opinion on everything and a need to express themselves, they like to be where the action is. They seek the company of beautiful people who are also active, talented, creative and outspoken. But looks are what they notice first, and they can easily form a relationship with the wrong kind of person, based on a few good times and the satisfaction of being seen with someone attractive and popular.

"3-4"s are not always easy to understand. They may call faithfully for a month or two and then suddenly stop for no apparent reason. When you call them, they seem to be always busy. Chances are it's nothing you did or didn't do, it's just that they have a need to break their routine once in a while. When they're ready, they'll be back, but they don't make commitments easily. They can be affectionate and jovial one moment, critical and temperamental the next. Their moods can swing from optimism and elation to depression and dejection. When they bottle-up their feelings they become prone to bodily ailments such as nervous stomach, rashes or headaches. Their partner may be perplexed as to whether he or she should get them to discuss their problems (and explain their peculiar behavior) or just leave them alone. Since "3-4"s love attention, the former solution is usually best so long as the dialogue doesn't start out sounding like the "third degree."

Creative and spontaneous, "3-4"s are good with children and make conscientious parents once they settle down. Domestic talents can appear when least expected. They have a practical, realistic side to their nature, and can be counted on to react quickly and appropriately when necessary.

"3-4"s seek variety in their work and interesting social surroundings. Frustrated artists at heart, they would like to be aesthetic, but usually end up doing something practical and useful instead. However, they are good at adding imagination to the task at hand, and are the least likely "4" to get caught in a rut. Self-expression is important to their well-being, and if they get stuck in a dull routine job they may be prone to ulcers (and other nervous disorders) unless they can make up for it by being socially or politically active on the side.

Reliable and versatile, "3-4" can be the chauffeur, for instance, who not only fixes the boss's car but his or her household appliances as well, and can even be counted on to occasionally help entertain the guests. Although conscientious about their work, they do expect some kind of compensation for their efforts, and some recognition and appreciation as well.

If you are the parent of a "3-4" child, you should bear in mind that even when he or she is a good student, the tendency is to hate school because it's a place where you *must* excel and where you are constantly being judged. These youngsters may even develop real or feigned illnesses such as stomach upsets in order to have an excuse to stay home. Other things seem so much more important and interesting than disciplined study—playing Cowboys and Indians, for example, or meeting a special friend at the movies, or rearranging their tin soldiers, or playing with their favorite truck (the one that makes the loud noise).

Like their adult counterparts, "3-4" children are social and outgoing but can be stubborn and argumentative when they feel insecure. They thrive on praise and need constant reassurance that they are loved and appreciated. From an early age, they are conscious of how they look and what they wear, and a "3-4" who has been taught that beauty is in the eye of the beholder and then is told he or she's adorable, may run proudly home to Mother proclaiming, "I have a beholder."

MOTIVATION
NUMBER

INNER-SELF
NUMBER

"Better three hours too soon than a minute too late."

—*Shakespeare*

EXPRESSION
NUMBER

Dependable, family-oriented "4-4"s may sow wild oats when young, but always have it in the back of their mind that they will settle down someday with their one true love. Hesitant to try anything unfamiliar, they are most likely to meet a partner through work or at a family get-together. They prefer the company of people who have similar backgrounds to their own, and can be quite rigid and prejudiced in their human relations. They seek security and a down-to-earth, conventional relationship with a warm, stable, dependable mate. Once they are attracted to someone they will expect to see them on a steady basis and will pursue them relentlessly. Their calls may be so regular that you can set a clock by them, and if they say they'll be there to pick you up at 8 P.M., rest assured they'll be there on the dot. Of course they'll expect you to be punctual too! If you want peace in the relationship, don't keep your "4-4" waiting!

Courtship with "4-4" may be more steadfast than exciting. Having a tendency to frequent familiar haunts, they may balk at the idea of trying a new place. Not ones to take chances or invite change, they can get stuck in a rut and be limited in their viewpoints. Their inability to relax and just enjoy themselves may make them seem somewhat dull and boring to a more adventuresome partner. But on the positive side, they will always be there when you need them. They are loyal, responsible and willing to work hard for that which they believe in. Family and community come first, and they can be counted on in any emergency to be a tower of strength for others to lean on.

"4-4"s want to be loved but have trouble expressing themselves or showing affection. They have a tendency to measure things in dollars and cents and to disregard the emotional and spiritual side of life. Consequently, they don't know how to respond appropriately and may unwittingly repel the very overtures they so desire. Sticklers for order, they can be demanding and critical and may, for instance, seem more concerned about the dust on the coffee table than their partner's broken heart. Under their calm and capable exterior, they may be smoldering with suppressed anger and frustration and they need an outlet such as boxing, sculpting, gardening or playing an instrument to help vent their pent-up feelings before they reach the boiling point and someone gets hurt.

At work, "4-4"s are happiest in a field that involves order, routine and a predictable future. Hard-working and determined, they are not bothered by difficulties or setbacks and their endurance and self-discipline enable them to see a job through to the end. They enjoy doing physical or practical things that result in a tangible, finished product—designing a bridge or making furniture, for example.

"4-4"s have a fascination with how things work. Anything mechanical is up their alley and they can do wonders with a hammer, screwdriver and saw. They also have a talent for working with figures, dealing with real estate, managing a small business, or even being involved in a community service. Whatever their field of endeavor, however, prestige and recognition are important to them and they may build up resentment if someone else gets credit for their efforts.

"4-4" children may seem slow to learn, but that's only because they're so methodical and must mull everything over before accepting it. Once they do absorb something, however, they are likely to retain it. They are not too keen on experimenting with anything new and can be picky eaters—preferring old standbys like hamburgers and french fries. They also dislike having their possessions tampered with. They have their own sense of order, and a wise parent will refrain from touching their belongings or rearranging their room without discussing it first. Although they may not always express their need for love and attention, they want it desperately and can be jealous of siblings or others who gain the limelight or receive recognition for something they feel they deserve. When feelings of inferiority, inadequacy, or frustration build up, "4-4"s may vent them in bullying someone weaker or having a temper tantrum. Involvement in some active sport such as handball or tennis could be a good safety valve.

5

MOTIVATION
NUMBER

8

INNER-SELF
NUMBER

"I'll walk where my own nature would be leading—It vexes me to choose another guide . . ."
—*Emily Bronte*

4

EXPRESSION
NUMBER

Although they may appear conservative and conventional, "5-4"s are turned on by the unusual and exciting. Adventure and new experiences beckon them and even when they do not participate themselves, they enjoy watching others who do. They are often attracted to someone who gives them a vicarious thrill—that daring ski jumper or talented figure skater, for example—and the relationship may last as long as they have something to admire.

"5-4"s want a partner who is fun-loving and stimulating but loyal and dependable too. Yet they themselves have an inner restlessness and may not be as reliable as their staid and stable appearance may lead you to assume. They resent any restraints or limitations on their freedom and can be quite stubborn when ordered around. If there are any commitments to be made, they want it to be their idea—not yours. Owing to the wide discrepancy between what they want and what they do, "5-4"s are not easy to understand. It is hard to predict when they will be dependable and when sporadic. They may meet someone they like and go out with them only once in a while, but over a long stretch of time, or they may have one whirlwind courtship after another. Quite often they are the ones chosen by their graduating class as the most likely to marry and settle down, yet show up at the fifteenth annual high school reunion party still single.

Earthy and sensual, "5-4"s are the "4"s most prone to overindulge—whether it be eating too much, drinking too much, or partaking of the pleasures of the flesh as if in a marathon. They can charm their way out of difficult situations, making it hard for anyone to stay mad at them for long. "5-4," for instance, is the man who forgets his partner's birthday but when she starts to get mad, lets drop how he drove to every hardware store in town looking for the part she needed for the dishwasher. Or, she might be the woman who burns the expensive steak her lover brought for dinner, but turns around and gives him a backrub he'll never forget.

Once they have decided to settle down, "5-4"s can be responsible about taking care of their home. They don't mind mowing the lawn or painting the garage or even washing dishes, and they can be depended on to drive the kids to Scout meetings. However, they expect to go bowling with the gang every Thursday night and not get asked a lot of questions if they're out late. Although they can be opinionated and stubborn, "5-4"s do not especially like to argue and may "clam up" rather than fight it out. Their mates may have difficulty getting them to relate their true feelings unless there are good channels of communication between them.

"5-4"s work well with their hands and have a knack for handling wiring and machinery. Lovers of the outdoors, they are often attracted to careers that allow them to be there—installing telephone lines or building roads, for example. They are also good at finding innovative ways of making money while putting out the least possible effort. For example, they have a keen eye for real estate bargains, and after making a few improvements can usually profit by reselling at a much higher price than they paid, or leasing at a high rent. Some call them wheeler-dealers, others say they're just lucky, but one thing's for sure, they do seem to get more than their money's worth. Although their maneuverings are honest and aboveboard, and they don't deliberately set out to take advantage of people, they always seem to end up with the long end of the stick. "5-4" would be the person who sells his or her car and a half-hour after the new owner takes possession the transmission gives out.

"5-4" children are attracted to the sensual and may love fondling a cuddly teddy bear, mushing their food around with their fingers, or insist on taking their own blanket with them when they stay overnight at Grandma's house, "because it's so soft." They show an interest in the opposite sex at a very early age and adults may be shocked at how observant they are.

"5-4"s are quick learners and usually do well in school. Although they may not always be the most well-behaved children in the class, their charming personalities help them get away with minor shenanigans. Versatile and imaginative, they enjoy acting and making up stories and they are good at organizing things and getting other children interested in their projects. Despite their popularity and independent appearance, however, these children are very tied to their family. They are especially attached to the parent of the opposite sex and enjoy having Mommy or Daddy all to themselves. They do not like to go away from home for any prolonged period of time (to summer camp for example), and resent having a babysitter.

| 6 |
| MOTIVATION
| NUMBER

| 7 |
| INNER-SELF
| NUMBER

| 4 |
| EXPRESSION
| NUMBER

"I am certainly not one of those who need to be prodded. In fact, if anything, I am the prod."
—*Sir Winston Churchill*

You are more likely to meet "6-4"s at work, running a marathon or through friends than in a social situation—unless it is a get-together at their own home. They may at first seem reserved and aloof, but can be quite friendly and endearing once they warm up to you. They are attracted to gentleness, sensitivity and refinement, and good manners are as important as good looks. If you have captured "6-4"'s eye and would like to fan the flames, there are several approaches you can take. Admire their possessions and achievements and flatter them (but only if you are sincere—astute, they are apt to sense false praise which is a real turn-off); ask for advice; or invite them over for a home-cooked dinner. "6-4"s love being wined-and-dined and one of the ways to their heart is definitely through their stomach. Whatever your approach, however, be patient, considerate and understanding of their moods. Don't try to dominate them or argue with them or push them around. They have a stubborn streak and may respond with hostility and anger when opposed. They need to do things in their own way and in their own time.

"6-4"s think they know what's best for everyone and can be quite dictatorial. Even when you don't necessarily agree with their viewpoints, you would do well to let them do their share of talking—they are quickly turned off by people who insist on monopolizing the conversation. And keep in mind, that even though their lofty ideals are not always appreciated, "6-4"s mean well. Concerned about how they appear to others, they have difficulty understanding why—when they work so hard at being charming and outgoing—they can't seem to help being critical, impatient and demanding as well. Somewhat limited in their viewpoints, they have a shaky self-image, which needs bolstering. When they feel inadequate or their sense of security is threatened, they may resort to outbursts of temper which can be as shocking and unexpected to them as they are to the person upon whom they are vented. "6-4"s do not purposely set out to hurt anyone and may find this aspect of themselves upsetting and confusing. Jogging, tennis or creating something with their hands can help alleviate some of their inner tension.

Genuine kindness and a sense of social responsibility are inherent in "6-4"'s nature. They want to take care of someone—to feel needed, appreciated and respected. Although they have trouble expressing their feelings and may find it easier to criticize than to compliment, they take great pride in their family—especially their children. Loyal and devoted themselves, "6-4"s are happiest with a faithful, homeloving, understanding spouse who does not get upset by their moods and who is willing to let them set the ground rules at home.

On the job, "6-4"s are hard-working and more than willing to accept their share of responsibility. They have high ideals and are happiest in a profession that combines practicality and usefulness with social responsibility or artistic expression. Dedicated workers themselves, they expect others to share their loyalty, self-discipline and willingness to put in a little extra without being guaranteed a reward.

"6-4" s' organization helps them adjust to the rigors and routine of a nine-to-five-type job situation and they can follow rules and be creative while remaining within boundaries. Their sense of responsibility is so strong, they would feel guilty if they did not push themselves. So intent are they on doing their part, they may not lift their heads from their desk long enough to notice that the sun is shining.

"6-4" children like school and are usually good students—absorbing slowly but surely. Eager to please, they are obedient and well behaved if given some disciplinary guidelines. Extracurricular activities also appeal to them and they enjoy being part of a group—whether it be the choir, the football team, or the corner street gang. Even at an early age they like to give advice and can be quite bossy. They also have a sense of humor and a sharp wit, which may be expressed anywhere from a stand-up comic routine to writing a weekly editorial for the school paper.

Like their adult counterparts, "6-4" children can be charming and endearing. They enjoy helping around the home and school and thrive on receiving praise and recognition for their efforts. When they have their minds set on something, however, they will be persistent in their efforts and go to great lengths to get it. If things don't go their way, they can be stubborn and fault-finding, and one who has seen their negative side may be quite surprised at how friendly and outgoing they can be when they are in a good mood.

7
MOTIVATION
NUMBER

6
INNER-SELF
NUMBER

"Talk to him of Jacob's ladder, and he would ask the number of steps."

—*Douglas Jerrold*

4
EXPRESSION
NUMBER

"7-4"s may appear earthy, practical and realistic, but what they are striving for is some form of refinement, exclusiveness or wisdom. Somewhat intellectually snobbish, they tend to shy away from what they consider to be average or mediocre people and select their close friends very carefully. They are attracted to someone they find mentally stimulating and who is conversant on a variety of subjects—music, literature and art, for instance. They like interesting discussions and can be appealed to more through their intellects than through their emotions.

Not the types to have several one-night stands, "7-4"s prefer warming up to a relationship slowly. Just because at first they don't call you every day doesn't mean they're not interested. It's just that they're set in their ways and tend to resist change or innovation. Very security-conscious, they find anything that interferes with their organized routine upsetting. If you are patient, dependability is bound to develop along with familiarity. Don't be critical or pry into their personal affairs. If they don't feel pressured to rush into anything, chances are that a once- or twice-a-month affair can turn into something much more . . . and it may happen much sooner than you think.

"7-4"s have a tendency to be critical, fussy and demanding, often concealing the loving, affectionate side of their nature and making them appear cold and aloof. But their iron hand, so to speak, is usually clad in a velvet glove. It may take a little longer to get to know them because of their reluctance to express their true feelings and their need to build up trust before they let anyone get close. They are most inclined to tie the knot with a partner who is cultured, intelligent and understanding about allowing them time alone to read, contemplate or dream, but who also encourages communication. If conflicts aren't discussed, the resentment "7-4"s build up can lead to moodiness, depression or the silent treatment. Country outings can be soothing to their nerves, and working in a garden may be a satisfying outlet for nervous tension. "7-4"s are devoted to their families and will make many sacrifices on the behalf of loved ones. A happy homelife is essential to their well-being.

At work "7-4"s are perfectionists and plodders. Conscientious and dedicated, they see a job through to the end and often work overtime without remuneration (although they may later resent having done so). However, they need to be allowed to do their job the way they feel is best and are difficult to persuade otherwise. Analytical and good with details, they prefer working on their own without having someone constantly looking over their shoulder or checking up on them. Not apt to skim the surface, they delve deeply into whatever project they are working on. "Why?" and "How?" are constantly on their minds. They are very thorough and will work tirelessly at gathering facts.

Being somewhat private and reserved, "7-4"s are unlikely to discuss details of their personal life at work. They do, however show concern for the common good and may often be found fighting for social causes such as better conditions in hospitals, schools, or animal shelters. "7-4"s are not ones to seek the limelight, but they do like to feel appreciated for their efforts.

"7-4" children, like their adult counterparts, can be shy, critical and reserved. They are easily misunderstood by parents and peers and often feel rejected by them. Selective in their choice of friends, they prefer those who are interesting and intellectually stimulating. However, they have trouble expressing their feelings and may sometimes find themselves snubbed by those whose company they seek. They have a methodical, analytical approach to things, which carries over into their play activities as well. Playing for the sake of fun is not enough. They seek to understand the theory behind winning the game and then go on to master and perfect it. Mental games such as crossword puzzles, Monopoly, and cards intrigue them. They also enjoy active games such as baseball and hopscotch, but while they are playing these, their mind is in a constant whirl as to the best way to throw the ball or kick the pebble out of the square.

8
MOTIVATION
NUMBER

5
INNER-SELF
NUMBER

"To work is simple enough; but to rest, there is the difficulty."

—*Ernest Hello*

4
EXPRESSION
NUMBER

The most likely place to meet the always-busy "8-4" is through work. But mountain resorts, health clubs, bowling alleys or beaches are also possibilities. In their free time, "8-4"s like to keep in shape and they love being outdoors. They can seem reserved and aloof when their mind is on other things, but when they meet someone they are interested in, they are charming and outgoing. Although your first impression may be that this is a hard combination to pin down, they do prefer the emotional security of a permanent relationship and can be dependable and reliable with someone they care for. Of course they expect their partner to act that way as well.

"8-4"s want to be in control of their affairs, and are happiest with a stable, fun-loving, faithful mate who is not overly possessive. Personal freedom is important to them and they don't want to be questioned about their whereabouts all the time. When the shoe is on the other foot, however, they have some double standards and can be jealous and demanding.

Despite their calm, controlled exterior, "8-4"s have trouble relaxing.

Determined and ambitious, they are real go-getters who can be quite persistent when they decide they want someone or something. Their charm and humor are great aids to their powers of persuasion and they are talented at making the best of what they have. Once the knot has been tied, they are loyal spouses but may be somewhat tyrannical and exacting with loved ones. They may hide feelings of anger and frustration from the outside world, but vent them on their families. They have a tendency to get so wrapped up in work that those close may feel they are more concerned with their job and the people they work with than with them. But they can be generous and genuinely appreciative of a mate who encourages their ambitions and gives them emotional support.

At work, "8-4"s are ambitious and have a talent for organizing and planning. They would like to build something of lasting value for which they can receive material security and recognition. Efficient and practical, they can follow rules and adhere to routine, as well as improvise when necessary. Loyal and disciplined, they are an asset to any organization, but can be demanding bosses—expecting everyone else to be as dedicated as they are.

Although "8-4"s prefer administering and delegating the detail and drudgery work to others, they usually end up pitching in with the groundwork. "8-4," may for example, be a contractor who starts out using a drill press and pouring concrete but who now gives the orders. His knowledge and reputation as a hard worker have earned him the respect of the employees who often think of him as one of them even though he's the boss.

Like their adult counterparts, "8-4" children have minds of their own. They can be charming at times, but also stubborn and hard to discipline. Patient and diligent when working toward something they want, they are good at figuring out how best to get it. They learn the value of money at an early age and soon find ingenious ways of making it. They may, for instance, take Mother's cookies to school and sell them to their classmates. Or loan a friend money to go to the movies and then charge him or her interest for it. If they resort to old standbys such as mowing lawns, raking leaves, shoveling snow, weeding gardens, or delivering papers, they can be counted on to do a good and efficient job.

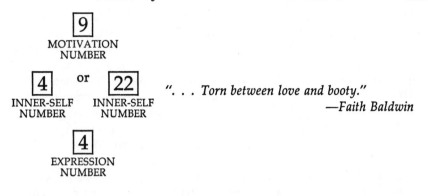

9
MOTIVATION
NUMBER

4   or   22
INNER-SELF   INNER-SELF
NUMBER   NUMBER

". . . Torn between love and booty."
—*Faith Baldwin*

4
EXPRESSION
NUMBER

"9-4"s enjoy meeting all kinds of people, but prefer to develop a relationship with someone they have a lot in common with. Although they would like to be forceful and extroverted, they are often slow to express their true feelings, and it takes a long time for them to build up trust in someone. They may have many acquaintances, but they confide in only a select few. More likely to go out with someone they've seen around for a while—at work or at a club, for example—than a blind date, they may nevertheless once in a while find someone so intriguing they'll find some excuse to strike up a conversation. They are attracted to members of the opposite sex who seem to share their ideals, and who appear dependable, sympathetic and responsive. Anyone pushy, selfish or overbearing will surely turn them off.

"9-4"s have broad, open-minded views, but these may be more theory than practice. Those with a "22" inner-self number especially, have a tendency to tout universal love, while being jealous and possessive themselves. They may believe one can love more than one person at a time, but when it comes to their own sweetheart caring for someone else they can't accept it. Prejudice in other people disturbs them, yet they too can be narrow-minded and rigid. "9-4"s themselves are often confused at this duality in their personality and neuroses or psychosomatic illnesses are not uncommon.

Generous and giving with loved ones, "9-4"s are subject to fits of depression if their devotion is not returned or appreciated. With them it's all or nothing. Incurable romantics at heart, they feel that a meaningful relationship is one where both partners spend as much time as possible with each other and there is potential for a permanent commitment. They will call regularly and expect their partner to be punctual and available at all times. They want no part of someone shallow or unreliable.

Financial security is very important to "9-4"s, and although they may dream of becoming artists or great humanitarians, they usually end up doing something routine and laborious such as working in a bank or insurance company. This conflict between what they would like to do and what they actually have the ability to do will be a constant source of frustration unless they work out a way of dealing with it. Doing office work in a nonprofit organization such as Human Rights, being a bookkeeper for a politician they believe in, or working backstage for a theatrical production will at least put them in an environment where common goals are supported. A creative hobby such as painting, sculpting or making pottery can also help make them feel fulfilled.

"9-4" children can be mischievous and impatient. They may love school but have difficulty sitting still and find themselves frequently reprimanded for talking in class or misbehaving. However, they can stay put when they are being entertained, and are happy watching television morning, noon and night. Activities that use up energy such as riding a tricycle, playing hopscotch or swimming, are much more to their liking than reading or doing puzzles. Although popular pastimes are the norm, once in a while they'll have an inspiration to do something different, such as slide down the banister backward or eat matches.

Like their adult counterparts, "9-4" children are sensitive and emotional. They need a great deal of love and understanding. Seeing someone else gain the limelight for something they would like to have done themselves may lead to jealousy and resentment. They expect to do things their own way and can become stubborn and subject to fits of temper when crossed. "9-4"s need a creative outlet, and painting, playing a musical instrument, acting or making objects out of clay can be most therapeutic.

| 11 |
| MOTIVATION NUMBER |

| 2 | or | 11 |
| INNER-SELF NUMBER | | INNER-SELF NUMBER |

| 4 |
| EXPRESSION NUMBER |

"To have striven; to have made an effort; to have been true to certain ideals—this alone is worth the struggle."

—Unknown

You are more likely to meet the idealistic "11-4" at an art gallery or an auction than at a disco or in a bar. Although they may not make the first overture themselves, they are receptive to anyone they find interesting or who they feel has something in common with them. They are drawn to people of substance who don't flaunt themselves or try to impress others. Easily turned off by showoffs, they can intuitively spot a phony a mile away. Sincerity and sensitivity are much more important to them than looks or bravura.

"11-4"s want love and affection, but—especially if their inner-self number is an "11"—they are very idealistic and may seek the impossible in a love relationship. Although they can be charming and generous with those they care for, they have trouble accepting people for what they are and may find normal run-of-the-mill relationships difficult. They are apt to be disappointed when situations and/or people don't live up to their expectations, and are prone to moodiness and depression when things go wrong.

"11-4"s are a combination of worldliness, common sense, sensitivity and imagination. They may present a purposeful, enduring front, but they sometimes find it hard to live up to it. Not wanting to face the harsh realities of life, they may use fantasy as a means of escape. When they feel too much is expected of them, they may try to shut themselves off from the risk of failure. They need someone warm, supportive and understanding by their sides who respects and admires them and makes them feel important and needed.

At work, "11-4"s are efficient and dependable and a loyal asset to any business. Practical and persistent, they can be counted on to see a project through to the end. Their greatest satisfaction comes from recognition for a job well done and from seeing a finished product they can be proud of.

Harmony on the job is important to "11-4"s and they are eager to settle any disputes that arise among coworkers so that petty quarrels may be avoided altogether. They work well in a group and enjoy getting involved in any company clubs or activities. As long as they get credit for what they do, and do not get lost in the crowd, they have no burning desire to be leaders.

Although they are diligent and hard-working, "11-4"s need to believe in a product or cause before committing their time or efforts to it. They may, for example, think twice before working for a company that pollutes the air, puts harmful chemicals in food, or sells land that's in swamps.

Also read the description for "2-4" that starts on page 96. "11" is such a high vibration that it is impossible to operate on it all the time. Children act like its lower octave—"2"—most of the time and adults operate on the "2" at least part of the time.

22
MOTIVATION
NUMBER

9
INNER-SELF
NUMBER

"Work hard, believe in what you do, and you'll succeed."

—Unknown

4
EXPRESSION
NUMBER

The most likely way to meet "22-4" is through work or friends. Though they may seem friendly and easy to approach, they tend to form close associations with only a select few. They have such high expectations that it usually takes a long time for strong ties to form. Since people tend to grow on them as they prove their worth, propinquity helps and "22-4"s are unlikely to pursue a long-distance romance where the initial attraction was merely physical.

"22-4"s are drawn to members of the opposite sex who are patient and loyal and who not only share their ideals but are willing to help them achieve them as well. They are visionaries who would like to put their dreams into practice, but they are realistic and down-to-earth too. They often feel they have a mission in life and may be so intent on fulfilling it that they neglect those close without really being aware of doing so. They need warmth and affection but have difficulty expressing their true feelings and can be jealous and possessive of those they love.

Although they appear calm and controlled, "22-4"s are subject to unpredictable fits of temper when things don't happen the way they planned. Security-conscious and routine-oriented, they may be reluctant to try new things or accept change. But a loving, appreciative partner who can be persuasive rather than bossy may succeed in dragging them out to have fun once in a while. "22-4"s don't really like the rigid side of their natures and will occasionally indulge in something different, like dancing classes or a weekend of sailing, if it's put to them in the right way.

At work, "22-4"s are diligent and methodical and would like to feel they are making a significant contribution to humanity. Accuracy and detail are their forte and they work best with things that are tangible and practical. They have a strong sense of system and organization and the planning ability to turn their ideas into reality. Determined and persistent, they do not like to be rushed or ordered around, and they are best left to work on their own. Their inventive minds often discover new ways of doing things, and of all the "4"s they are the most likely to come up with a better mousetrap. They are good at figuring out how to perform a task more cheaply, more efficiently, and in a shorter time than it's been done before.

Also read the description for "4-4"s starting on page 100. "22" is such a high vibration that it is impossible to operate on it all the time. Children act like its lower octave—"4"—most of the time, and adults operate on the "4" at least part of the time.

VII
Freedom and Change: The Number 5

"5"s experience life through their senses. Willing to try anything once, they thrive on finding new and different things to do. Restless and easily bored, they are in constant pursuit of adventure and sensual pleasures. They seek frequent change, whether it be in their relationships, job or environment. In fact, it is not unusual for them to drop out at some point of life to do their own thing for a while and they may get involved with strange schools of thought or odd life-styles.

Fun-loving and full of youthful curiosity, "5"s learn best from their own experiences. Freedom to do as they please is important and they can be quite selfish about having their own way. Not known for their willpower, they may lack self-discipline and emotional control. They have a tendency to repeat mistakes—especially in areas involving physical pleasures. "5"s are prone to overindulge in the sensual—eating, drinking, gambling, sex, and failure to accept responsibility for their actions is also common. Hyperactive and high-strung, they may overtax themselves to the point of physical or nervous breakdown. Carelessness and a tendency to let their mind wander may make them accident-prone.

Able to do more than one thing at a time, "5"s are versatile and resourceful. Bored by old ways and repetitive situations, they enjoy stirring things up a bit—whether it be starting a fight or opening up a new approach to something. However, they may not stick around long enough to see the end result. Clever and innovative, a "5" often is a "jack of all trades, master of none." "5"s have trouble concentrating on details and seeing a job through to the end, and although they can do many things well, their tendency is to scatter their energy in too many directions. "5"s enjoy a challenge and have a need to gain the advantage over others in some area of their life. They have a keen sense of competition and a willingness to speculate and gamble. They can be quite manipulative and opportunistic—using people and then discarding them.

"5"s enjoy a good time and are often the life of the party. Popular and open-minded, they are able to relate to anyone and have a need to mingle with a variety of people—friends, acquaintances, and strangers. Although they may be interesting and entertaining companions they are not particularly loyal. They have a wandering heart and a weakness for the opposite sex. Not anxious to settle down and be faithful to one person, "5"s shun responsibility and domestic ties. If, however, they do decide to give it a try, they are happiest with an active, stimulating, physically responsive mate who is willing to accept their need for freedom and won't try to pin them down.

Prone to many emotional ups and downs, "5"s can be thoughtless, irritable, and temperamental. However, they do not let any one thing upset them for very long and will not hesitate to break a relationship they find dull or binding. Jealousy or possessiveness on the part of their mate will only make them fly faster into someone else's arms. "5"s are definitely not easy to live with. Rather than try to figure them out, a wise partner will learn to be adaptable and make any necessary allowances or adjustments him or herself. The reward for sticking it out may well be an active, eventful, exciting life full of unexpected surprises.

COMPATIBILITY GUIDE

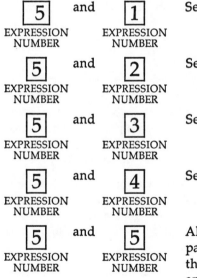

| 5 EXPRESSION NUMBER | and | 1 EXPRESSION NUMBER | See page 33 (chapter III). |

| 5 EXPRESSION NUMBER | and | 2 EXPRESSION NUMBER | See page 53 (chapter IV). |

| 5 EXPRESSION NUMBER | and | 3 EXPRESSION NUMBER | See page 73 (chapter V). |

| 5 EXPRESSION NUMBER | and | 4 EXPRESSION NUMBER | See page 94 (chapter VI). |

| 5 EXPRESSION NUMBER | and | 5 EXPRESSION NUMBER | Although this combination may seem passionate, exciting and adventuresome, there is likely to be lack of purpose and an unwillingness of either partner to accept responsibility. A close personal relationship may be characterized by many breakups and reconciliations. |

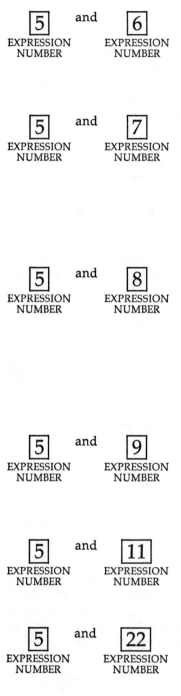

5 and **6**	Poor combination unless "6" enjoys being the homemaker and does not mind "5"'s absences. More likely, "6" will find "5" too restless and irresponsible; "5" will find "6" a "stick-in-the-mud" and feel "smothered" by it.
EXPRESSION NUMBER / EXPRESSION NUMBER	

5 and **6**
EXPRESSION NUMBER   EXPRESSION NUMBER

Poor combination unless "6" enjoys being the homemaker and does not mind "5"'s absences. More likely, "6" will find "5" too restless and irresponsible; "5" will find "6" a "stick-in-the-mud" and feel "smothered" by it.

5 and **7**
EXPRESSION NUMBER   EXPRESSION NUMBER

Good business combination—"7" working behind the scenes; "5" dealing with the public. In a close personal relationship, however, there is conflict between "5"'s constant need to be with people and "7"'s desire to be alone. "5" has trouble understanding "7"'s need for privacy, and "7" finds "5"'s inquisitiveness irritating.

5 and **8**
EXPRESSION NUMBER   EXPRESSION NUMBER

Productive business combination—"5" bringing in financial opportunities, "8" cashing in on them by lending good judgment to "5"'s promotional schemes. Although "5" is impressed by "8"'s money and efficiency, and "8" finds "5" stimulating and refreshing, there could be conflict in a close personal relationship between "5"'s irresponsibility and "8"'s practicality.

5 and **9**
EXPRESSION NUMBER   EXPRESSION NUMBER

Good business, friendship, or marriage combination. Though there may be some conflict between "9"'s romantic ideas and "5"'s self-indulgent approach, both are active, adventuresome and outgoing, and enjoy similar interests.

5 and **11**
EXPRESSION NUMBER   EXPRESSION NUMBER

Good creative combination—ideas will be plentiful but may lack practicality. In a close personal relationship, however, "11" may find "5" undependable and irresponsible.

5 and **22**
EXPRESSION NUMBER   EXPRESSION NUMBER

Good business combination—"22" providing something substantial for "5" to sell and promote. In a close personal relationship, however, "22" may find "5" too flighty and impractical.

Following are all possible combinations of a "5" expression number with the different motivation and inner-self numbers.

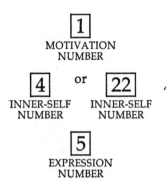

1
MOTIVATION
NUMBER

4 or 22
INNER-SELF INNER-SELF
NUMBER NUMBER

5
EXPRESSION
NUMBER

"Nothing ventured, nothing gained."
—W. S. Gilbert

"1-5"s are nonconformists and their love of a challenge does not falter even in the love department. A "1-5" could, for instance, be an American tour guide who, while showing a group of German students around, singles one out and makes up his mind to get to see her alone, no matter what. The fact that he lives in New York and she lives in Frankfurt merely makes it more interesting, and he'll worry about how they'll get to see each other again later.

"1-5"s have great vitality and energy and are attracted to active, fun-loving, intelligent people who have minds of their own. They shy away from those who seem gloomy or boring. If you have captured their eye and would like to fan the flames, be witty and interesting, but a good listener too. Let them make the decisions and take the lead. Be willing to accept them the way they are, and learn to be subtly persuasive rather than forceful so they will get the impression that things were their idea rather than yours. Don't criticize them or try to pin them down, and above all, don't try to rush them with romantic suggestions of settling down together. Keep in mind that any first appearances to the contrary, "1-5"s have a need to be independent and do not like to feel trapped or pinned down. One of the fastest ways to turn them off is to ask them to account for every minute of their time. Freedom to do things their own way is one of their prime goals in life and they appreciate a partner who shares their belief in the importance of each person doing his or her own thing.

Even if you've had a fantastic time on your first date with a "1-5" and you're sure the feeling was mutual, don't expect him or her to call you again right away or to sweep you off your feet. "1-5"s don't usually plunge into a heavy relationship. They prefer a partner who is hard to get rather than one who is possessive or overly eager to settle down, so if you feel you *must* get in touch anyway, keep it light and don't pry into what they've been doing or ask why you haven't heard from them. Instead of calling, you could, for instance, send a funny appropriate cartoon with a note saying it reminded you of that scene in the movie you saw together where you both laughed so hard people turned around and glared at you. Or, if it's their birthday or some holiday, you could send a well chosen humorous card with a little reminder that you're still around.

Although they may appear to have many friends, "1-5"s are essentially loners. Their search for intellectual as well as physical stimulation leads them to mingle with a variety of people. Curious and adventuresome, they enjoy trying new things and are attracted to the sensual—good food, silk sheets, running barefoot in the sand. Very often they are trend-setters or leaders of the crowd. If their inner-self number is a "22," they will be even more restless, and once they get out of school, it is unlikely they'll hang around the town they grew up in because they sense a whole new world out there beckoning.

Intelligent, versatile and creative, "1-5"s are full of original ideas, but may not finish what they start. They enjoy action, movement and change, and have a talent for finding new, improved ways of doing things. Routine does not appeal to them and they would much prefer working at something unique and different. If, however, circumstances force them into a nine-to-five job, it will most likely be one that allows them a certain amount of freedom to carry out their duties their own way without being constantly watched. It is not unusual for them to have a job on the side such as tending bar, or working in an amusement park.

Like their adult counterparts, "1-5" children are creative, original nonconformists who want to stand out in some area. Their natural curiosity and quick minds make them good students and they are usually at the top of their class. Because they are so versatile, they usually try different, better ways of doing things and may have trouble understanding why adults want them to do it their way. Their spirit of adventure and inventiveness makes them popular, but although others are drawn to them, they themselves do not necessarily seek their company. When "1-5"s set out to the fishing hole, for example, several youngsters may tag along, which is fine with them, but they would have been just as happy to go alone.

2
MOTIVATION
NUMBER

3
INNER-SELF
NUMBER

5
EXPRESSION
NUMBER

"The supreme happiness of life is the conviction that we are loved."

—*Victor Hugo*

"2-5"s do not like to be alone, and the most likely place to meet them is somewhere there are people—a party, a resort, an adult-education class, a convention. Your first impression is apt to be that they are popular, outgoing and hard to pin down, but appearances to the contrary, they are really quite sensitive and dependent. Nothing can throw them into a depression faster than being dateless when the weekend comes around. And yet this happens much more often than you may expect. A potential date who sees all the attention "2-5"s get and who notices all the members of the opposite sex flirting with them may never get around to asking them out because he or she'll assume they are already busy.

"2-5"s may come across restless, fickle or unreliable, but underneath it all is loyalty and a desire to please. They want to be dependable and considerate, and may be confused at this conflict between what they want and what they do. Frustration can make them subject to moodiness and dejection. They are attracted to people who are warm and communicative and whom they can count on. They enjoy togetherness, and if they are interested in someone will be reliable about calling and setting up dates. They can become quite possessive and may brood for days on end after a lover's quarrel. The way to their heart is to be supportive, available, and willing to share many different activities, ranging from traveling to sports or attending a class one night a week.

Once they have settled down, "2-5"s enjoy children and make good parents. However, they enjoy socializing and going out so much they may let the housework slide. Eventually it will get done, but a compulsively tidy mate may find the disarray annoying. As with everything else, they prefer that tending to the home and the kids be a joint effort.

"2-5"s are not career-oriented types who would put getting ahead before family concerns. Competitive or cutthroat jobs that require a tough exterior and an aggressive spirit are not suited to their fragile egos and sensitive temperaments. At work, as in their private lives, they want to feel needed and appreciated, and of all the "5"s, they are the most willing to cooperate and handle details. They want to please, and getting along with bosses and co-workers is important to them. No matter how much they like their job, if they don't have good personal relationships, they'll be miserable. Versatility and a need to express themselves in many different ways causes them to often have an outside interest such as a side job, a hobby, or just keeping busy with the family. They may, for instance, teach exercise or dancing classes one night a week, be the secretary of their garden club, or sew clothes for their kids. Music is a good outlet for them too. They have a good sense of rhythm and often show a talent for playing an instrument. They have a facility with languages, and communications can offer them many job opportunities from bilingual secretary to editor in a publishing house.

"2-5" children are sensitive and shy. They cry easily when frustrated and need a great deal of reassurance. Craving affection, they enjoy being hugged and cuddled, and parental absence causes much pain. They love animals, and having a pet is a good way for them to learn responsibility. Supervision is necessary, however, for although they mean to do everything they're supposed to, they can be unintentionally distracted and forget to walk it or feed it on time.

Like their adult counterparts, "2-5" children do not like being alone. Group activities appeal to them and they usually join several clubs or teams at school. Band, Glee Club, drama group or sports team—wherever their friends are, "2-5" will also be. They enjoy things with a beat—marching, tap dancing, drumming, disco music—and since these are all good means of venting frustration, they should be encouraged.

Enthusiastic about school, "2-5"s usually prefer languages and the arts to math or science, but they are motivated to do well in all subjects. Versatile and resourceful, they can often do more than one thing at a time—amazing the parent who sees them memorizing a poem for English class while watching television.

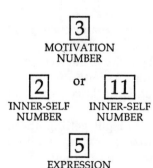

MOTIVATION NUMBER: 3

INNER-SELF NUMBER: 2 or 11

EXPRESSION NUMBER: 5

"Some think the world was made for fun and joy and so do I."

—Unknown

You are most likely to meet "3-5"s at the local hangout or at a social event. Expressive and enthusiastic, they can talk circles around anyone and enjoy doing things with flair. Although usually charming and endearing, they can occasionally be immature and irresponsible as well. They need to be the center of attention and will usually manage to gain the limelight in one way or another. Guess who, for instance, had too much to drink at the last office party and kissed the entire female staff? Yes, it was "3-5"! And guess who was the first to suggest an outing to a nude beach last summer? Right again (it *was* "3-5")!

Talented but restless, "3-5"s tend to have scattered interests. They may know something about everything yet not know anything thoroughly—start a myriad of projects, yet not finish any of them. Impulsive and changeable, they have trouble concentrating on any one thing for long. But they do want to be admired and they like being seen with the in crowd. If you look as though you might fit in—or make them look good—you have a good chance of capturing their attention. Beauty in their surroundings and associates is important and you'll rarely find a "3-5" with a partner who is not good-looking. If, however, their inner-self number is an "11," looks won't be enough. They will be more discriminating and refined in their tastes, and will look for intellectual stimulation as well.

Difficult to pin down, "3-5"s can be erratic and unreliable even with people whose company they enjoy. They have a tendency to take loved ones for granted when the going is smooth and to make promises for the future only when they fear they are about to lose those they love. If you want to keep their interest, try not to seem always available. Keeping them guessing or playing hard to get can sometimes work wonders.

"3-5"s have a youthful exuberance and fun-loving nature that enables them to relate well to children. If they decide to settle down, they enjoy having a family and can be good parents. However, they can also be jealous of a spouse who pays more attention to the little ones than to them. Although usually optimistic and enthusiastic, they are ruled by their emotions and may be prone to wild mood swings and fits of temper when things go wrong. Not always easy to live with, they need an understanding, stable, attractive mate who enjoys doing things on a whim and who doesn't demand domestic perfection.

At work as in their private lives, "3-5"s dislike routine and have trouble concentrating on any one thing for very long. Although creative, versatile and full of ideas, they tend to lose interest quickly. They need variety in their job, contact with people, and preferably a chance to be in the limelight as well. So important is prestige that they might be tempted to accept a job with a lower salary if it gave them a better office and a more impressive title.

"3-5"s enjoy positions that let them talk and socialize. Their enthusiasm and charm make them well suited to dealing with the public. They also enjoy working with children—teaching or nursing, for example. Having a comforting nature, they are good at turning little ones' tears into smiles by putting everyday tragedies such as broken dolls or scraped knees into a broader perspective.

Like their adult counterparts, "3-5" children are restless and talkative. They want to be the center of attention and may show off or exaggerate to be noticed. Although they are usually optimistic and enthusiastic, they may become moody and temperamental when they feel rejected or inadequate. They need help channeling their energies and encouragement to follow through on what they start, or they may waste their talents by scattering themselves in too many directions. They have trouble paying attention and are too impatient to concentrate on details, yet are prone to fits of temper when things don't turn out right.

Active and energetic, "3-5"s enjoy sports which involve showmanship such as figure skating, gymnastics or horseback riding. They should be encouraged to express themselves through some creative outlet—drama or writing for example—and to develop at least one skill. Whether it turns into a career later on, or remains a hobby, it could be a source of fulfillment throughout their adult life.

| 4 |
| MOTIVATION NUMBER |

| 1 |
| INNER-SELF NUMBER |

| 5 |
| EXPRESSION NUMBER |

"I am better than my reputation."

—*Schiller*

While they may come across footloose and fancy free, "4-5"s really seek a stable, dependable relationship. You are most apt to meet "4-5"s at work or through friends, but they do enjoy being active and outdoors, and a nearby lake in the summer or a ski slope in the winter are also good bets. Once they meet someone who has that certain chemistry they will pursue him or her steadily right from the start—which, in view of their independent, nonchalant manner, might come as a surprise to the object of their affections. They *want* a certain amount of routine in their lives. Security is important and they need to feel sure of themselves, their partner and their position. Only then do they feel free to travel and do the crazy, unusual things that are so much a part of them.

"4-5"s are attracted to members of the opposite sex who are fun-loving but stable, loyal and domestically inclined. They enjoy being wined and dined, and one of the ways to their heart is definitely through their stomach. Once a commitment has been made, they want to be catered to, and can be jealous, possessive and demanding. On the positive side, however, they are faithful, reliable and willing to work hard to benefit their loved ones too.

Earthy and sensual, "4-5"s enjoy good food, good clothes and good sex. Home is their castle, and although they enjoy going out to movies, theater, parties or dancing, they want a pleasant place to come back to. Structure is important to their well-being, and they are happiest with a warm, practical mate who makes them feel comfortable, who is a good cook, who entertains their family and friends, and who adheres to a certain amount of schedule in daily activities.

At work, "4-5"s are practical and willing to follow a routine, but they are also able to express themselves in an enterprising, inventive way. Responsible and hard-working, they believe in being prepared, and do not get flustered or caught offguard by unusual questions or situations. "4-5," for instance, is the convincing salesman who is equipped with all the facts. Or the real estate agent who knows all the mortgage rates, school situations, distances to shopping centers, going prices of comparable homes, and so on. Their adaptability comes in handy no matter what their profession, and they have enough determination to make any job work out if they really want it to.

Like their adult counterparts, "4-5" children may appear independent and adaptable but are very security-conscious and set in their ways. Parents are often surprised at how stubborn their kids can be about some things when they are so easygoing about others. "4-5," for instance, is the child who insists on carrying a baby bottle full of juice around with him long after he has learned to drink from a cup, or who can't be parted from her cuddly but raggedy-looking teddy bear when she starts kindergarten.

"4-5"s usually do well in school—especially when it comes to subjects they enjoy. However, they have a knack for getting others to do unwanted errands, chores or homework for them, and classmates may be amazed at how easily they can get out of doing something they don't like. A curious combination of conformity and rebelliousness, "4-5"s will respond well to rules and regulations as long as they are given a certain amount of freedom and independence as well.

5
MOTIVATION
NUMBER

9
INNER-SELF
NUMBER

5
EXPRESSION
NUMBER

"The things that haven't been done before,
Those are the things to try. . ."
                              —*Edgar Albert Guest*

"5-5"s are true free spirits. Freedom to do their own thing is important to them and they enjoy excitement, adventure and variety in their life. You might meet them anywhere from the beach to the county fair, from an adult-education class to the local hot-dog stand. Their inquisitive nature makes their interests limitless and your best bet for capturing their attention is to be in their line of vision—that is, have a talent or interest in something they like, and let them know it. If, for instance, they are lusting to go on a scuba-diving trip your company is offering, make sure you go too—and do a little homework in advance. When they find out you can identify all the fish and the coral you see, they may end up lusting after you too—providing there's chemistry there to start with.

"5-5"s are attracted to exciting and sensual people who provide intellectual as well as physical stimulation. They are easily bored with anyone they can take for granted, and the best way to keep their attention is to add novelty to the relationship and to keep them guessing—at least once in a while. Don't expect them to cater to your every whim or to stay always by your side. Constantly on the go, they are hard to pin down. Their mind soon wanders somewhere else, and although they may be enjoyable company, they have inconsistent temperaments and are not very dependable.

"5-5"s enjoy being surrounded by people and are often the life of the party, but they are unlikely to pledge allegiance to anyone. Not especially loyal, they seek variety in their relationships as in everything else. Although they might sweep you off your feet, their charm may be superficial and should not be taken too seriously. They do not like to feel pressured or restricted in any way, and suggestion works much better than telling them what to do. "5-5"s want to make commitments—if any—themselves, and if they finally decide to settle down it will be by their own choice—not because of another's maneuverings. Since sensual pleasures and new experiences are so appealing to them, it is possible that even when the knot has been tied, they will occasionally stray from home. They are willing to try unusual life-styles, and with their "anything goes" attitude, an open marriage may be more successful than a more traditional one.

At work, versatile and clever "5-5"s have a talent for improvising and for finding new, improved ways of doing things. They dislike routine and detail and have trouble sticking with any one task for very long. Resourceful and full of innovative ideas, they are the most likely combination to be a "jack of all trades, master of none." People-contact is important to their well-being, and they are happiest working at something unusual or different which provides action, change and stimulation. Dealing with the public, investigating, seeking new solutions to things, or undercover work are all fields they find enjoyable. And whatever they enjoy, they are good at. Constantly on the go, and not known for their loyalty, "5-5"s would not hesitate to grab what they might consider a better or more interesting opportunity—even if it were with a rival company.

"5-5" children are curious, restless and easily bored, and have trouble staying with any one project for very long. Anything exciting or risky beckons them—climbing the tallest tree, jumping off the highest diving board, going on the "scariest" ride in the amusement park, or taking a flying leap on their skateboard. They love the feeling of speed, whether it comes from riding their bicycle as fast as it will go, skiing down a steep slope, or just racing in the wind. Lively and energetic, they need plenty of exercise and physical activity, and they enjoy sports—especially those that are competitive. However, they prefer tennis, swimming or skating to being on a football or baseball team. Somewhat loners, they are more interested in perfecting their own skills than in cooperating with a group of people or being loyal to a team. Quick to learn, they usually do well in school but often get impatient with the establishment's way of doing things.

6

MOTIVATION
NUMBER

8

INNER-SELF
NUMBER

"Love has always been the most important business in my life . . ."

—*Stendhal*

5

EXPRESSION
NUMBER

Charming and outgoing, "6-5"s enjoy entertaining or being entertained. Social life is very important to them and they like to have a lot of friends. This is one combination that does not mind going on a blind date or trying a singles' bar or dance. Their attitude is likely to be "nothing ventured, nothing gained." Yet though they may appear flirtatious, restless, or fickle, they really want a steady, long-term relationship, and appearances to the contrary, settling down with a home and family is important to them. Without someone special to care for, they feel insecure and unfulfilled.

"6-5"s are attracted to members of the opposite sex who seem loyal, affectionate and outgoing, and who share their love of home and can provide emotional security. Once infatuated, they will pursue the relationship right from the start. There's no playing hard to get or "I'll see you around" attitude with them. Domestic urges are almost as strong as sexual attractions, and they are eager to play house for real. Resourceful and sometimes artistic, they enjoy putting their talents to use in creating a harmonious abode for themselves, and will expect their partner to take an interest in this as well. However, they believe a home should have a lived-in feeling, and they don't put much emphasis on fastidious housekeeping.

Idealistic and romantic, "6-5"s have a strong belief in fair play but don't always adhere to it themselves. As long as they feel a mutual bond of trust, understanding and love, they are willing to allow their mate the freedom to pursue separate interests. However, they can be quite manipulative too. They often end up turning things to their own advantage, sometimes making those close feel used and abused. "6-5"s themselves can be quite upset and confused by this conflict between what they want and what they do, and find it hard to admit to their shortcomings. They do not like having their faults pointed out to them, and can be disbelieving and defensive when they are.

At work as in their private lives, "6-5"s are creative, expressive, and people-oriented. They enjoy dealing with the public and giving advice—whether it be as receptionists at a convention directing people where to go, salesmen telling prospective customers which shade is most becoming, or social workers counseling runaway children. Committed to their work, they have a deep sense of responsibility and are willing to put in long hours when necessary. Whatever their field of endeavor, they feel they know what's best for everyone and do not hesitate to voice their opinions. They are skilled at influencing others and getting them to do things their way.

"6-5" children have dual natures. They can be charming and outgoing at times; bossy and argumentative at others. Although they are not too fond of routine chores, they are willing to help out at home, especially if it involves cooking or serving guests at one of their parents' parties. They like being at the center of things and feeling important. Other children may flock to them for advice, which they are more than willing to give since they, like their adult counterparts, feel they know what's best for everyone. They are quick to rush in and intercede when they feel someone is being wronged, and are easily hurt when their help is not appreciated.

"6-5" children enjoy the outdoors, rougher sports, and—male or female—would rather play with boys than girls. Unafraid of voicing their opinions to anyone, they are likely to be the ones chosen when someone is needed to be spokesman for the gang.

MOTIVATION
NUMBER

INNER-SELF
NUMBER

"A person needs at intervals to separate himself from family and companions . . ."
—*Katharine Butler Hathaway*

EXPRESSION
NUMBER

"7-5"s are enigmas. Although they may appear friendly and outgoing, they can also be aloof and hard to approach. Selective in their choice of friends, they are attracted to members of the opposite sex who are interesting or outstanding in some way and who share their interests. They seek intellectual stimulation and find petty chitchat boring. Very difficult to win over or hold, the way to "7-5" s' heart is through their mind. Your best bet for capturing their attention is to be conversant on a variety of subjects from world affairs to current plays, movies or TV shows, to the latest books. One of these topics is bound to be of interest to them. And avoid trying to manipulate them into a relationship or asking personal questions about their private lives. Courtship is apt to be sporadic, and unless you happen to go away on a vacation together, it is unlikely that they will spend more than a few hours at a stretch with you. Even then, they will want to be alone at least part of the time.

"7-5"s have a need for privacy, and potential or even actual mates must understand that when they say they are going to spend the night reading, they probably mean it. And if they are fibbing, they are doing so out of principle—because you're prying. They insist on keeping a part of themselves hidden, and nobody, absolutely nobody, can penetrate that invisible shield they put up. (Don't even try unless you want to surely turn them off.) Of all the combinations, "7-5"s are one of the most likely to want to get away from it all, and their escapism may take many forms—from sleeping too much to overindulging in food, drink, sex or drugs.

"7-5"s can be self-centered and critical but a wise partner will disregard this fault-finding aspect of their personality, realizing that it's nothing personal—it's just that nothing, no matter how perfect to other eyes, is ever quite right for them. They are not the greatest candidates for family responsibility or settling down, but if they do decide to make a commitment, their intended better not stall or put the decision off. "7-5"s are apt to change their mind—especially if they feel rejected—and may quickly turn their interest somewhere else.

At work, "7-5"s are perfectionists—more interested in specializing in some area than in dealing with other people. Whether bosses or employees, they like to do things their own way and they do not like to be asked a lot of questions. If they have to associate with others—as salesmen or teachers, for instance—they would prefer to deal with top management or the very brightest students.

"7-5"s are drawn to anything unseen, unknown or mysterious, such as the occult, which their curious minds can investigate, and their ability to probe and analyze makes them natural detectives. Their intuition comes in handy in business as well as in their personal lives, and more often than not they make a decision because it feels right.

"7-5" children are hard to understand. Adults in their environment may feel they spend too much time alone or that they are old beyond their years. Like their adult counterparts, they crave privacy and they resent being questioned about anything personal—not because they're doing something wrong, but just on principle. Somewhat loners, they feel different from most of their peers and are very selective in their choice of friends. Although they usually know they will be successful someday, they want to excel in some area and may feel insecure and full of ungrounded fears. They appreciate reassurance that they are loved and acceptable the way they are.

"7-5" children resent being told what to do by someone who just happens to be older and bigger but not necessarily wiser, and they may do just the opposite as soon as they are able—just out of spite! If, for example, they are forced to go to bed early every night, they may later on develop irregular sleeping habits and upon reaching adulthood, be real night owls. Or, if they have been forbidden to play with a certain ethnic group, they may wind up marrying someone of that nationality when they're older. They can't wait to grow up!

MOTIVATION
NUMBER

INNER-SELF
NUMBER

EXPRESSION
NUMBER

". . . It's as easy to marry a rich woman as a poor woman."

—*Thackeray*

Although they may appear charming and outgoing, "8-5"s can also be calculating and manipulative. Concerned with their image, they are impressed by power, wealth and prestige, and often marry someone they feel can enhance their station in life. Their philosophy is likely to be that it's just as easy to fall in love with someone rich as it is to fall in love with someone poor. When they meet a person who fits their specifications, they are unlikely to let different backgrounds or religions stand in the way of the union. Persuasive and persistent, they do not take "no" for an answer and will pursue the object of their affections relentlessly.

Active and energetic, "8-5"s enjoy working-out and keeping fit. You are as likely to meet them in a swimming pool or on the handball court as at work or through a friend. They are attracted to members of the opposite sex who are sophisticated and, like them are interested in climbing to the top. Although they have trouble expressing tender feelings and may appear more interested in their career, they can be generous and responsive to someone who appreciates and admires them, and who not only believes in their ambitions but is willing to help them achieve their goals as well. But, there is also a stubborn and inconsiderate side to their nature which is brought out by anyone who opposes them. A lover who has outlived his or her usefulness may be shocked at how unfeeling "8-5"s can be toward anyone who stands in their way.

Once they have settled down and tied the knot, "8-5"s consider their family a reflection of themselves and may be rough on a child they consider a whiner or a sissy. They are happiest with a loyal, devoted, encouraging mate who offers moral and emotional support and who allows them to make the important decisions in the relationship (or at least lets them *think* they're the boss).

At work, as in their private lives, "8-5"s aspire to a position of prestige and power. They would like freedom to do things their own way. Hard-working but restless, they prefer an active busy job to one involving dull routine. They are rarely satisfied with the latter and may do it only as a last resort to pay their bills—planning all the while to do something better. Clever and enthusiastic, they are good at organizing people and finding more efficient ways of doing things. They have a keen business sense and may discover unique ways of making money—investing in real estate or a product few others would consider, for example.

"8-5" children, like their adult counterparts, are expert at getting others to let them have their way. They can, for instance, get Mother to let them stay up past their bedtime to watch TV by convincing her the program will help improve their grade in Social Studies, by promising to fold the laundry for her while they're watching, and so on. Constantly on the go, they are full of restless energy that needs an active outlet. Sports usually appeal to them and they prefer those in which they do well. Lively and competitive, they need to stand out in some area and will work hard to gain recognition. Good at organizing their peers, they are likely to be class leaders or captains of the team and, in fact, these activities are often more important to them than studying. "8-5"s need a great deal of love and attention, and above all, the reassurance that they are important in some way.

9
MOTIVATION
NUMBER

5
INNER-SELF
NUMBER

5
EXPRESSION
NUMBER

"Live life . . . every golden moment of it."
—Unknown

"9-5"s are sociable and outgoing and enjoy being around people. They live broad, active, adventuresome lives, which may seem routine to them but usually appear enviable and exciting to others. Easily bored, they need an active social life and, when possible, frequent changes of scenery such as a weekend skiing in the mountains or a few days at the shore. You are more likely to meet them at a party or on a cruise than in a library or at a lecture.

"9-5"s are attracted to members of the opposite sex who are interesting and fun-loving, and they tend to shy away from anyone who seems gloomy or boring. Full of restless energy, they are not about to sit around sympathizing with tales of woe. Although they themselves can talk a blue streak, they are not usually good listeners and are apt to hear only what they want. Chances are that unless you share their diverse interests and are able to keep up with them, you will not hold their interest for long. Romantics at heart, they can be jealous and possessive of their current heartthrob, but will quickly tire of anyone who plays hard to get or who keeps them guessing too long. Their attention can quickly shift to someone new, and they often have a "love them and leave them" reputation.

Ruled by their emotions, "9-5"s can be quite dramatic—attracting attention to themselves by their behavior. Kindhearted and generous, they have a "what's mine is yours and what's yours is mine" attitude toward money and possessions and have no qualms about draining their partner's resources as well as their own. Although they are usually cheerful and outgoing, they can also be irritable and tense—especially if they feel restricted or tied down in any way. Impatient when things don't go their way, they can have quite a temper when crossed.

"9-5"s have leadership ability and are good at dealing with the public. They do not like to feel confined in some insignificant routine job, and they seek work that has a purpose of some kind. Money isn't always a major consideration and they may volunteer much time to an endeavor they feel is worthwhile—directing a drama group, or fund-raising for a worthy cause, for example. They are often drawn to politics where they can fight for something they believe in, get on a soapbox and be noticed.

Although willing to work hard, "9-5"s have a tendency to get restless and need frequent breaks. Vacations are important to them and they may be tempted to take more time off than they are allotted, even if it's without pay. So great is their need for a certain amount of freedom to make their own decisions that they may impulsively quit a job rather than give in to rigid thinking.

"9-5" children have active imaginations and are easy to entertain. Full of restless energy, they enjoy playing ball or hide-and-seek with their friends in the playground. Avid readers of fairy tales, adventure stories, and—as they get older—romances, they can also get lost in flights of fantasy at a show, the ballet, or a trip to the museum. Music is another love, and even before they can read, they may be able to pick out which records they'd like to hear by learning to recognize the labels.

"9-5"s find learning new things exciting but they may not enjoy the pressure and rigidity of a formal classroom situation. Although a certain amount of routine makes them feel secure, strict authority leads to nervousness and inner tension. Unless their humanitarian spirit has been dampened by bigoted adults, they are compassionate and broad-minded, and from a very early age they may be champion of the underdog. "9-5"s cannot be forced into a model, but yearn to be loved and accepted for what they are.

MOTIVATION
NUMBER

INNER-SELF
NUMBER

EXPRESSION
NUMBER

"Life is so very short and very uncertain; let us spend it as well as we can."

—*Unknown*

The most likely place to meet "11-5" is at work or through friends. Although they may seem extroverted, easygoing and flirtatious, they are sensitive and even shy. Wanting to make a good first impression, they are eager to appear agreeable, and at a swim party, for instance, may pretend to enjoy sitting on a swimmer's shoulders (as he or she walks deeper and deeper into the water) even though they may be scared to death and haven't had the nerve to tell anyone they can't swim. Or, they might blow a week's salary on dinner at a restaurant that turned out to be much more expensive than they thought, rather than suggest eating somewhere else. (It would be too humiliating to admit they couldn't afford it.)

"11-5"s are free spirits who want someone else to be free with. Parties, dinner out or the theater all hold appeal, and even though without the opportunity to do these things they would feel restless and tense, they don't really enjoy doing them alone. Love, affection and companionship are essential to their well-being and they seek to share their lives with someone outgoing, dependable and responsive who has similar ideals. However, they have trouble accepting others for what they are, and can easily become disappointed and depressed when a partner fails to live up to their expectations. Often, without realizing it, their relationships are based on physical attraction and they may go through a series of unhappy affairs before settling down. Each time they feel "this one will be different," but all too often they pick the same type over and over again.

Intuitive and idealistic, "11-5"s are drawn toward work they feel is meaningful or that conveys a message of some kind—education, counseling, film production or photography, for example. People fascinate them and they prefer a job that involves contact with others to one where they are off by themselves. However they do need freedom to carry it out their own way without constant supervision. Pettiness is a turn-off and they try to avoid getting involved in it. But they do have a knack for troubleshooting and diagnosing business ills and may sometimes act as mediators, trying to pacify two opposing sides.

Also read the description for "2-5," which begins on page 119. "11" is such a high vibration that it is impossible to operate on it all the time. Children act like its lower octave—"2"—most of the time, and adults operate on the "2" at least part of the time.

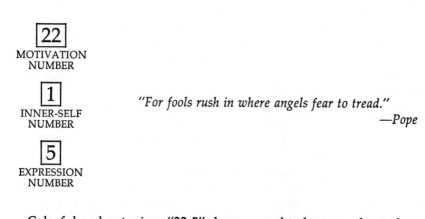

22
MOTIVATION
NUMBER

1
INNER-SELF
NUMBER

5
EXPRESSION
NUMBER

"For fools rush in where angels fear to tread."
                                                          —*Pope*

Colorful and outgoing, "22-5"s have a need to be around people and to lead an active, varied social life. They may, however, have difficulty forming strong emotional bonds with one person unless they have something else in common such as work. Although you could meet this combination at a social gathering or participating in a sporting event, they are more likely to be attracted to someone they see on their job who has some quality they admire. "22-5" could, for instance, be the scientist searching for a cure for cancer who falls in love with his or her brilliant lab assistant; or a pilot who is drawn to the stewardess on his flight who speaks six different languages.

Despite their unconventional and often erratic behavior, earthy "22-5"s really need some security and stability. Yet their impulsive ways often defeat their aims and it can sometimes take superhuman patience and understanding to put up with them. They may, for instance, in the midst of a serious relationship with someone special they hope to settle down with, suddenly for no apparent reason go off to some exotic place with a new acquaintance. This conflict between what they want and what they do can lead to great inner turmoil and pain.

Even when they have tied the knot, "22-5"s are not always easy to live with. They have high expectations of their spouse and demand not much less than domestic perfection. They are happiest with a versatile, domestically oriented, responsive mate who is their intellectual equal and who is willing to let them have the final say as to how things should be run. Expecting to be the boss at home, they can be subject to explosive outbursts of temper when crossed.

At work, "22-5"s would like to accomplish great things, but unless they have learned to discipline themselves they may scatter their energies to such a degree that they never make their dreams a reality. When creating something grand is on their minds and no practical results seem to be manifesting, they can become extremely depressed and fraught with inner tension. Discrepancies between what they want and what they do only serve to confuse them.

Creative but restless, "22-5"s are happiest in action-packed jobs—situations that call for flexibility and quick decision-making, such as head of an emergency room, or a commodities broker on the floor of the stock exchange, for example. They find dull routine irritating, and regimentation such as punching a clock goes against their grain. Much as they want order and efficiency, they need a certain amount of freedom to do things their own way as well. Flexible hours are preferable and an atmosphere that gives them the feeling of having a certain amount of power spurs them on.

Also read the description for "4-5," which starts on page 122. "22" is such a high vibration that it is impossible to operate on it all the time. Children act like its lower octave—"4"—most of the time and adults operate on the "4" at least part of the time.

VIII
Service and Responsibility: The Number 6

Affectionate and domestically inclined, "6"s seek emotional harmony and strive to bring comfort and happiness to those close to them. Homeloving and service-oriented, they need someone to take care of and to do things for. They can be very possessive and overprotective, and are often blind to the faults of those they love.

It is difficult for "6"s to see any viewpoint other than their own, and they insist they're always right, no matter what the issue. Honest, straightforward and often blunt, they feel they know what's best for everyone and can be quite the domestic tyrants. They have a remedy for everything, and a desire to right all wrongs (according to their own standards). They enjoy giving advice and are often asked to intercede in disputes. However, so great is their sense of justice that they may be quick to jump in even when they aren't asked, and they are liable to take offense if criticized for meddling.

"6"s take their responsibilities (whether domestic, social, or career) seriously and are always there when needed. Kind, sympathetic, and sometimes too trusting, they find it hard to say "no" and are prone to fall for a sad story. They have a tendency to put others before themselves and to get so wrapped up in their problems that they neglect their own well-being. For example, although home, family and children are so important to them, "6"s are the most likely number to stay unmarried because of loyalty to an aging parent whose care they feel responsible for. Unexpressed resentment often builds up, however, making them moody, picky or quarrelsome.

Friendly, congenial and responsive, "6"s relate easily to others. Their charm and persuasiveness enables them to sell just about anything they believe in. They are drawn to fields concerned with the welfare of other people—catering, housekeeping, medicine or counseling, for example. But just as often they use their artistic and creative talents at home, producing harmonious surroundings for their loved ones. They enjoy decorating, cooking, entertaining and bringing the family together to celebrate special occasions. Sentimental and romantic at heart, they also enjoy remembering special occasions with a gift or card.

Great believers in teamwork, "6"s do not like doing things alone and prefer feeling socially involved in some way. They love mixing and mingling with people and being part of a group. Charming and outgoing, they enjoy socializing and making others feel at ease. For instance, perfect hosts or hostesses, they will try to seem interested in the conversation of their guests even if the topic does not interest them at all. They have a strong sense of loyalty—friendships are dear to them—and most of their relationships are long-lasting.

COMPATIBILITY GUIDE

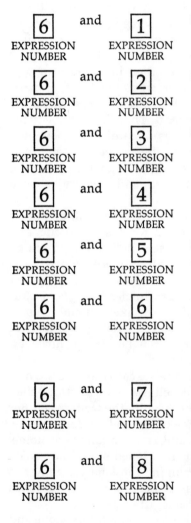

6 and 1 EXPRESSION NUMBER / EXPRESSION NUMBER		See page 33 (chapter III).
6 and 2 EXPRESSION NUMBER / EXPRESSION NUMBER		See page 53 (chapter IV).
6 and 3 EXPRESSION NUMBER / EXPRESSION NUMBER		See page 73 (chapter V).
6 and 4 EXPRESSION NUMBER / EXPRESSION NUMBER		See page 94 (chapter VI).
6 and 5 EXPRESSION NUMBER / EXPRESSION NUMBER		See page 116 (chapter VII).

6 and **6**
EXPRESSION NUMBER / EXPRESSION NUMBER

Good combination providing each shares the other's ideals. Otherwise they may try to remake each other and a great deal of compromise and adjustment will be called for.

6 and **7**
EXPRESSION NUMBER / EXPRESSION NUMBER

Conflict between "6"'s need to interact with others and "7"'s desire for privacy may make this a poor, mutually irritating combination.

6 and **8**
EXPRESSION NUMBER / EXPRESSION NUMBER

Good combination for business, or marriage. Both are responsible, practical and stable, and "8" appreciates "6"'s ability to create harmony and entertain guests.

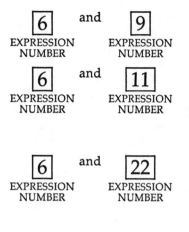

| 6 and 9 | Creative, artistic, humanitarian combination—good for business, friendship or marriage. |

6
EXPRESSION
NUMBER
and
9
EXPRESSION
NUMBER

Creative, artistic, humanitarian combination—good for business, friendship or marriage.

6
EXPRESSION
NUMBER
and
11
EXPRESSION
NUMBER

Good business or marriage combination. Both are creative and idealistic, and seek love, peace and harmony. "11" can broaden "6" 's horizons, and "6" can add balance to "11" 's life.

6
EXPRESSION
NUMBER
and
22
EXPRESSION
NUMBER

Socially responsible "6" and humanitarian "22" work well together as a team to benefit others. In a close personal relationship, however, "6" may find "22" inhibiting and there can be an angry clash of wills at home.

Following are all possible combination of a "6" expression number with the different motivation and inner-self numbers.

1
MOTIVATION
NUMBER

5
INNER-SELF
NUMBER

"Respect the other fellow's opinion, but always act on your own."

—Unknown

6
EXPRESSION
NUMBER

Although "1-6"s are willful and have minds of their own, they often join community organizations or groups that provide intellectual stimulation or an opportunity to put some skill to use—a chess club, a study group, a tenants' association or a choir, for example. These are the best places to meet them since they are attracted to members of the opposite sex who share their interests or who possess some talent they admire. "1-6," for instance, can be the singer who falls in love with one of the dancers at the Folklore Society, or the first grade teacher who ends up dating a divorced parent he or she meets at the PTA.

Once you have captured "1-6" s' attention, the way to their heart is to make them feel important—recognize and admire their achievements, seek their advice on some issue (and, of course, be sure to let them know how good it was later on). Don't be critical or pushy or tell them what to do—no matter how yielding or willing they seem—or you may be in for an unexpected surprise. Remember that "5" inner-self!

"1-6"s need a certain amount of freedom, but seldom voice this need until they reach their boiling point and give vent to an unexpected outburst of temper. Even when they are romantic and dependable, never take them for granted, and make sure there are good channels of communication open between you so you can prevent problems later on. They may, for instance, seem to want to spend all their free time with you and do all the things you want to do, while beneath the surface (and unbeknownst to you) resentment is building up at all the adjustments and sacrifices they feel they are being called upon to make. One day, out of the clear blue, and for no apparent reason at all, they may pick a fight with you, angrily accuse you of being too demanding and selfish, and break off what seemed (to you) like a beautiful relationship.

Restless yet responsible, independent yet devoted, "1-6"s may themselves be confused at these different aspects of their personality and wonder how it's possible to feel them all at the same time. They are happiest with a patient, understanding mate, who can accept them for what they are and who lets them have their own way.

At work, "1-6"s need a worthwhile goal on which to focus their enthusiasm. Creative and energetic, they are happiest in some area where they can combine leadership with service—politics, medicine or education, for example. Stable and responsible, they have good judgment, innovative ideas, and the ability to lead a group along new and adventuresome paths.

Although they may appear conservative, they have a yearning to do something pioneering or unusual and they may, for instance, be a minister who volunteers to do missionary work in Africa, or a doctor who joins the Peace Corps, or a chef who seeks a job on a cruise ship that sails around the world.

"1-6" children are independent thinkers, eager to fend for themselves without parental interference. Neither whiners nor crybabies, they have friendly, endearing personalities and a good sense of humor. Although outgoing and adventuresome, they take their responsibilities seriously both at home and at school. They have few qualms about displaying their talents and like to be praised for their excellence—whether it be a good report card or a star performance in a school play.

Children of many interests, "1-6"s like active sports but can be just as happy listening to records, drawing pictures, playing checkers or relaxing in a rocking chair. They have a tendency to be impulsive and not always look before they leap. Consequently they may be the team member who hits the baseball through Mrs. Miller's window. Although they are often part of a group or team, they are just as happy to be alone. Domestic activities interest them and a favorite plaything could well be a toy stove. Pretend cooking may quickly turn into helping Mother with culinary creations.

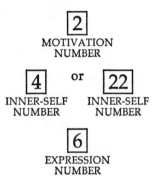

| 2 |
| MOTIVATION NUMBER |

| 4 | or | 22 |
| INNER-SELF NUMBER | | INNER-SELF NUMBER |

"A helping hand, an eager heart, he's always there to do his part."

—*Unknown*

| 6 |
| EXPRESSION NUMBER |

Loyal and devoted themselves, "2-6"s are attracted to members of the opposite sex who seem warm, dependable, reassuring, and who are willing to settle down as well. Practicality is another plus, as "2-6"s are not big spenders. Although they can be romantic and attentive and willing to go out, they are easily turned off by someone who always insists on going to expensive places or who is extravagant in other ways. Home-cooked meals once in a while or a walk in the park are appreciated.

The most likely place to meet "2-6" is at work or at a club, but once in a while chance meetings do occur. "2-6" can, for instance, be the woman who walks into a pet shop because looking at the animals will cheer her up, and leaves much happier . . . the salesman who tried to sell her the two parakeets (who, by the way, were kissing each other), asked her to go to the movies with him Friday night.

Ideal homemakers, "2-6"s want someone to care for and to share their dreams with. To them, life without love is not worth living. But they are cautious in their approach and may wait for the person they are interested in to make the first move rather than risk rejection. They are unlikely to pursue someone who seems indifferent to their advances.

Peace-loving, adaptable and perceptive, "2-6"s are willing to compromise in order to create harmony. Good listeners and considerate hosts or hostesses, they go out of their way to make their guests feel comfortable, and they have a tendency to be self-sacrificing for those close. So hard do they try to please, they often seem passive (unless they have a

"22" inner-self number) and, considering them to be easy pushovers, others may take advantage of them. Extremely sensitive and emotionally vulnerable, they are easily hurt and can be subject to moodiness and depression when they feel unappreciated. Yet an enthusiastic thank you and a compliment are sufficient rewards for the little favors they are constantly doing for loved ones.

At work, "2-6"s are creative, tactful and diplomatic, and work well with others. New employees find them most willing to show them the ropes of a job and get them involved in the group. As long as they feel needed and appreciated, they are the combination most willing to stay in the background and make some personal sacrifice to further the success of a group.

"2-6"s are good at details and are willing to follow instructions. They have a talent for putting themselves in the other person's position and seeing things from their point of view. Humanitarian work, teaching, and diplomacy are their forte and they are extremely reliable in whatever area they choose.

Like their adult counterparts, "2-6" children are friendly and kindhearted. Willing to help out at home or at school, they want to feel needed and appreciated and can become resentful and moody when they don't. Tears are common and Mother may be perplexed as to why. These children crave affection and without it feel lost and abandoned.

Home and security are important to "2-6"s and they are usually unquestioning followers of rules. Although they might get involved in childish pranks if their friends are all doing it, they're not apt to play hooky or forget to do their homework or talk back to the teacher. At play, they are eager to be part of a group and, subject to peer pressure, will put up little defense if they fear their popularity is at stake.

"2-6" children love animals and will show heartrending devotion to a pet if they're fortunate enough to have one. They like to cuddle and may also become attached to a teddy bear or favorite doll, which they insist on having near them before they go to sleep.

3
MOTIVATION
NUMBER

3
INNER-SELF
NUMBER

6
EXPRESSION
NUMBER

"Even though the hour is late, it takes more determination than I've got to walk away from a party that is going well."

—*William Feather*

"3-6"s are never at a loss for words. Although the most likely place to meet them is at a social event or a community affair, they are good at finding pretexts for striking up conversations with intriguing strangers who catch their eye. "3-6," for instance, could be the man who sees an enchanting girl at the tie counter in Bloomingdale's and asks her opinion as to which one his father might like best—the stripes or the blue? Or, the woman who asks the handsome-looking man in the hotel lobby to take her four-year-old nephew to the men's room for her. Good looks are what attracts them first, but they are also looking for a personality that complements their own. If, for instance, they are the quiet type (which is unusual), they may date someone talkative and extroverted. If they're loquacious and outgoing, they may be attracted to a shrinking violet. Either way their main concern is that their partner be loyal and devoted and able to make them look and feel good.

"3-6"s like being the center of attention and have a need to be admired and appreciated. Spontaneous and outspoken, they want to be socially active and to have someone to voice their opinions to. They can be convincing talkers and are good at winning arguments—sometimes twisting logic or purposefully overlooking details. Generous, affectionate and romantic at heart, they want to enjoy life and prefer going out and doing things to sitting home by the fire. Entertaining or being entertained is a significant part of their life, and when they are home, they like having their house filled with guests. Although not the best organizers in the world, they are good cooks and are also particular about the appearance of what they serve—that sprig of parsley or twist of lemon must be in just the right place.

"3-6"s are somewhat high-strung, but once they settle down, they make good spouses and parents. They adore children and lavish lots of love and attention on them. They enjoy playing with them, teaching them things, and showing them off, and will see to it that they are always dressed nicely for school. On the other hand, "3-6"s can be jealous and possessive of their mate and often have double standards— for instance, it may be okay for them to flirt, but not for their partner.

Not ones for cutthroat business, "3-6"s prefer working in some creative field where they can express their artistic talents. Harmonious surroundings are important to them and they derive much personal gratification from being popular with their coworkers. Charming and outgoing, they work well with other people and with children and they make excellent teachers. They also excel at getting ideas or messages across in an imaginative, expressive way. Generous and caring, they make a point of becoming personally involved with those they work with, and "3-6" may, for instance, be the boarding-school counselor who buys a bathrobe and slippers for the little boy or girl who doesn't have any.

Always conscious of beauty in things as well as people, "3-6"s often end up making one or the other attractive—designing homes and apartments or clothes and jewelry, painting pictures or making up faces, sculpting statues or styling hair. Music or acting may also appeal to them and they enjoy performing, whether it be for one or one thousand. Drama may or may not be part of their profession, but it is certainly part of their everyday life.

"3-6" children, like their adult counterparts, want to be seen and heard and should not be stifled. Their creative talents need to be channeled into something constructive, such as art, music or drama. They love to talk and may frequently have to be admonished to be quiet and pay attention in school. Their attention spans are relatively short and they have difficulty sitting still for long periods of time. However they are curious and imaginative and do well at things that interest them.

"3-6"s are expressive and beguiling. Very often they use their charm (innocently or on purpose) to get what they want. For example, "3-6" is the little girl who dresses up in her mother's best clothes and makeup, and as Mother is about to scold her, puts on her most endearing smile and says, "I hope I'm as pretty as you are when I grow up." Very often "3-6" children are spoiled rotten.

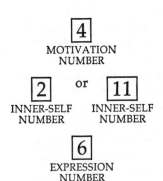

MOTIVATION
NUMBER

INNER-SELF   INNER-SELF
NUMBER   NUMBER

EXPRESSION
NUMBER

" 'Mid pleasure and palaces though we may roam, Be it ever so humble, there's no place like home . . ."

—John Howard Payne

You are most likely to meet "4-6"s at work or through friends. They like having a good time but they feel more comfortable hanging out at a friend's or having people gather at their house than going out a lot or trying something unfamiliar. Security is important to them and they are more likely to date someone whose background is similar to their own. They are attracted to members of the opposite sex who are practical, reliable, affectionate, appreciative, homeloving, and preferably from the right side of the track, and they rarely stray far from their own age group. Once you have captured their attention they will be steady, regular and dependable, but though you can expect them to be generous with their time, don't expect them to be equally so with money. Extravagance turns them off, and a home-cooked meal in a romantic setting appeals to them far more than dinner at some exclusive restaurant.

Once a relationship is in progress and some commitment has been made, don't expect to spend much time alone together. "4-6"s usually have many friends they see on a regular and frequent basis and they will expect you to fold them into your life as well. They are also close to their families and if you want to win "4-6" over, be prepared to win Mama and Papa over as well.

"4-6"s have dual personalities and their true selves are seldom revealed before marriage. They place their best foot forward to the world—appearing charming, benevolent and outgoing. At home, however, they can be critical and demanding and given to fits of temper. This duality may be even more pronounced if they have an "11" inner-self number. They may put their loved one on a pedestal during courtship only to become picky and fault-finding once the knot has been tied.

"4-6"s enjoy country living and would prefer a home in the suburbs to an apartment in the city. If, however, circumstances do not allow this, they need to escape—at least on holidays. Home is their castle and they like taking care of it, working for it, and entertaining in it. Fastidious housekeepers themselves, they expect their mate to pitch in with the chores. They expect clothes to be hung up right away, no dishes left in the sink, and may easily get annoyed if anything is disturbed (such as a guest towel rumpled by their mate before company arrives).

Practical and economical, "4-6"s like handling the family finances themselves and give freely of their sound advice to more extravagant members. They expect their spouse to know how to balance the checkbook and hairbrained get-rich-quick schemes are as likely to bring on heart palpitations as are a partner's infidelities. Dependable "4-6"s take responsibilities and commitments seriously and expect their mates to do likewise. They expect their spouse to share their values and to be as devoted and willing as they are to make sacrifices to see that the children have the attention and things that they need.

At work, as in their private lives, "4-6"s are responsibility-conscious and willing to work hard. Honest and persevering, they strive to be fair and square in all their dealings. Routine and regular hours do not faze them and they do not mind working overtime if necessary. Security is important to them and they usually scrutinize benefits and long-term growth potential when choosing a company to work for. Not apt to gamble, they would be unlikely to start out in their own business unless it were a sure thing.

Enthusiastic and reliable, "4-6"s are good at getting others to cooperate in whatever project they undertake. They are often attracted to careers that benefit people in some way and may serve on school boards or political parties either as employees or as volunteers. If they have an office job, their duties must be clearly defined and they need to feel that they are a necessary part of the whole (department, firm, or whatever).

"4-6" children have trusting natures and respect adult authority. They are therefore vulnerable to misinformation—even if it is said in jest. If Father says that the moon is made out of blue cheese they will accept it and defend it as truth in the face of anyone who doubts them. They can become very disillusioned and feel betrayed if adult behavior is proven anything but honorable. Parents should be careful what they say around their "4-6" child and assure him or her that they too are human and can make mistakes.

Obedient and responsible most of the time, "4-6" children can also be stubborn and obstinate. Since they are sensitive to criticism, it is important to let them feel that their efforts are appreciated even when they are being disciplined or corrected. They want to be noticed and to feel needed and important in some way.

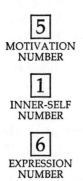

5
MOTIVATION
NUMBER

1
INNER-SELF
NUMBER

6
EXPRESSION
NUMBER

"My heart is warm with the friends I make, And better friends I'll not be knowing; Yet there isn't a train I wouldn't take, No matter where it's going."
                 —Edna St. Vincent Millay

"5-6"s need to be involved with other people and frequently meet prospective partners just plain going from "A" to "B." They may, for instance, stop to help someone who has a flat tire on the highway or who is trying to fight off some drunk at a bar. Or, they may notice an intriguing person standing in front of the bakery drooling over some pastries in the window and respond with a "they sure look good, don't they? Want to try one of those éclairs?" They are attracted to members of the opposite sex who are fun-loving, sexy, and intelligent, and provided the chemistry and excitement don't abate, courtship is likely to be constant and steady right from the start. Otherwise it could be chalked up as an interesting page in their diary marked with a star for new love interests that failed. Since the pursuit is often more fun than the catch, don't let "5-6" take you for granted. Keeping him or her guessing once in a while and adding a little novelty to the relationship now and then can do wonders where keeping the flames fanned is concerned.

Curious and enthusiastic, "5-6"'s are responsive to anything sensual, different or unusual. They often have the travel bug and feel an inner restlessness and irritability when confined, which may be confusing to them. Although they feel committed to their loved ones and would never actually abandon their responsibilities, they do need a certain amount of freedom to pursue their own interests and may daydream of greener pastures and release from home ties and duties. If they can afford it (once they have settled down), they are the combination most likely to turn family vacations into something exciting and adventuresome that everyone can enjoy together—whether it be skiing on the local slopes, surfing in Hawaii, or sunbathing at Saint-Tropez.

At work, "5-6"'s are charming and persuasive and good at finding ingenious solutions to things or selling their innovative ideas. Shrewd when it comes to business, they can make money in many areas others would never think of and can turn a losing operation from the red into the black by making the right contacts, deals and investments.

People-oriented "5-6"'s have a talent for marketing and often deal with consumer products. They may be involved with anything from distributing food to building houses to making toys. Quite often responsibility upon responsibility is heaped upon them and they may feel as though they are so swamped with work they have no time to have fun. Striking a balance between toil and leisure is important for their peace of mind.

Like their adult counterparts, "5-6" children are friendly and outgoing. Active and full of restless energy, they enjoy activities such as swimming and dancing, which feel good and can also be done with a team. They need a certain amount of freedom and can become quite rebellious if severe restrictions are placed upon them. They know they're reliable and feel harsh discipline is both unnecessary and unfair.

Curiosity about new things and a sense of responsibility about getting their work done on time make "5-6"'s good students. They are full of ideas and other children are drawn to them for advice as well as companionship. If they have any younger brothers or sisters, they like telling them what to do. They also enjoy other advantages of being older, such as being able to stay out later or being the first to learn how to drive. "5-6" children often fantasize about the day when they can be their own boss and not have to answer to anyone.

6
MOTIVATION
NUMBER

9
INNER-SELF
NUMBER

6
EXPRESSION
NUMBER

"I may have my faults, but being wrong ain't one of them."

—James Riddle Hoffa

Friendly, gracious and outgoing, "6-6"s are usually popular with members of the opposite sex. However, they may have trouble settling down to a steady relationship. They are great romantics and quick to fall in love, but too much togetherness leads to fault-finding and pickiness on their part. "6-6"s are one of the hardest combinations to please, and whereas they may at first put a prospective lover on a pedestal, it may soon crumble.

Beauty and harmony in their surroundings are important to "6-6" s' well-being and they are attracted to people who are affectionate, soft spoken, homeloving and appreciative. Behavior that is coarse or vulgar in any way will surely turn them off and they don't like to be criticized or contradicted. They are happiest with a partner they can control as well as cater to—someone who will let them be right. But if the relationship gets too comfortable or turns into a boring rut, they may turn elsewhere for stimulation.

"6-6"s need someone to take care of but it doesn't have to be a lover or a family of their own. They can also be parental toward friends and coworkers. They are genuinely concerned for others and feel they have to protect them (whether by seeing that they eat right or dress warmly enough) and may have a tendency to be worrywarts. They are often reputed to have a remedy for everything from a broken romance to the common cold and they love giving advice. No matter what the issue, they always feel they are right and that only their opinion counts, and they can create resentment in others when their ideas on how to right wrongs or on how to better manage one's life are unsolicited.

Single or married, "6-6"s enjoy taking care of a home, decorating, cooking and most of all entertaining. They have a talent for playing host and making their guests feel at ease. They are noted for their culinary skills as well, and an invitation to a "6-6" dinner party is rarely refused.

At work, as in their private lives, "6-6"s want to feel needed, trusted, respected and appreciated for their efforts. In return, they are willing to take on responsibilities that others flee from and will go out of their way to improve situations and to create order and harmony out of confusion. Idealistic and service-oriented, they would like to be in a position that gives them the opportunity to advise, comfort or protect others. This desire to help people, combined with their good insight into human behavior, often leads them into careers concerned with the welfare of others—teaching, counseling or social work, for instance. They are also interested in community affairs and may take an active part in local politics. They have a tendency to get emotionally involved with their work, and if not careful, may get mixed up in messy company politics and gossip.

"6-6" children can be friendly and charming at times, bossy and obstinate at others. Having other children to play with is important to them. They begin giving advice very early in life and, like their adult counterparts, have a thing about always being right. Convinced that they know it all, they often learn lessons the hard way.

Often creative and talented, "6-6"s should be encouraged to vent some of their energies and frustrations into some form of artistic expression. Giving them responsibilities is also a good way to keep them out of mischief. Caring for a pet, weeding a garden, delivering papers, are all tasks they can perform.

Interested in food and its preparation, "6-6" children enjoy helping Mother prepare meals—especially dessert. When it comes time to clean up, however, they are quick to disappear.

7
MOTIVATION NUMBER

8
INNER-SELF NUMBER

"To associate with other like-minded people in small purposeful groups . . ."

—*Aldous Huxley*

6
EXPRESSION NUMBER

You are more likely to meet "7-6"s through work or friends than at a social event. It's not that they don't like entertaining or being entertained, but they prefer small, select, intimate groups to anything that resembles a crowd. "7-6" could, for instance, be an editor who starts a relationship with an author he or she finds particularly attractive as well as talented; or a graduate student who falls for one of his or her professors. Like anyone who has a "7" motivation, "7-6"s seek both looks and brains. Physical compatibility is a must, but so is intellectual rapport.

"7-6"s can be difficult to understand. Although they may appear outgoing and charming, they are reluctant to express their true feelings. Appearances to the contrary, they often feel insecure and lack confidence in themselves and exuberance may be a coverup for sensitivity. They need time to warm up to a situation and are often reluctant to show a new love interest too much attention right away. A "7-6" man, for instance, may at first wait two or three weeks between calls; and a "7-6" woman might be turned off by a man she's just met who tries to see her every night—she's apt to feel he's coming on too strong. Male or female, they dislike being rushed into anything and like a partner to grow on them. They do not like people prying into their private lives—especially someone they've just met. First dates should be kept on an intellectual level. Interesting discussions on books or plays, for instance, are apt to endear you to them a lot faster than flattery or a bunch of personal questions or, heaven forbid, a pass.

Once a commitment has been made, "7-6"s have high standards and a strong sense of responsibility. They may, however, have trouble adapting to their partner's habits and idiosyncracies. They themselves need a certain amount of privacy in a relationship but are not always willing to give it to loved ones. They may be jealous and possessive and resentful of having to adjust to a partner's life-style (preferring that the adjustment be to theirs instead). Devoted spouses and conscientious parents, they run efficient households but are not always eager to listen to viewpoints of family members which differ from their own, and they can be demanding and critical at home.

At work, "7-6"s want to be experts in some area. They are happiest in a career that is mentally stimulating, influential, and which provides a service for others while at the same time allowing them a certain amount of independence. They like to reason things out and in their search for meaning in everything, they are often drawn to psychology or one of the esoteric sciences such as astrology or tarot. They have a talent for applying the knowledge they gain from their studies to practical everyday life, and can be a great help to others.

Shrewd and analytical, "7-6"s can handle office work with skill and accuracy, but they do not like to deal with company politics or the pettiness that goes on in most offices. They need to feel that they are doing something important and prestigious and they like to do their work their own way, without someone looking over their shoulder. Form and design are likely to catch their fancy, and they can create beauty from the crudest of materials. They also have a knack for choosing what goes best with what. "7-6," for instance, is the interior decorator who selects the perfect table for that odd corner and just the right drapes to match the living-room furniture; or the valet who makes sure to pack appropriate clothes for his or her boss's ski week in Switzerland and orders the most stylish tuxedo for the black-tie ball.

"7-6" children, like their adult counterparts, need a great deal of love and understanding. Although they may appear outgoing, they are very sensitive and may have crying fits for what appears to be no reason at all. At other times they may compensate for feelings of inadequacy by being boisterous and bossy. Parents should consider the possibility that obnoxious behavior could merely be a means of getting attention. They should be encouraged to excel in some area and be given moments of privacy when they seem to want to be left alone.

Eager to learn, "7-6"s are conscientious about getting their homework done and usually do well in school—at least in subjects which interest them. They like to play games with their friends too, and often are successful in getting them to do things their way. Although they hate being asked a lot of personal questions, they like to have one special pal with whom they can share special secrets which they wouldn't tell anyone else. Impressed by image, "7-6"s often join fan clubs or select organizations and can become cliquish when they let themselves get too wrapped up in their own small groups.

8
MOTIVATION
NUMBER

7
INNER-SELF
NUMBER

"With affection beaming in one eye, and calculation shining out of the other."

—*Dickens*

6
EXPRESSION
NUMBER

"8-6"s want to settle down and have a family but are unlikely to marry for love alone. Early in life they set a goal for themselves, and although they are attracted to members of the opposite sex who are good-looking, dependable and intelligent, they will rarely pursue the relationship unless he or she can in some way enhance their station in life as well. They enjoy things that are impressive—a palatial home, expensive cars and clothes and may confine their dating to people of one or two professions they admire (with family wealth being a possible compensating exception). Since they expect to have children who will carry on their line, so to speak, they may in extreme cases, have even more stringent requirements. They may, for instance, be looking for someone who not only belongs to the right religion, class and socio-economic background, but who has blue eyes or black curly hair as well.

Once they have found someone who fulfills all their requirements, "8-6"s will pursue him or her relentlessly and probably sweep them off their feet. They can be generous and lavish with their attentions during courtship, but are apt to become more practical, demanding and involved with home or career once the knot has been tied. They take responsibility seriously and expect their mate to do likewise. Loyal, devoted and appreciative of a warm, understanding spouse who allows them to make all the important decisions and who helps them achieve their goals, "8-6"s are unlikely to turn to extramarital affairs, but if they do, they will never let any interfere with their happy homelife.

At work, "8-6"s want positions with authority and prestige. They are good at organizing and making important decisions, but prefer to leave the details to others. Creative and dynamic, they often use their executive skills to benefit people in some way—hospital administration, investment counseling, or store management, for example, and they have a talent for making money through food—whether it be catering parties, owning a fruit stand or managing a supermarket. Sales or marketing may also interest them, and their outgoing personality is certainly an asset should they select one of these areas.

Whatever their chosen field, "8-6" s' drive for power and their willingness to work as hard as necessary to get it, usually leads them into a job where they are boss. Their judgment when delegating responsibility is usually good, and they try to always be fair. However, they are often impatient with those who are slower than they are, and may even have a cruel streak that rears its ugly head once in a while.

"8-6" children are active and into everything, and a parent may often exclaim, "I wish I had his [or her] energy." Friendly and outgoing, they enjoy sports and being part of a team—preferably the captain. They enjoy organizing things and are likely to be active in school politics, newspaper or yearbook when they get older. Although schoolwork may not seem so interesting to them as extracurricular activities, they usually study hard because they feel they must and because they fear failure.

"8-6"s learn responsiblity at an early age, and with the proper guidance and discipline can be most helpful with domestic chores. They want recognition and appreciation for what they do, however, and very early learn the value of money. Financial handouts are never refused. (A compliment or a big hug and kiss wouldn't be either!)

MOTIVATION
NUMBER

INNER-SELF
NUMBER

"The true nobility of life is honest, earnest service."
—Unknown

6

EXPRESSION
NUMBER

Charming and outgoing, "9-6"s enjoy being the center of things—whether it be giving advice or sharing the latest gossip. They love to solve problems and may find themselves getting more personally involved in those of other people than they expected. They can, in fact, get so carried away with telling people what to do or how to handle a situation that they may sometimes be considered meddlesome. Relationships are paramount in their lives, and if you ever come across someone you think is a "9-6" and he or she is a loner, you had better ask them to check their birth certificate—you're probably working with the wrong name.

Whether they like it or not, "9-6"s are often on the move—flying somewhere on a business trip, taking a train to visit a sick aunt, or driving the kids to hockey practice. You are more likely to meet them at work or through friends, or even in an airport or a parking lot, than reading a book in the library or strolling leisurely through a museum. They are drawn to members of the opposite sex who are attractive, intelligent and fun-loving and are all for long romantic courtships. They enjoy going out to theater or dinner and they also like entertaining and being entertained. Open-minded and tolerant, they are the most likely "6" to marry someone of a different background—be it religion or nationality—and wide age differences are not unheard of. They do, however, expect their mate to be loyal, dependable and domestically inclined.

Once they have settled down, "9-6"s are devoted spouses and parents. They can, however, be quite demanding and even intolerant if things aren't done their way. Married or single, they love togetherness and will eagerly look forward to sharing vacations, backyard barbecues, or summer Sunday afternoons at the pool with those they love.

"9-6"s have a tendency to worry too much and can fret about anything—whether or not the house looks presentable enough for company, whether they are dressed properly for an occasion, or whether or not the Scout troop will return safe and sound from their camping trip, for example. They want to do so many things there just aren't enough hours in the day. Every now and then they may feel confined by home and responsibilities and dream about having more freedom and time to themselves, but even if a marriage is unhappy, it would take an awful lot for them to end it—especially if there are children involved.

"9-6"s want to do something worthwhile, but because they have so many interests they may have difficulty choosing one for a career. A job that involves travel to far-away places would appeal to them as would some aspect of the performing arts. Equally as good on a soapbox, they are often drawn to politics, fighting for a cause. Since they usually have a broad understanding of life and are blessed with the social graces, they can work harmoniously with others.

Being responsible is an asset and "9-6"s often move up the corporate ladder rapidly because they can handle many duties efficiently. If they happen to be born into a family business, chances are they learn responsibility early. They could, for instance, be the ten-year-old who starts helping Mother operate the cash register a couple of hours after school each night, and little by little learns the business inside out. Being family-conscious anyway, they are likely to want to remain in the business.

"9-6" children can be bossy and aggressive, but they also have a soft side that is easily moved by a person or an animal in plight. Romantic and idealistic, they spend a lot of time daydreaming and affairs of the heart concern them early. They enjoy sharing their secrets with best friends and often record accurate details of daily events in a diary. They usually like school and their sense of responsibility coerces them to do their homework, but they look forward to the end of classes when they can go outdoors. Likewise, they can be helpful with domestic chores, but will probably put up a fuss at first, if they feel confined to the house. They would, for instance, prefer raking leaves to doing dishes, or shining shoes out in the backyard to cleaning up their room.

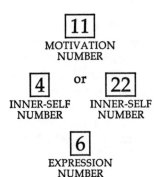

11
MOTIVATION
NUMBER

4	or	22
INNER-SELF		INNER-SELF
NUMBER		NUMBER

6
EXPRESSION
NUMBER

"Back of the Job—the Dreamer Who's making the dream come true!"

—Berton Braley

"11-6"s want to love and be loved and they dread living alone. Yet it is not easy for them to find someone who measures up to their standards. They are idealistic in love as well as in everything else and have high expectations of a partner—especially when they have a "22" inner-self number. Status and potential are important and they are more impressed by titles such as Doctor or Chairman of the Board than they are by good looks or charming dispositions. They can be quite manipulative and often try to remake others to suit their ideals. If, for instance, a prospective partner doesn't have an important position when they happen to fall in love, "11-6" will do everything possible to help him or her get one—even if it means working two jobs to put him or her through school. Emotional and romantic, they can be martyrs for loved ones—sacrificing their own well-being for theirs. Resentment and disappointment, however, tend to build up if he or she fails to live up to their hopes and dreams.

"11-6"s are sensitive and easily influenced by their surroundings, and they tend to take on the moods and attitudes of those who are close to them. Physical ailments can often be traced back to emotional upsets. When their efforts to create harmony for loved ones are not appreciated they are easily hurt. Little things bother them too much and they have a tendency to dwell on "poor me" thoughts.

Although honest in matters of importance, "11-6"s want to be charming and well liked and may resort to white lies in order not to hurt another person's feelings. They may, for instance, call up with all kinds of elaborate excuses for getting out of a date rather than come straight out and tell you they've met someone else; or, rather than fire a cleaning lady they are dissatisfied with, they may tell her they are going away on a long trip and will get in touch with her when they return. They know how painful it is to be rejected and are reluctant to look like the bad guy (or gal).

Idealistic, creative and reliable, "11-6"s take pride in their work, and whether it be wiring a house or sewing drapes, they want the end result to come out perfectly so others will admire it. They need encouragement, reinforcement and praise, and feeling important and appreciated is as much a consideration as salary—if not more so.

"11-6"s love giving advice—whether it be on how to invest money, how to paint, or how to get out of a depression. They are also good at promoting and selling products they believe in. They can be very persuasive with prospective customers. Good at details, they leave no stone unturned, know all the arguments, and will turn on the charm until the expected sale goes through.

Also read the description for "2-6," which starts on page 139. "11" is such a high vibration that it is impossible to operate on it all the time. Children act like its lower octave—"2"—most of the time and adults operate on the "2" at least part of the time.

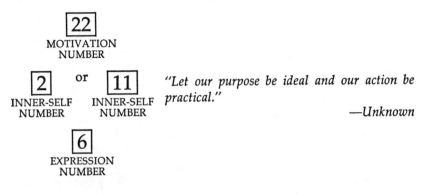

22 MOTIVATION NUMBER

2 or **11** INNER-SELF NUMBER   INNER-SELF NUMBER

"Let our purpose be ideal and our action be practical."
—Unknown

6 EXPRESSION NUMBER

The most likely place to meet "22-6" is at work or through friends. They want someone to share their life with but will rarely put family concerns before career. They have high expectations for themselves and expect a partner to be supportive. Without the satisfaction of accomplishing something worthwhile—something creative and beneficial to others—they feel miserable and unfulfilled. They are attracted to members of the opposite sex who are practical, affectionate and intelligent and who share their ideals. They expect to be catered to and they also need a certain amount of freedom to pursue hobbies and/or career. Domestic urges are strong, however, and once they are attracted to someone, it won't be long before living together, if not marriage, will be discussed.

Idealistic and humanitarian (especially if they have an "11" inner-self number), "22-6"s have a strong sense of social responsibility. Homeloving, but also community-oriented, they may burden themselves with too many social obligations and take it out on those close by being irritable, demanding and critical.

At work as in their private lives, "22-6"s are idealistic and practical. They want to accomplish great things to benefit humanity in some way and are always looking for new forms of expression and ways of applying them. Artistic and imaginative, they are often drawn to the creative arts. They also have a desire to help others and may be drawn to fields that are concerned with their welfare, such as improving educational facilities, medical research, or urban planning. In an office situation they will find innovative ways of making work interesting and are good at organizing coworkers. Whatever their chosen career, they are much happier giving orders than taking them and make very demanding bosses.

Also read the description for "4-6," which starts on page 142. "22" is such a high vibration that it is impossible to operate on it all the time. Children act like its lower octave—"4"—most of the time, and adults operate on the "4" at least part of the time.

IX
Introspection and Perfection: The Number 7

"7"s are the intellectuals, the scientists, the analysts—always searching for reasons why. They love nature, quiet places and investigating life's mysteries. Skeptical, secretive, reserved and proud, they are complex people who are not easily understood or appreciated. Not easy to get to know, there is much more to them than appears on the surface. Loners who suffer within, their outer calm often belies inner turmoil, tension, conflicting emotions and a fear of rejection. Although they may appear cold, aloof or unfeeling, they have sensitive natures and need warm, understanding mates who can provide emotional support, be their intellectual equals and respect their need for privacy. Life with a "7" can be perplexing—their elusive nature being a cause for friction and misunderstandings in their personal relationships. They themselves, however, are always asking questions and can be very disturbed by evasive answers.

Perfectionists at heart, "7"s would rather not do something at all if they could not do it well, and they tend to be equally demanding of others. Although sensitive to criticism themselves, they are often critical, impatient or irritable with those close who may, in turn, find "7"s analytical approach to everything annoying. Quality is much more important to them then quantity and they would rather have a few good outfits than ten closets full of cheap clothes. When it comes to choosing friends, they are just as selective and discriminating, and prefer intellectual equals. They admire those who stand out from the crowd in some way and would rather have a few close friends than many acquaintances.

"7"s do not enjoy small talk and may appear uncommunicative unless they feel the conversation is about something worthwhile. *If* they are in the mood, and *if* they like the people, "7"s can be the life of the party, but when stuck in a situation where this is not the case, they can turn off entirely and retreat into a corner or to the nearest door for a fast exit. "7"s need harmony in their domestic and personal relationships. They dislike conflict and will withdraw in the face of petty bickering and upheaval.

Being a mental number, "7" does not always have a great deal of physical vitality. More than any other number, it is important for him or her to get sufficient rest. "7"s enjoy solitude and need time to be alone with their thoughts—preferring to observe rather than to participate. A good education is important to them, as is the opportunity to specialize in some area—whether it be medicine, a literary field, mechanics or the occult. Moody and easily depressed, they may seek escape from the stark realities of life through drink, drugs, sleeping a lot, or getting lost in a world of books. Peace and quiet is essential to their composure.

COMPATIBILITY GUIDE

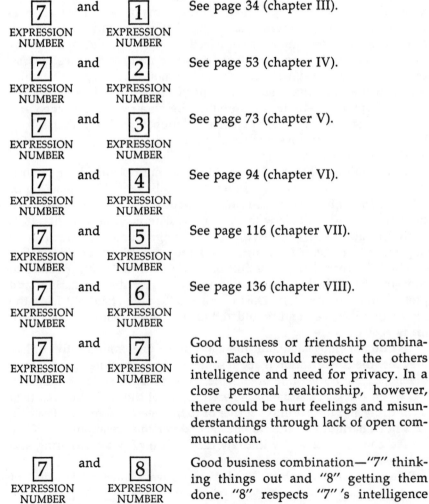

| 7 and 1 | See page 34 (chapter III). |
| EXPRESSION NUMBER EXPRESSION NUMBER | |

| 7 and 2 | See page 53 (chapter IV). |
| EXPRESSION NUMBER EXPRESSION NUMBER | |

| 7 and 3 | See page 73 (chapter V). |
| EXPRESSION NUMBER EXPRESSION NUMBER | |

| 7 and 4 | See page 94 (chapter VI). |
| EXPRESSION NUMBER EXPRESSION NUMBER | |

| 7 and 5 | See page 116 (chapter VII). |
| EXPRESSION NUMBER EXPRESSION NUMBER | |

| 7 and 6 | See page 136 (chapter VIII). |
| EXPRESSION NUMBER EXPRESSION NUMBER | |

7 and **7**
EXPRESSION NUMBER   EXPRESSION NUMBER

Good business or friendship combination. Each would respect the others intelligence and need for privacy. In a close personal realtionship, however, there could be hurt feelings and misunderstandings through lack of open communication.

7 and **8**
EXPRESSION NUMBER   EXPRESSION NUMBER

Good business combination—"7" thinking things out and "8" getting them done. "8" respects "7"'s intelligence and ability to handle details. "7" admires "8"'s ability to organize. They do not, however, have many personal interests in common.

7	and	9
EXPRESSION NUMBER		EXPRESSION NUMBER

"7"'s desire to perfect himself is in conflict with "9"'s desire to work for humanity. Although "9" can broaden the scope of "7"'s ideas, in a close personal relationship, "9"'s tendency to wander may give rise to "7" having ungrounded inner fears.

7	and	11
EXPRESSION NUMBER		EXPRESSION NUMBER

Good business combination—both are intuitive and detail-conscious. In a close personal relationship, however, escapism or false pride on "7"'s part may create a problem, and "7" could find "11"'s need for companionship confining.

7	and	22
EXPRESSION NUMBER		EXPRESSION NUMBER

Good business combination—"7" adding mental stimulation and analytical thoughts, "22" putting them into practical form. In a close personal relationship, however, there may be lack of personal understanding for one another's needs.

Following are all possible combinations of a "7" expression number with the different motivation and inner-self numbers.

1
MOTIVATION NUMBER

6
INNER-SELF NUMBER

"The more I get to know about people the better I like my dog."

—Lamartine

7
EXPRESSION NUMBER

Loners in the true sense of the word, "1-7"s often appear cool and aloof but they can warm up to someone they find interesting. You are more likely to meet "1-7"s at a lecture or in a museum than at a social event. Selective in their choice of friends, they are drawn toward members of the opposite sex who are good-looking and smart and who don't monopolize the conversation. They need mental as well as physical stimulation and will rarely cement a relationship with someone who is not their intellectual equal. They are often attracted to people who are different in some way—much older or younger, perhaps, or from a different background. "1-7," for instance, is the man from the city who goes camping along the river in a beautiful country setting and meets a girl who lives there. Seeing her as untainted by urban living he may be inclined to have a long-distance romance with many letters and a few phone calls going back and forth between visits.

"1-7"s want to be looked up to and respected. The way to their heart is through their intellect rather than their emotions. They like a partner to be witty, uncritical, independent and conversant with a wide variety of subjects. Not liking to feel restricted in any way they are quickly turned off by anyone who seems pushy or possessive. A companion is expected to be discreet and unostentatious, to respect their privacy and to refrain from showering them with a multitude of personal questions.

In all areas of their life, quality is more important to "1-7"s than quantity, and they do not have to be surrounded by people or things in order to feel content. In fact, time to be alone to do their own thing is so important to them that they may prefer one-night stands or sporadic relationships to feeling restricted or pinned down. Self comes first, and they are not always considerate of the feelings of others although they can be generous and appreciative of someone who lets them have their own way. This is not the combination of a homemaker, and if "1-7"s decide to settle down, they are unlikely to be homebodies. They may spend as much time away from the house as in it, and should there be any children, they will expect their spouse to shoulder the brunt of the responsibility.

On the job, intellectual, analytical and shrewd, "1-7"s are the specialists, the authorities—preferably in some scholarly or scientific area. They find fulfillment through work that offers a mental challenge of some kind, and a satisfying career is essential to their well-being. They would prefer to be their own boss; not ones to punch a clock or have someone constantly looking over their shoulder, they would enjoy freelancing or a job where they could choose their own hours. At any rate, they are happiest working alone or in an area where they are given freedom to do things their own way.

"1-7" children may seem quiet and withdrawn but they don't miss a thing! Even at an early age they are surprisingly observant. Having, for example, detected an anatomical difference between his or her mother and a popular television star, "1-7" is the five-year-old who comments, "Mommy, you're prettier than Wonder Woman but she has bigger hearts." Parents need to be careful about what is said or done in front of their "1-7" child or they may be in for some embarrassing surprises.

Like their adult counterparts, "1-7" children do not like to be asked a lot of questions, but they demand many answers. They have analytical minds that go a mile a minute, and no subject is beyond their scope of interest. Perceptive and extremely bright, they seem to mature emotionally faster than many other youngsters, possibly owing to their burning desire for independence.

MOTIVATION
NUMBER

INNER-SELF
NUMBER

EXPRESSION
NUMBER

"Fond as we are of our loved ones, there comes at times during their absence an unexplainable peace."
—Anne Shaw

"2-7"s may, at first, come across reserved or shy, yet they can be charming and friendly once they warm up to someone. There is a gentle, kind sympathetic side to their nature and they feel frustrated and confused when others don't see them the way they picture themselves and accuse them of being cold and aloof. Very sensitive and easily hurt, they are prone to periods of depression and moodiness when they feel misunderstood. You are more likely to meet them at work or through friends than in a crowd. They like social activities, but prefer small, select, intimate groups, or dinner for two rather than anything rowdy or packed.

"2-7"s want to love and be loved and settle down with someone special. Full of romantic fantasies, they may imagine themselves to be madly in love with everyone they date, but infatuation would be a more accurate term. Emotional compatibility is more important to them than looks, and they are attracted to members of the opposite sex who are patient, loyal and reassuring, and who enjoy doing things together. Although courtship will be steady and dependable, they want privacy as well as companionship. Once in a while "2-7"s have a need to be silent or alone and will appreciate a partner who is understanding and secure enough not to nag them about it or give them the third degree. They are willing to give their partners a certain amount of freedom too, but will never forgive infidelity.

Very observant and detail-conscious, "2-7"s are also intuitive and assume that those close to them are equally so. Consequently, they are not always easy to get along with. They may, for instance, be overaccommodating to the needs of a lover and then be sorely disappointed if they don't feel appreciated. Hurt and resentment build up when their partner fails to live up to their expectations. Yet it is difficult to know what they really want as they tend to keep their true feelings hidden.

Once they have settled down, "2-7"s can be devoted parents and spouses as long as their need for privacy is respected and they are not required to account for every minute of their time. Easily distracted, they may have difficulty concentrating when they hear a spouse talking on the phone, watching TV, or puttering around the kitchen. They need a separate room or corner of their own they can return to when they want to be alone and undisturbed.

At work, "2-7"s do not demand big impressive titles, but they do need a position with some prestige attached to it and where their mental alacrity will be appreciated. Their interest in analysis and research and their willingness to work behind the scenes make them excellent assistants or troubleshooters—picking out important details, reading between the lines. Careful and perfectionistic, they are also good with figures or proofreading or editing material, and they excel at delicate artwork such as ornate carving, etching or embroidery. Cooperative and willing to please, they are happiest in pleasant surroundings and working with people whose company they enjoy.

"2-7" children may appear calm and collected, but are sensitive, emotional and easily hurt. Self-conscious and often insecure, they want to please and can be devastated if their efforts are rejected. Although they may seem aloof and hard to understand, they want to be liked and are very concerned about what others think. Easily frustrated, they may withdraw in the face of tension—even to the point of refusing to talk to anyone except a favorite pet they claim is the only one who understands them. They love animals and may find it easier to communicate with them than with people.

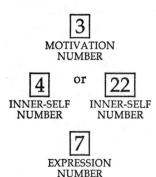

3
MOTIVATION
NUMBER

4   or   22
INNER-SELF   INNER-SELF
NUMBER   NUMBER

7
EXPRESSION
NUMBER

"The problem of attracting the whole world's attention without incurring the ridicule of anyone has never yet been solved."

—*Anonymous*

Appearances are important to "3-7"s and they want to be seen in the company of interesting people. You are more likely to meet them through friends or at a social event than sitting alone in a bar. Concerned about their own image as well as that of their partner, they are attracted to members of the opposite sex who have good looks and good taste. Anyone flashy or gaudy is apt to turn them off. "3-7"s love to be admired and appreciated, be it for their appearance or their brains, and the way to their heart is through flattery and compliments. Romantic and attentive when they begin an affair, they can be generous with compliments, gifts and nights on the town. Budget permitting, they don't skimp on luxuries such as dining out in fine restaurants, a beautiful car or travel. But they are cautious not to overdo. Their attentions can, however, stop as suddenly as they begin, and without any explanation, either—unless there are good channels of communication open between you. They have a tendency to keep problems bottled up inside, and without some creative or physical outlet for venting frustrations, tension and anxiety can build up to unhealthful levels. A wise partner will learn how to encourage "3-7" to talk about what's bothering him or her without prying or sounding like the third degree.

Difficult to get to know well, "3-7"s have two sides to their personalities. All at the same time they can be social and reserved, serious and fun-loving, so near and yet so far. They often appear aloof and hard to approach, but are friendly and outgoing with those they warm up to. Selective in their choice of friends, they may have many acquaintances but only a few are allowed to get close.

Appearances to the contrary, "3-7"s are willing to settle down once they have found the right person. They need to express their ideas and voice their opinions, and someone to share their thoughts with is essential to their well-being. But although companionship and social life are important to them, they need a little time each day to be by themselves just to think, to reflect, and to regenerate their energy. They need a patient, understanding partner who knows when to draw them out of their shell and when to leave them alone. Not always easy to live with, they can be critical and argumentative with those close, and although usually optimistic and enthusiastic, they can be moody and withdrawn when feelings of inadequacy overcome them. They enjoy children and can be loving, devoted parents as long as there is help from their spouse and no great demand put on their time.

"3-7"s need outlets for self-expression and, especially if they have a "22" inner-self number, a satisfying career and/or hobby is essential to their feelings of self-worth. They are happiest being in a profession that is mentally challenging and preferably in an exciting and glamorous atmosphere. Literary by nature, writing or editing often attracts them, as do the performing arts. But they may express themselves in a stylized way that would appeal to a specialized audience rather than to the masses.

Intuitive and sensitive, "3-7"s surroundings are very important to them, and when the setting is right, they can be most enthusiastic and cooperative about carrying out their responsibilities and obligations. But don't give them an orange crate for a desk! Dingy, shabby surroundings are not conducive to their productivity.

"3-7" children have tremendous energy that needs an outlet. Self-expression is important to them and they need reassurance and praise for their efforts. Like their adult counterparts, they enjoy having an appreciative audience and being the center of attention, and even at an early age, looks are important to them. They are very conscious of their appearance and the image they cut. Charming and outgoing when they want to be, they can also be hard to approach. They are selective in their friendships and enjoy being part of a clique. They are usually popular with the in crowd at school and are often elected to some office—student council president, homecoming queen or captain of the swimming team, for example.

| 4 |
| MOTIVATION NUMBER |

| 3 |
| INNER-SELF NUMBER |

| 7 |
| EXPRESSION NUMBER |

"I never say the things I meant to say and am overwhelmed afterwards with the things I should have said and could not."
                                        —*Gamaliel Bradford*

"4-7"s are a curious mixture of extroversion and aloofness, and although they may seem social and outgoing, they are hard to approach. The most likely place to meet them is at work or through friends. Selective about whom they associate with, they prefer to choose their friends among people of similar backgrounds and interests to their own. They want security and stability and have a tendency to resist change and innovation. When considering a potential mate, status and intellectual compatibility are more important than looks. But patience, warmth and understanding are what keep the flames glowing. Appearances to the contrary, they are very sensitive. They have trouble expressing their emotions and may appear unfeeling when in reality they feel very deeply and have a great need for love and affection.

Once someone catches "4-7"'s eye they will pursue him or her relentlessly. Patient and determined, they are willing to work hard for what they want—and a desirable partner is no exception. Dependable and generous with their time and attentions, they can, nevertheless, suddenly stop calling with no explanations offered should they lose interest in the relationship.

A comfortable, stable homelife is essential to "4-7"'s well-being, and though they can be exacting and domineering, they make devoted parents and spouses. They are happiest with loyal, appreciative, practical mates who will allow them privacy when they need it and who won't be put off by their moods.

Although they may sometimes do things in a unique way (for the most part unintentionally), "4-7"s prefer tradition and routine. Skeptical, pessimistic and not apt to take chances, they may tend to ignore any flashes of perception or intuition because they don't fit into the ordinary world. On the job, they are hard-working, systematic, organized and efficient. They have high expectations of themselves as well as those they work with, and although willing to pitch in with the groundwork, can be demanding, critical bosses. Analysis and research appeal to them and they excel in highly technical fields where they can be the authority. Their analytical minds plus their natural curiosity about people and what makes them tick, can draw them into some branch of psychology or anthropology.

"4-7"s seek bare facts and unvarnished truth. Patient and persevering, they can handle routine and follow the rules as long as they are not demeaning. Precision appeals to them, and long hours and small details do not upset them when they are involved in work that they find stimulating or that they can carry out in their own way.

"4-7" children tend to be well behaved, studious and willing to abide by rules, but they can also be stubborn and resistant to change. If their parents move, for example, and they have to go to a new school, leaving behind the friends they feel comfortable with, they can become so upset that they actually get physically sick. Security and reassurance are important to them and variations in schedule or departures from the expected give rise to inner tension and fear. Like their adult counterparts, they need order and structure in their environment. "4-7" is, for instance, the child who pours all his or her mother's perfumes into one bottle so that the bureau looks neater.

| 5 |
| MOTIVATION NUMBER |

| 2 | or | 11 |
| INNER-SELF NUMBER | | INNER-SELF NUMBER |

| 7 |
| EXPRESSION NUMBER |

*"I keep six honest serving-men
(They taught me all I knew);
Their names are What and Why and When
And How and Where and Who."*

—*Kipling*

"5-7"s like to be where the action is and you can just as easily meet them at work or in a bar as walking a dog, hanging out with the gang down by the local pizza stand, or placing a bet at the track. They may seem sweet and innocent when you meet, but don't let first impressions fool you. There's no one more willing to try anything different or unusual at least once. Restless and easily bored, they enjoy taking chances and their intuition and good hunches often lead them into gambling. They are also responsive to the sensual, and want to feel unhampered to pursue their many and varied interests. A companion is likely to be included, but only one who understands their need for personal freedom and does not try to be possessive. The key to their heart is to keep adding novelty to the relationship, to be a good listener as well as conversationalist, to respect their privacy when they want to be alone, and to be headache-free and raring-to-go whenever they are. Anyone dull or rigid will turn them off as surely as someone who expects them to constantly account for their whereabouts. Although they have a need to keep their own affairs private, they are most curious about others and can sometimes be quite tactless about the questions they ask or the statements they make.

Appearances to the contrary, "5-7"s are full of intense feelings and passions. Fond of the opposite sex, they may overindulge in sensual pleasures, but once a commitment has been made they can be faithful and dependable. They are attracted to people who are interesting and unique in some way and who can provide physical as well as mental stimulation. Once they set their sights on someone, they will pursue him or her relentlessly and the chase is often more appealing to them than the catch. "5-7"s are quite willing to pursue a long-distance romance or to travel several miles to meet a date. They thrive on change and adventure, and any obstacles that need to be overcome only make it all the more intriguing.

Once they settle down, "5-7"s enjoy children and can be loyal, devoted spouses and parents so long as they don't feel tied down by responsibilities. If they feel fenced-in, however, inner tension and nervousness build up and they can become most irritable and critical of those close.

At work, "5-7"s accept no boundaries, and there's no way they will even be comfortable operating within strict routine or limitation. Although enthusiastic about work they find mentally stimulating, they have a tendency to look for shortcuts and to become restless and impatient with petty details. Nine-to-five office-type jobs are too stifling for them. Some variety and challenge are necessary in order to hold their interest and make them do their best.

Curious about the "whys" and "wherefores" of just about everything, their minds are always open to new ways of doing things and they often come up with innovative ideas others may block because they deviate from what the establishment has proclaimed true.

Like their adult counterparts, "5-7" children are restless and adventuresome, and have a great deal of energy that needs a physical outlet. Not liking to feel restricted in any way, they enjoy sports and playing outside in the street or playground away from parental supervision. Self-discipline is difficult for them and they have a tendency to be sloppy.

"5-7" children have vivid imaginations and inventive minds, and they often get by on their wit. Since they are easily bored, they may not be inclined to stick with things—even those they're good at. They need encouragement to develop their talents whether these be writing poetry or short stories or inventing simple communication devices with empty tin cans. Since they are eager to please, it does not take much effort to give them some incentive. With "5-7" children, a little praise goes a long way.

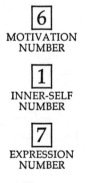

| 6 |
| MOTIVATION NUMBER |

| 1 |
| INNER-SELF NUMBER |

| 7 |
| EXPRESSION NUMBER |

"Away from the world and its toils and its cares,
I've a snug little kingdom up four pair of stairs"
—Thackeray

The best place to meet "6-7" is at work, at a class or at a club—someplace where you can bump into each other regularly and frequently. Although they may appear reserved, independent and aloof, they can actually feel quite insecure and they do not like to live alone. Having someone they can count on to be there in times of emotional stress is essential to their well-being, and they will place qualities of reliability and devotion above looks, wealth or status. In fact so great is their need for loyalty and devotion, "6-7"s often fall for someone who grows on them because he or she is always there when needed—to drive them to the market when their car won't start, to pick up their clothes from the dry cleaners or to hold their hand when they're sick. The most domestic of the "7"s, they dream of a cozy abode to come home to every night, and they want someone special to be there to share it with them.

Idealists who want harmony in their everyday life but often despair of finding it, "6-7"s are attracted to members of the opposite sex who are warm, sensitive, supportive and encouraging. They try to put their best foot forward to the world, and once they warm up to someone they can be charming, gracious and romantic in the pursuit. Grievances or resentments will probably remain hidden during courtship, but once the knot has been tied, they can be irritable, critical and short-tempered with those close. They want to be the boss at home!

When "6-7"s settle down, they can be devoted parents and conscientious, hospitable spouses. They enjoy puttering around the house and entertaining select groups of friends. They will go out of their way to cater to those they love and are easily hurt if not appreciated. But quite often there is an inner conflict between what they want and what they do, and they may feel isolated and misunderstood. For instance, they may want to have children but be terrified of the thought of giving up so much of their free time to raise them. They may want peace and harmony in their surroundings but have a hard time keeping their own temper in check. Patience and understanding on the part of a wise mate plus good channels of communication can help keep frustration and inner tension at a minimum.

At work, "6-7"s are happiest in positions that have clout or that allow them to specialize in some area. They have individualistic ideas and expect to be able to do their job their own way. Since they are so responsible, they are often the person in the office who gets the most work dumped on them—everyone *knows* it will get done if "6-7" has the assignment. As long as long hours don't interfere with their home-life, they will endeavor to accommodate their bosses, but family comes first, and "6-7"s will rarely neglect their spouse or children for a chance to make a few extra dollars on overtime.

Idealistic and sensitive, "6-7"s like to think that their work benefits others in some way and, therefore, they are often found in teaching or counseling fields. They like giving advice but will usually refrain from butting in or getting too personally involved with people at the office, unless they feel encouraged to.

"6-7" children, like their adult counterparts, want to be open and friendly, but may frequently feel isolated or misunderstood. They do not realize that they sometimes appear secretive and aloof instead of as sociable as they think. Sensitive to the moods of others, they enjoy giving comfort and advice, and may be found settling disputes between parents or among friends. Usually obedient, they are responsible when given chores to do, but the manner in which they are assigned is important. They don't like being dictated to.

Young "6-7"s have a system for everything. Their room may look a mess, but they know where all their belongings are and do not like anything to be touched or moved around. As they grow older, this ability to mentally organize everything becomes a great asset. In a lecture, for instance, they instinctively know what is important enough to write down, and their notebook is often borrowed by friends who don't have this ability.

7
MOTIVATION
NUMBER

9
INNER-SELF
NUMBER

"O for a Booke and a shadie nooke,
eyther in-a-doore or out . . ."

—*John Wilson*

7
EXPRESSION
NUMBER

You are more apt to meet "7-7"s at work, a concert, a fashion show or even on a business trip than at a party or a club. They may come across cold and aloof and hard to approach, but they are full of emotions and can be very warm when they *want* to be. Selective in their choice of friends, they gravitate toward those who are their intellectual equals. Intelligence and status are what capture their eye, and although they do not come on strong, once they spot someone or something they want, they can be subtly aggressive in their pursuit. They will court a potential partner eagerly and dependably so long as they don't feel trapped or manipulated in any way.

"7-7"s are not social butterflies and will make it quite clear that they do not want to associate with those they consider less evolved. This attitude is not necessarily due to an inflated ego as much as to a feeling that time would be much better spent at home reading a book than attempting to communicate with people with whom they have nothing in common. Appearances to the contrary, however, they do need affection and companionship. So long as they have privacy when they need it, and enough help to allow them needed time to rest and be alone, they are willing to make a commitment and can be good parents and loyal spouses. They are not always easy to live with though. Perfectionists at heart, they are demanding not only of themselves but of those close. Quick to find fault, they are easily depressed when overcome with feelings of inadequacy and they can become moody, fussy and full of complaints. They are happiest with a stable, sympathetic, loving spouse who is mentally stimulating, and who knows instinctively when to cheer them out of a blue mood and when to leave them alone.

"7-7"s are bookworms, abstract thinkers, seekers of knowledge, and perfectionists—very demanding of self and others. Prone to bouts of melancholy, ungrounded fears, and negative thoughts, they may seek to escape from life's uglies by one means or another. Born skeptics, they are always looking for proof and answers, and are very curious as to what makes others tick. Evasive answers upset them, yet they themselves are very private and reluctant to reveal their true self to others. Intrigued by the mysterious and the occult, they are often involved in matters which contain a certain element of secrecy.

"7-7"s want to perfect themselves and be specialists in some area. Mental stimulation often compensates for other setbacks or disappointments in their life, and they often find their greatest self-fulfillment and satisfaction through a job they feel devoted to. They excel in highly technical fields and do best in any type of scientific or research work. Having a strong intellectual bent, they are often attracted to something scholarly, such as teaching or writing. Careers that have an abstruse or secretive element, such as metaphysics or espionage, also appeal to them, but if they do not have the opportunity to specialize in some area, they may vacillate and hop from one thing to another, finding them all disappointing.

Detail-conscious, methodical and responsible, "7-7"s prefer working independently without having someone look over their shoulder or tell them what to do. However, when they are boss, they can be demanding and critical, and not nearly so willing to give their employees the breathing space that they themselves require.

"7-7" children often appear secretive, withdrawn and aloof too, but appearances to the contrary, they are extremely sensitive and full of repressed emotions. Reluctant to reveal their real feelings, they may not always be truthful. They are prone to inner fears of inadequacy and, more so than any other combination, it is important for them to have a good education so they can gain confidence by becoming proficient in some area.

Not physically-active children, "7-7"s need time alone and a lot of rest. Unless the preoccupation is mental, they usually prefer observing to participating. They resent adults pushing them into things they don't feel like doing—playing rigorous sports, for example—and they will avoid people whose company they do not find enjoyable or interesting. "7-7"s are the youngsters most likely to retreat to their room—book in hand—when company arrives. Privacy is important to them, and because of this they are often misunderstood. It is not uncommon for them to seek escape from the harsh realities of life through an excess of reading, fantasizing or sleep.

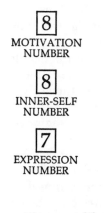

MOTIVATION
NUMBER

INNER-SELF
NUMBER

EXPRESSION
NUMBER

"He who has his thumb on the purse has the power."
—*Bismarck*

The most likely way to meet "8-7"s is through work or friends, and your first impression of them will probably be quite accurate. Status-conscious and ambitious, they have big ideas, expensive tastes and an unalterable desire to be in control—whether of their careers or their relationships. They are so concerned with their image and the impression they are making on others, they can be quite compulsive and have trouble relaxing. They are attracted to members of the opposite sex who are attractive and intelligent, and who preferably have social standing and prestige as well. Unless someone can be a credit to them in all areas, they are unlikely to pursue the relationship. When they meet someone who fits all their requirements they will pursue them relentlessly. They can be generous and lavish with their attentions and money but have little sympathy or tolerance for those who don't live up to their expectations. Often they are prone to fiery outbursts of temper if anyone tries to manipulate them or push them around; and when they feel a relationship has outlived its usefulness, they will not hesitate to break it off.

Whether or not the other person's feelings are hurt will be one of the furthest things from their mind.

Shared goals and ideals are so important to "8-7" it is not uncommon for them to wind up picking a mate who is also a best friend or a colleague. Although they can be loyal, indulgent spouses and parents, career comes first and they are under constant self-imposed strain and pressure. They may stay late at the office day after day seeming cold and uncaring—too involved with work to devote much time to their family. A wise mate, however, will recognize the tension they are under and help them unwind and relax rather than add to it by nagging or complaining.

At work, "8-7"'s aspire to positions of power and influence. Ambitious and self-confident, they are drawn to executive and administrative careers. They have good judgment, shrewdness, and analytical ability, and their interest in the financial affairs of others may lead them into some area of financial administration. Expansive and far-sighted, they have a talent for managing and making important decisions, and prefer doing the organizing while having someone else work out the details (although they can handle details too if they have to). Unable to relax, they have a tendency to become workaholics—putting themselves under constant pressure and strain. Forceful and persevering, they know exactly what they want and will pursue it methodically, undaunted by any obstacles.

Active and competitive, "8-7" children like sports and other outdoor activities. They also enjoy organizing things and are often leaders at school. As they grow older, mental games have as much appeal as physical sports, and they are likely to become more interested in being chairman of the debating club than making the basketball team. Selective in their choice of friends, they like to feel that those they associate with, like themselves, are special in some way and may be instrumental in forming exclusive groups or cliques.

"8-7" children can be bossy and compulsive; they are often tense and high-strung, and may have trouble relaxing. Since they are so demanding of themselves, they feel they have to excel in whatever they undertake, and should they fail in *anything*, they feel guilty and defeated. Parents should make it clear to them that they are loved just the way they are, and that they don't constantly have to prove themselves.

MOTIVATION
NUMBER

INNER-SELF
NUMBER

EXPRESSION
NUMBER

"... *the mind is restless, turbulent, strong, and
unyielding ... as difficult to subdue as the
wind.*"

—*Unknown*

You are more likely to meet "9-7"s at an encounter group, a concert or
a party than at a health club or a marathon. They are idealistic, romantic
and highly emotional, but have trouble showing their feelings and may
appear reserved or aloof. They do, however, have active fantasy lives
and may dream of attaining the ultimate experience in some area—
whether it be spiritual enlightenment or love.

Trusting, good-natured, warmhearted and tolerant, "9-7"s are looking for something they can identify with in everyone—for what people
have in common rather than their differences. And these same qualities
are what they themselves are attracted to in members of the opposite
sex. Emotional and intellectual compatibility rank much higher than
looks. Their attitudes toward love, however, transcend the conventional. They need a certain distance between themselves and their partner,
and if there are too many demands on their time they will retreat.
When, for instance, courtship begins, they can be most attentive—
calling three or four times a week with interesting things to do, but
should their partner insist that they not only be together on Thursday
and Saturday, but on Friday and Sunday as well, they may get so
uptight they stop calling altogether for a week or two (or even a
month).

"9-7"s do not like to feel fenced-in or tied down to one person. They
can love more than one at a time and truly love them all. Social life and
outside interests are important to their well-being and they are quite
skillful at arranging their affairs the way they want them. They crave
excitement, adventure and variety, and if they feel confined in any way
(be it by job, marriage, or life-style), they will get restless and impulsively seek stimulation elsewhere. They are happiest with a fun-loving,
romantic, broad-minded mate who understands their need for freedom
and will not try to pin them down.

At work, "9-7"s are more concerned with the mental than the material world. Cutthroat business deals are not their forte and they're much
more comfortable in a field that helps humanity in some way. Matters

that have the potential of universal application appeal to them much more than working on a narrow one-to-one wavelength. Curious about everything, they want to make broad contacts with all kinds of people, and even though they may handle a very specialized area of work, they do not like to feel confined. They need to be involved in something expansive and would be miserable chained to a desk or a dull routine job. Idealistic and enthusiastic about anything they believe in, they make good teachers, mystics or religious leaders.

Like their adult counterparts, "9-7" children often have active imaginations and a vivid fantasy life. Interested in people and places that are far-away or different, they may select friends among those children who are exotic or unique in some way. Good at expressing themselves, they usually do well in school—especially in those subjects that call for creative or verbal skills, such as writing, art, photography, social studies or drama. However, when their mind isn't on the lesson or they're just plain bored, they can get into mischief. Good-natured, enthusiastic and often impulsive, they have an adventuresome nature and do not like to be restricted or told what to do. They may rebel against strict authority—especially if they feel confined. Why Mother gets upset when they take off for parts unknown (like Johnny's house) without telling her where they're going is hard for them to understand.

| 11 |
MOTIVATION
NUMBER

| 5 |
INNER-SELF
NUMBER

*"Oh, how hard it is to find
The one just suited to our mind!"*
                                   —*Thomas Campbell*

| 7 |
EXPRESSION
NUMBER

You are most likely to meet "11-7"s through work or friends, but lectures, concerts and cultural events are also good possibilities. They may at first seem reserved, aloof and hard to approach but they can be friendly and outgoing when they warm up to someone. Particular about the friends they make, they gravitate toward those who are mentally stimulating and who share their ideals. And while they are attracted to a good body, unless there is a special talent or an interesting personality to go along with it, they are unlikely to pursue the relationship. Romantic and idealistic, they may have difficulty finding someone who can live up to their standards. They can feel frustrated and confused when others accuse them of living in an ivory tower. Despite appearances to the contrary, they are very sensitive and want to love and be loved. They are often torn by an inner conflict between wanting companionship and craving solitude at the same time. Not easy to live with or understand, they are happiest with an intelligent, talented, patient, understanding, loyal mate who does not get upset by their moods, who provides emotional support, and who allows them privacy when they need it.

Once they have settled down, "11-7"s can be devoted parents and spouses, but they are unlikely to stick out a bad marriage for the sake of the children. Self-sufficient when they have to be, they may have too much pride to even accept child-support payments. They recognize the importance of a good education and will make undue sacrifices to put a child through college.

Although a compatible companion is essential to their happiness, "11-7"s are not really domestically oriented and housework ranks low in importance to them. They enjoy lively discussions around the dinner table or working on hobbies together, for instance, but without intervention from other members of the family, dishes could remain in the sink for days. Usually perceptive and observant, they may know the titles and locations of every book in the house, but return a blank stare when asked the color of their bathroom.

Inspired and intuitive, "11-7"s are drawn to mental or technical fields where they can be specialists and contribute ideas for others to put into practice. They are excellent with detail, and can handle figures with efficiency and alacrity, but they can get bored if the job is routine. Intellectual stimulation is essential to their sense of well-being and accomplishment, and they are happiest in a position that calls for mental expertise while giving them an opportunity to constantly learn something new—job-related or not. They are willing to work hard toward a goal, but have difficulty tolerating office pettiness and unnecessary bureaucracy. In spite of a desire to please, if they receive little recognition or are not treated with respect, they will be miserable in that job.

Also read the description for "2-7," which starts on page 159. "11" is such a high vibration that it is impossible to operate on it all the time. Children act like its lower octave—"2"—most of the time and adults operate on the "2" at least part of the time.

22
MOTIVATION
NUMBER

3
INNER-SELF
NUMBER

7
EXPRESSION
NUMBER

"To follow knowledge like a sinking star beyond the utmost bound of human thought."

—*Tennyson*

You are more apt to meet "22-7" through work or friends than at a race track or a bar. Not content to lead simple lives, they have a need for variety, adventure and excitement, and are attracted to people who are interesting and mentally stimulating. Beauty and brains are both prerequisites for capturing their fancy, but although they are earthy and sensual, relationships based on sex alone might soon bore them.

"22-7"s can be friendly and outgoing with those whose company they enjoy, but can also be reserved and aloof. Imaginative and inquisitive, they enjoy observing others but may be reluctant to reveal anything personal about themselves. They have a strong need for privacy, and people who make excessive demands on their time or who seem to pry into their private lives can quickly alienate them.

Once they become interested in someone, they can be steady and dependable, but nevertheless, they are also sometimes difficult to understand. Full of inner tension and turmoil, they can be critical and demanding and seem to fly off the handle at seemingly insignificant things. They have low stress thresholds and are prone to unpredictable mood swings—charming and enthusiastic one day, depressed and withdrawn the next. A wise companion will be patient, understanding and supportive, and wait for a mood to blow over instead of taking it personally or making an issue of it.

"22-7"s have high aspirations and are driven to make something of themselves. So-called ordinary jobs are not satisfying to them unless they are stepping-stones to an important position. They are dreamers, yes, but not unrealistic ones, and are willing to work diligently toward their goals.

It is important for "22-7"s to have a good education. Always searching for reasons "why," they may become interested in philosophy, religion or the occult sciences, and pioneer their own theories on these subjects. Or, analytical and intrigued by science, they may excel in technical fields such as engineering or oceanography. They recognize the value of knowledge, and will endure undue hardships in order to go to college—even putting themselves through by working during the day so they can attend classes at night. Whatever field they choose, they want to be the best in it and will endeavor to offer something new and creative of themselves.

Also read the description for "4-7," which starts on page 162. "22" is such a high vibration that it is impossible to operate on it all the time. Children act like its lower octave—"4"—most of the time, and adults operate on the "4" at least part of the time.

X
Power and Efficiency: The Number 8

"8"s are go-getters. They know what they want and will go all out to get it—overcoming any obstacles in their path. Often they have the attitude that rules are made for others, not them. (If you see someone stepping off the curb to cross the street before the light changes to green, chances are he or she is an "8.") The end often justifies the means, and they can be impatient, intolerant and even cruel.

"8"s do not like to be reliant on others and have a need to be financially independent. Material security and a sense of accomplishment are essential to their well-being. They have a great drive to achieve, and even when they appear easygoing there is an underlying aggressive streak. Concerned with the physical and material side of life, they are never passive where money is concerned. They aspire to positions of power and influence and enjoy things on a grand scale. Financial success and recognition are important to them, and they find smallness or pettiness of any kind irritating. Mechanical or routine jobs do not appeal to them, and they don't like being told what to do. Good at managing and organizing, they want to take charge and do the directing themselves. They need to be their own boss. Of all the numbers, "8" is the most likely to be a self-made success, and may sometimes appear tough, ruthless, and difficult to approach.

Natural-born executives, "8"s have good judgment, business expertise, and the ability to take charge of any situation. Expansive and far sighted, they can size up people and situations and are good at making important decisions and delegating authority. They mean to be just but may sometimes come across bossy and dictatorial. Ambitious and manipulative, they enjoy financial wrangling and contact with the business world. They find competition stimulating and work well under stress. Always busy, they do not like to waste time or money, and may have trouble resting or relaxing. They have great vitality, forcefulness and physical endurance and often excel at sports—either incorporating them into their career (as an athlete, coach, or director of a sports club, for example) or using them as an outlet for some of their pent up energy and aggression.

Earthy and fond of the good life, "8"s believe in living as well as possible. They may overindulge in food or sensual pleasures, but only so long as it does not interfere with their career. When the honeymoon is over, so to speak, "8"s are not easy to live with and they can be quite demanding and domineering. Home is their castle and their expectations that it be a place of peace, quiet and order, can be a strain on the rest of the family. They want things done their way, and can be overbearing and unyielding to the desires of those close.

"8"s worry about what others think of them. They put a good deal of stock in appearances, and want to make a good impression. Although they may be temperamental at home, they are careful to control their emotions and impulses in front of the rest of the world. Very concerned with the image they project, they admire people of power and position. They respect dignity and shy away from people who lack personal pride. Honest, frank, and often blunt, they can be loyal, dependable friends as long as they get respect and allegiance in return. "8"s can be generous, but they want everyone to know about it. If, for example, they loan someone money, all their friends will hear about it. Or if they make a donation to charity, they'll broadcast that too. At home, however, they are not so ostentatious, and can be thrifty and abstemious. So driven are they toward the pursuit of money and/or recognition that it may become an end in itself leading them to neglect all else. They may put so much energy into their job that they have too little time or are too weary to enjoy the so-called fruits of success. "8"s may, for instance, have a library full of books they have every intention of reading, but never get around to actually doing so.

When "8"s allow their workaholic obsession to interfere with their personal life, it can cause problems at home. They may be too busy for sentiment and seem uncaring and cold. Yet they may be deeply in love and expect their partner to understand that they have the best interests of their family at heart and to stand by them all the way. When this is not the case, they may seek refuge in the arms of a more understanding friend. It is not uncommon for "8"s to indulge in extramarital affairs, but they are careful to be discreet. They are happiest with a loyal mate who is a credit to them, who shares their ambitions and who is willing to work alongside them toward common goals.

COMPATIBILITY GUIDE

| 8 | and | 1 | See page 34 (chapter III). |

EXPRESSION   EXPRESSION
NUMBER   NUMBER

| 8 and 2 | See page 53 (chapter IV). |

EXPRESSION NUMBER · EXPRESSION NUMBER

| 8 and 3 | See page 73 (chapter V). |

EXPRESSION NUMBER · EXPRESSION NUMBER

| 8 and 4 | See page 94 (chapter VI). |

EXPRESSION NUMBER · EXPRESSION NUMBER

| 8 and 5 | See page 116 (chapter VII). |

EXPRESSION NUMBER · EXPRESSION NUMBER

| 8 and 6 | See page 136 (chapter VIII). |

EXPRESSION NUMBER · EXPRESSION NUMBER

| 8 and 7 | See page 156 (chapter IX). |

EXPRESSION NUMBER · EXPRESSION NUMBER

8 and 8
EXPRESSION NUMBER · EXPRESSION NUMBER

This combination can be successful or explosive, depending on the willingness of each person to compromise, and to give-and-take with each other.

8 and 9
EXPRESSION NUMBER · EXPRESSION NUMBER

Good business combination—"9" inspiring "8", "8" turning "9"'s ideas into profits. In a close personal relationship, however, "8" may find "9" impractical and emotional. "9" may find "8" self-centered and too wrapped up in work.

8 and 11
EXPRESSION NUMBER · EXPRESSION NUMBER

Good business combination—"11" providing ideas and inspiration; "8" putting them into practice with great efficiency. In a close personal relationship, however, "8" may find "11" impractical and unrealistic; "11" may find "8" materialistic and insensitive.

8 and 22
EXPRESSION NUMBER · EXPRESSION NUMBER

Good combination for business, friendship or love. In a close personal relationship there could be a clash of wills between these two strong-willed numbers, but they are both materialistic and share common interests and goals.

Following are all possible combinations of an "8" expression number with the different motivation and inner-self numbers.

1
MOTIVATION
NUMBER

7
INNER-SELF
NUMBER

"I came, I saw, I conquered."

—*Julius Caesar*

8
EXPRESSION
NUMBER

Work is the most likely place to meet "1-8"s since they put so much energy into their career they may not notice someone anywhere else. Aggressive and ambitious, they find little time to nurture their intimate relationships unless their partner happens to be pursuing the same goals and can be a helpmate to them. They may appear impatient, abrupt or aloof, and are not always easy to approach or get close to but they can be warm and charming when it serves their purpose. Bundles of energy, they are always on the move and most members of the opposite sex have difficulty keeping up with them.

Although they would prefer to have a special someone in their lives, "1-8"s are often content to live alone. They have an independent streak and will not tolerate dissent from a partner. For example, if a mate gave an ultimatum such as, "Either get rid of the dog or I'll move out," they would probably let the partner leave. They have definite likes and dislikes and aren't always tactful when proclaiming them. Love affairs tend to be stormy and full of strife, but somehow "1-8"s thrive on that. Passive partners bore them and rarely earn their respect. Tempers can flare but "1-8"s bounce back quickly, and five minutes after a heated argument they can be calmly discussing another subject.

"1-8"s are status-conscious and expect their partner to have prestige and travel in the right social circles. They have a good sense of humor and a healthy sex drive and have little patience with prudishness or so-called Victorian attitudes. Trend-setters at heart, they may seem unconventional at times, and they don't particularly care what the masses think.

Ambitious, strong-willed, and able to lead, "1-8"s are born executives. They have tremendous powers of concentration and place a high premium on success. Impatient with those who are slower than they are, they have little tolerance for idleness and make demanding bosses. They strive to pioneer their new ideas and are always working toward progress and change. They often find themselves laboring on some proposal to convince others that new equipment, programs, products or whatever would be worthwhile and would show up on the bottom line. Refined and sometimes aloof, they are careful to keep everything professional and in good taste.

Both quality and quantity are important to "1-8"s and they expect to have attractive surroundings in their workplace—fine furniture, windows, carpet—whatever goes with a position of status. Their drive to get to the top is strong and they are willing to work hard to move themselves up the corporate ladder. They would feel unfulfilled with a dull or menial job and if they see no other way out of a dead-end position, they will either quit and join another firm or branch off and start their own business.

Like their adult counterparts, "1-8" children find it hard to sit still. Restless and spirited, they are also impatient and head-strong, prone to outbursts of temper when crossed. They do not like being told what to do and can be rebellious and defiant if they do not find it reasonable. Independent and often self-sufficient, they never think of themselves as children, but rather as young adults who happen to be in small bodies temporarily.

Even as children, "1-8"s find satisfaction in work and usually do well in school—taking pride in doing their homework creatively and efficiently. Very competitive, they enjoy being the best in everything and enjoy sports as well as activities such as bike-riding or hiking, which they can do alone. They are outgoing and show leadership qualities early in life, and may run for class office or captain of a team or club.

MOTIVATION
NUMBER

INNER-SELF
NUMBER

"And, of all the best things upon earth, I hold
that a faithful friend is the best."
—Edward Robert Bulwer Lytton

8

EXPRESSION
NUMBER

Charming, outgoing, "2-8"s often find themselves in group settings; business meetings, church or synagogue functions, clubs, adult-education classes, or even social get-togethers are all likely places for meeting them. If your first impression is that they like to have someone special by their side, you are probably right. They need a meaningful relationship. Without a partner they feel a definite void in their lives and are subject to loneliness and periods of depression. Ambitious and hard-working they want to feel their efforts are for someone special—such as a family—and they will accumulate for their children's education or for a better home. They are attracted to members of the opposite sex who are loyal, practical, appreciative and homeloving, and who are willing to stand by them and encourage them toward their goals.

During courtship, "2-8"s tend to be steady and dependable and may sweep you off your feet with their lavish attentions. But if you want to avoid faux pas in your newly formed relationship, you should be aware right from the start that appearances to the contrary, "2-8"s are prone to little idiosyncracies which may seem insignificant to you, but which could be quite major to them. Don't make the mistake of fluffing off something they obviously dislike or find silly. If, for instance, they tell you they can't stand polka dots, don't buy that polka-dot dress you saw in the window to wear when you go on your date; if they tell you it bothers them when you chew gum, at least refrain from chewing it in their presence; and if they tell you they detest onions, serve them in a separate dish so you can add them to your own salad while they enjoy theirs plain. Little considerations such as these can make all the difference between a pleasant evening or one of tension and awkwardness—a long-term relationship versus a one- or two-night stand.

Once they have settled down, "2-8"s can be faithful, generous spouses and devoted parents. However, their loving natures and desire to please may sometimes be hidden by possessiveness and/or by aggressive, determined, independent behavior. They may, for instance, without thinking, make an important decision without consulting their mate, or dictate how something should be done without considering their partner's feelings on the subject. Patience, understanding and good channels of communication are all necessary ingredients for keeping the peace in this relationship.

At work, "2-8"s have difficulty acting as a manager or someone in charge. Although they have the ability to use good judgment, and can size up people and situations in a minute, they tend to personalize things that happen at work and somehow sentiment still creeps in even when they're making executive decisions.

Observant and good at details, "2-8"s have a talent for sensing when things are out of balance. They make good mediators or trouble-shooters, and they do well in group administrative work where a sympathetic ear is sometimes every bit as important as efficient organization. Working in a family or small business is also appropriate since they would enjoy the closeness of everyone involved. Related or not, they would feel that everyone at work made up one big, hopefully happy, family. In such a situation emotionalism may not seem as out of place and is more likely to be excusable.

"2-8" children may appear tough and cool but they have a great need for affection and for friends. A loving relationship with their parents is essential for their well-being and they may appear to be so close to their mother that crueler children may call them a Mama's boy or girl.

Observant and perceptive, "2-8" children usually do well in school. They have good memories and enjoy getting their work done on time. They also like sports and being part of a team, and are good at organizing their friends and at getting a game going.

3
MOTIVATION
NUMBER

5
INNER-SELF
NUMBER

8
EXPRESSION
NUMBER

"Keep up appearances whatever you do."
—*Dickens*

"3-8"s love being the center of attention. They also have a strong desire for status and success and will look for a mate who can enhance their position in life. Looks are what first captures their eye, and when they feel attracted to a member of the opposite sex, they are never at a loss as to how to approach them. "3-8," for instance, is the woman who goes up to the handsomest man at the pool and gives him a line about how familiar he looks; or the optometrist who flirts with all the pretty girls who come to him for glasses and asks out the ones who don't budge when their knees "accidentally" touch; or the woman who spots a man she'd like to meet while working in her office and arranges to photocopy something while he's using the machine so she can strike up a conversation while waiting her turn . . . and invites him to a party. They like to keep their relationships light and fun-oriented and will shy away from anyone who tries to manipulate them or pin them down. Big turn offs are a lover getting possessive or pouting because they don't spend enough time together or because he or she went out with someone else. "3-8"s need a certain amount of freedom and will be faithful only if it suits them—not just to make someone else happy.

Colorful and outgoing, "3-8"s need to express themselves and want an audience to voice their opinions to. Looks and an active social life are important to them and since they themselves can be quite vain and fashion-conscious, they prefer to be seen in the company of beautiful people. Nothing escapes their notice, and if their partner wears a new outfit or gets a hair cut, they are bound to comment on it.

Restless and interested in many things, "3-8"s are not apt to remain sedentary for long. Even if they do settle down with one person, they are likely to continue having many activities and hobbies outside the home. They can be affectionate and charming when they want to be, and have a talent for making depressed partners see a silver lining among those dark clouds.

Whatever their line of work, "3-8"s need to feel important. They want recognition for their talents and achievements, and since they enjoy having an audience they are often attracted to the performing arts. Money and status are important and they rarely go into a profession out of love alone. It's more likely they'll choose a career from those that pay the best salaries and have the most prestige.

Efficient and good at delegating responsibilities, "3-8"s have a talent for running a business. They don't like to handle details themselves, but are good at finding someone else who does. Dynamic and multifaceted, they are full of ideas and opinions and should they get stuck in a menial position or with an overbearing boss, they will soon come up with some scheme for getting out of such an unpleasant situation. Being so restless, they are happiest in a job that allows them to travel, attend conferences, be on committees, or anything else that interrupts routine and lets them get out of the office now and then. They are hard workers but get bored easily and will rebel if not treated well.

Precocious and energetic, "3-8" children may have trouble concentrating on any one thing for long, and they need help to direct their talents into something that can be useful in adult life. Like their adult counterparts they are social and outgoing and enjoy being the center of attention and are usually popular at school. Should they not receive the limelight they think they deserve, they may resort to bragging and can be very selfish. If, for instance, they bring home a friend who captures their parents' attention, they are likely to come down with a stomachache or some other imaginary illness just to divert their parents' attention back to themselves.

Even at an early age, "3-8" children are concerned about their looks. They love bright colors and big shapes—whether in clothes or toys.

Colorful blocks and stuffed animals appeal to them and a "3-8" may well be the seven-year-old who's caught cutting the big red dots out of Aunt Mary's dress when she comes to stay for the weekend.

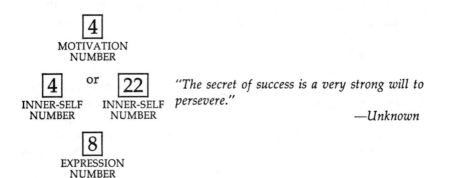

4
MOTIVATION NUMBER

4	or	22
INNER-SELF NUMBER		INNER-SELF NUMBER

"The secret of success is a very strong will to persevere."

—*Unknown*

8
EXPRESSION NUMBER

You are more likely to meet "4-8"s at work or through friends than at a social event. They enjoy parties, but prefer get-togethers with people they know rather than large crowds of strangers. Earthy and practical, they seek the physical and material comforts of life and want a solid relationship that provides security as well as love. They are attracted to members of the opposite sex who are warm, affectionate, and physically good-looking, and if they are stable, responsible and homeloving as well, the spark in "4-8"'s heart can easily turn to flame. Once they become interested in someone they are steady and persistent in their efforts to win them over and will not take "no" for an answer. Courtship will be regular and dependable but not extravagant. Generosity is not their forte, and "4-8"s are more giving of their time than their money.

Though they enjoy being admired, "4-8"s are not prone to flirt once they have found their true love—or even before. They tend to stick to one person at a time and an "it has nothing to do with our relationship" statement from a partner who is seeing someone else as well will not be acceptable. They expect their lover to be as faithful and as devoted as they themselves are and are turned off by flamboyant or coquettish behavior. They are unlikely to commit themselves to someone whose values differ greatly from their own.

Once they have settled down, "4-8"s can be critical and demanding. Order is important in their everyday life and they would be miserable living with a slob. Little annoyances like overstuffed drawers or dirty dishes left in the sink can be the cause of much bickering and "4-8"s do not hesitate to lay down the law of the household. Hard-working and materialistic, they have many financial concerns and expect thriftiness at home. Routine is also taken for granted, and they can be quite tenacious and stubborn about adapting to change. They have a tendency to repress their emotions and may be subject to periods of depression. A wise spouse will see to it that they don't get stuck in a rut and will know when and how to present them with a frivolous idea, encourage them to see an amusing movie, or maybe take a crazy class—just for the fun of it.

At work, "4-8"s can usually make the most of whatever comes their way. Though not very imaginative, they are good at organizing, managing and planning and, if they are boss, they may feel torn between delegating the work out to others and wanting to do it themselves. They have sound business judgment and try to be fair and square in their dealings, but can sometimes come across as impossibly demanding and hard to please. Their prime interest is in making more and more money and their energies are ever geared toward making greater profits. Not apt to take risks, "4-8"s would be unhappy in any job that did not offer a stable income, but they would be more than willing to work long hours—if their time were well compensated for.

"4-8" children develop an interest in money at an early age and usually handle it very well. Their abundant ideas on how to make it include anything from a lemonade stand by the bus stop to putting on plays in the garage and charging twenty-five-cents admission. They also enjoy sports, the outdoors and rough-and-tumble games. Playmates are usually their own age and background and they rarely, if ever, make friends with anyone who seems different in any way.

Although order and neatness are important in their lives, "4-8" children rarely volunteer to help parents clean the house. If asked to do so, however, they willingly do their share. Routine is important to them, and disturbed by changes, they may close themselves off from possibly rewarding experiences by their lack of adventure. Although they don't show their emotions easily, they are sensitive and may harbor grudges. They are quick to use their fists and to strike out when hurt.

MOTIVATION
NUMBER

INNER-SELF
NUMBER

EXPRESSION
NUMBER

"We speculate to accumulate."

—*Unknown*

You are more likely to meet "5-8"s on a business trip, on a hockey team, or through friends than in a library or a museum. Active and outgoing, they enjoy anything sensual or unusual and are attracted to members of the opposite sex who are responsive and adventuresome, who share their fun-loving bon vivant spirit, and who are able to spread a dollar a long way. Restless and unwilling to be pinned down (unless it's by their own choice), they need a certain amount of freedom in a relationship and can be quickly turned-off by anyone rigid or clingy.

"5-8"s own interests come first and, although not particularly loyal, they would be discreet about their affairs. Having a lover is important to them and once they have their sights on someone, they are determined in their pursuit. However they like a challenge and are apt to be more turned on by someone who adds novelty to the relationship by keeping them guessing once in a while than by someone they can take for granted. Manipulative and appealing when it's in their best interest, they can turn on the charm to such a degree that their partner will be quite surprised at the cool, callous side of their nature that becomes apparent once the affair is over.

"5-8"s have a tendency to rate potential relationships in terms of dollars and cents. Questions like, "What will I get out of it?" or, "How much will it cost me?" cross their mind, and if the price is higher than the benefits they may forget the whole thing and seek another fish in the sea. On the other hand, the way to *their* heart is to be as generous with your bank account as with your compliments and to be ready and willing to go to "in" places and come up with interesting things to do.

At work as in their private lives, aggressive and competitive "5-8"s are good at getting what they want. They have good insight and are versatile and imaginative in finding solutions. Always thinking of ways to make money, they will, for example, give up an afternoon of leisure to sell green carnations at the St. Patrick's Day parade. They're good at taking advantage of a situation and making things pay off.

Perceptive, efficient and able to make quick decisions, "5-8"s have leadership qualities and if given a choice will often go into business for themselves. But although they are hard-working, they are happiest in a job that allows some flexibility. People-oriented and smooth talkers, they can sell just about anything—including themselves.

Charming but manipulative, "5-8" children are usually popular and good at getting their own way. They have an independent streak and may be a bit rebellious at times. However, they can usually get away with it. Even at a young age, they have a knack for using compliments and cute expressions that can make a parent who feels like giving them an angry spanking want to give them an affectionate hug instead. They're also good at changing the subject or making their shenanigans sound less mischievous than they really are.

Although they are restless and have trouble sitting still for long, "5-8" children do well in school in subjects that interest them. Curious, versatile and competitive, they do best whenever they feel challenged. They tend to shun responsibility, but learn easily with fair, understanding discipline. The best incentive to get them to do something is money (they quickly learn its value). And one of the worst threats parents can make is to deprive them of their allowance.

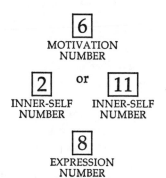

| 6 |
| MOTIVATION NUMBER |

| 2 | or | 11 |
| INNER-SELF NUMBER | | INNER-SELF NUMBER |

| 8 |
| EXPRESSION NUMBER |

"His bark is worse than his bite."
                    —*George Herbert*

Dependable and responsible, "6-8"s seek harmony and security through their relationships. Of all the "8"s, they are the ones most likely to marry someone from their home town—especially if they have a "2" rather than an "11" inner-self number. "6-8," for instance, is the man who marches down the aisle with the girl whose pigtails he used to pull in the fourth grade, whom he used to meet in the halls between classes in high school, and with whom he'd go to the drive-in during summer vacation. Having little experience with other relationships could be a problem later on if they start pondering what it would be like with someone else. They may be guilt-ridden for thinking such thoughts, but if their mate seems to constantly be arguing with them about something or other, their minds do wander.

Married or single, "6-8"s are homeloving and domestically oriented and are attracted to members of the opposite sex who share these qualities as well. They are attached to their families and enjoy entertaining, and a prospective partner will be expected to give "6-8" 's friends and relatives at least equal time. Good cooks, they take pride in having elaborate dinner parties and will often try to impress a new lover with a romantic home-cooked dinner.

Once they settle down, "6-8"s are unlikely to stray far from home, and will usually want to have children. They are loving parents and spouses, but can at times be demanding and critical—especially if they have an "11" inner-self number. They expect their family to be a credit to them and their idea of settling an argument is to announce that things should be done their way. If anyone accuses them of being unfair, their first reaction is surprise, because they really believe that they know best—for all concerned. They like the idea of being involved in the community and can usually be found on some committee or other—whether it be the PTA, local politics, or a fund-raising event. When teachers need parents to chaperone a school function, "6-8"s are apt to be the first to volunteer. They enjoy doing things as a family and are happiest with a loyal, affectionate mate who has similar values to their own.

At work, "6-8"s may appear tough and detached, but are really idealistic and sympathetic underneath it all. Although they possess leadership qualities, they may not be so well suited for management positions in cutthroat businesses as are some other "8"s because of their tendency to allow sentiment to affect their judgment.

What "6-8"s are well suited for is managing something in which they have a personal interest, such as a child-care center, animal shelter or greenhouse. Their love for food could also inspire them to go into any one of several careers—managing a restaurant, catering, running a bakery, delicatessen or cooking school, writing cookbooks, or importing and exporting gourmet foods. Well organized, responsible and willing to work hard, they also have a good sense of balance and are capable of delegating duties efficiently. "6-8," for instance, is the office manager who not only knows what everyone is working on and what status each project is in, but who also keeps track of everyone's birthday (and arranges a small celebration), and who provides a listening ear and, if necessary, aspirin and a Band-Aid as well.

"6-8" children may seem sensitive and shy one minute, tough and a bully the next. They like being included in everything and often exhibit obnoxious behavior just to get attention if they think they're being ignored. Parental approval is important to them and they can be very responsible if they think carrying out certain duties will please their folks and return their love. "6-8"s may have a tendency to be sloppy, but are willing to help with household chores, especially if they involve cooking. They love to eat and find comfort in food, which could lead to a weight problem at an early age.

"6-8" children are good at organizing their friends into sports teams or groups. They like telling them what to do and enjoy giving advice. Interested in school politics, they often run for class office and can usually be found on some committee or other. They also enjoy taking an active part in social activities such as being in charge of handling refreshments for the school dance.

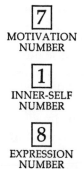

7
MOTIVATION
NUMBER

1
INNER-SELF
NUMBER

"I do everything for a reason. Most of the time the reason is money."

—*Suzy Parker*

8
EXPRESSION
NUMBER

Whether you meet "7-8"s at work or through friends, they would want a chance to check you out and get used to you for a while before asking you out. Particularly choosy about friends, they may seem difficult to approach and even harder to get to know well. Although they can be outgoing with people they like, for the most part they are reserved and aloof. They tend to hold things inside and keep a part of themselves hidden. They need a certain amount of privacy. Don't pry into their personal affairs or try to pin them down. They are attracted to members of the opposite sex who are intelligent and communicative, and who can be a credit to them. If they have money and status as well, so much the better. But no matter what they have to offer, "7-8" is unlikely to pursue the relationship unless they share the same values and are willing to help "7-8" achieve his or her goals.

Although they enjoy stability, the comforts of home and the security of a special relationship, "7-8"s tend to be career-oriented and may not enjoy being saddled with the responsibility of bringing up children. They need freedom, independence and time to themselves, and will balk at attempts to restrict or confine them in any way. Demanding and critical of themselves as well as others, they are not the easiest combination to get along with. They are impatient with anyone slower than they are and will not tolerate arrogance or inconsiderateness. They tend to brood and become depressed over real or imagined imperfections, and the most cutting remark one can make to them is that they are stupid. However, they are hard to intimidate and very rarely lose a verbal battle. They excel in communication skills and know how to get their point across.

Ambitious, determined and efficient, "7-8"s want to specialize in some area. At work they are not satisfied with a job that doesn't have status or power attached to it, and not for long will they remain at the bottom of the ladder working their way up. Shrewd and intuitive, they know how to get what they want, and if their aims include increasing company profits, they can be tremendous assets to any firm. Analytical and perceptive, they make good troubleshooters, and they also do well in technical fields that demand specialized skills.

"7-8"s have individualistic ideas and are not apt to adhere to rules such as clock-punching. Indeed, company regulations may be so offensive to them that they may decide to go into business for themselves. They need mental challenge and stimulation and get easily bored with routine work.

Curious about what makes people tick, "7-8"s are often drawn to psychology and the behavioral sciences. Teaching may be rewarding for a while, but it usually doesn't have enough prestige, nor does it pay well enough to attract them forever. Although they have goals that transcend material rewards, they take it for granted that they will be included.

"7-8" children are often looked up to by their friends for their brains. Even at a young age they keep their emotions under control and often appear mature beyond their years. Sociable when they want to be, they are choosy about their friends. To many of their peers they seem unapproachable, someone to be respected from afar, not someone to become chummy with. Instead of team sports, they prefer pastimes they can enjoy by themselves, such as putting a puzzle together or riding a bicycle. They prefer activities that call for perfected detail—playing the piano, ballet, swimming, diving, ice-skating or gymnastics, for example.

Curious and full of questions, "7-8"s appreciate school for what they learn. Good students and voracious readers, they may sometimes, however, declare that they get more out of their books than a dull classroom where they do "silly" things. They are usually well behaved, but only because they feel they have to be. Resentful of authority, they look forward to adulthood as a time when they won't have to answer to anyone anymore.

MOTIVATION
NUMBER

INNER-SELF
NUMBER

EXPRESSION
NUMBER

*"Don't be afraid to take a big step if one is indicated.
You can't cross a chasm in two small jumps."*
　　　　　　　　　　　　—David Lloyd George

Social, outgoing and full of energy, "8-8"s are more likely to be met at a neighbor's barbecue, at a friend's wedding reception, or on a tennis court than in a library or a museum. They are attracted to members of the opposite sex who are earthy but dignified, easygoing but strong, practical but not cheap. And, if they can enhance "8-8" 's station in life, so much the better. Once they are interested in you, they are steady and dependable in their pursuit and a prospective partner should have little doubt as to how "8-8" feels about them. Generous and lavish with their attentions, they do, however, expect to be in control of the relationship and to have the last say in matters of importance. Any attempts to push them around or tell them what to do will be met with resentment.

"8-8" men tend to be chauvinistic; women tend to be more career-minded than family-oriented—unless they can run the family like a business. But male or female, they are active and demanding and others may find it exhausting trying to keep up with them and wonder how they manage to accomplish all that they do. Married or single, they are materialistic and expect to have all the creature comforts of home. They want the biggest and the best of everything, and would like to have the power and status that often accompany the good life. A partner is expected to share their values and help them achieve their goals.

Once they have settled down, "8-8"s will be devoted to and appreciative of a patient, understanding mate who provides a peaceful, harmonious atmosphere and can help them relax and unwind. They will do anything for their families, but are not above getting involved in a discreet affair when away on business, for example, or if they feel unhappy at home.

Superefficient and hard-working, "8-8"s are well suited for the business world. They have tremendous willpower and the drive to keep working for a goal even in the face of obstacles. Thriving under competition or challenge, they often choose to own their own business. Sports also attract them and if they don't become a coach or a professional athlete, they often play on a company or a community team. Although they have executive ability and are good at organizing, they are not particularly imaginative. Stubborn and difficult to sway, they would rather stick to the tried-and-true. They are comfortable with the proven methods they're used to, and are not apt to experiment with new or innovative ways of doing things.

"8-8"s can be charming and manipulative when it serves their purpose and they may believe, in many cases, that the end justifies the means. Good at seeing the overall picture in any program or business deal, they have a talent for delegating the necessary responsibilities in order to see a project through. Having to deal with minutiae irritates them and if they have any say in the matter, someone else will do the nit-picking.

"8-8" children, like their adult counterparts, are powerhouses of energy and can be active, demanding, exhaustive youngsters. Headstrong and stubborn, they want things done their way. They may, for instance, keep their belongings organized a certain way and not like them to be shifted around on cleaning day. They have volatile tempers and their anger is easily sparked. Quick with their fists, they demand respect from their peers.

Even at an early age, "8-8"s are conscious of the value of money and the things it can buy. They are strongly motivated to earn it, to be financially independent, and to be powerful and influential someday. Born leaders, they have a talent for getting others to do things for them, and they can organize anything from a baseball game to a fan club. Active sports appeal to them and are a good way for venting frustrations and excess energy. They are usually athletic and a valued member of any team.

| 9 |
| MOTIVATION NUMBER |

| 8 |
| INNER-SELF NUMBER |

| 8 |
| EXPRESSION NUMBER |

"Success is getting what you want. Happiness is wanting what you get."

—Unknown

You are more likely to meet "9-8" at work or through friends than at a social event or on a cruise. Thoughts of travel, adventure and romance do beckon them, but they may not always find time for such pursuits. They are often so caught up in their careers that those close to them may feel they are indifferent to their feelings even when this is not really so. If at first they seem harsh, tough or abrasive, don't let that fool you. Underneath it all they are compassionate and easily moved. Generous at heart, they may shower loved ones with gifts to make up for the time they cannot spare.

"9-8"'s are attracted to members of the opposite sex who are friendly, communicative, broad-minded and tolerant, and who can enhance their position in life. Although they admire practicality, pettiness or miserliness will surely turn them off.

Once "9-8"'s become interested in someone they will be steady and dependable callers, but they don't want to feel pushed into anything or manipulated in any way. They want to be in control of their relationships and be the ones to decide if and when a commitment should be made. And they tend to be more demanding than accommodating. They may, for instance, call off a date because something unexpected comes up at work—and expect their lover to be understanding—but would get quite upset at a partner who is not always available when they want him or her to be.

"9-8"'s have an inner restlessness and a need for personal freedom. Often they are torn between wanting to settle down with one person and fear of making a commitment. Idealistic and romantic at heart, their need for love may be insatiable and they may go through phases of having several lovers in succession. If, however, it turns out that none of them is really satisfying, a period of depression and bitterness could follow.

"9-8"'s have tremendous potential to do something beneficial for humanity. Not only are they efficient organizers, but they also have good imaginations and a dramatic flair. Idealistic and gifted with foresight, at work as in their private lives, they set far-reaching goals for themselves and become intent on pursuing them. Ambitious as well as dedicated, they work hard for what they believe in and can fit an amazing amount of activity into one day.

Since they have such excellent supervisory and management skills, "9-8"'s may be moved up the corporate ladder and placed in charge of a section or department that they really have no interest in managing. This could create some inner conflict as they are not happy in the business world unless they feel their work is creative or humanitarian. "9-8"'s need a goal or cause to dedicate themselves to, and in order for their profession to be satisfying, they must *feel good* about what they do.

"9-8" children have a tremendous amount of energy and want to be active practically every waking moment. They don't have the patience to sit still for long periods of time, and would rather participate in active sports or play with toys that move or do something. When asked if they like school, they are likely to answer, "It's okay." It gives them an opportunity to meet new friends and learn useful things (such as how to count money). They are well behaved if they think the rules are fair, but will rebel and begin to resent authority if they feel it is tyrannical or unnecessary. "9-8"s have leadership qualities that often go beyond school activities. Rather than run for a class office that doesn't interest them, they may decide, for example, to form their own club, make themselves the president, establish the dues, activities and meeting place, and so on.

MOTIVATION
NUMBER

INNER-SELF
NUMBER

"A good hope is better than a bad possession."
—Anonymous

EXPRESSION
NUMBER

You are most likely to meet "11-8"s through work or friends. Although they may appear cool, detached or aloof, they are emotionally vulnerable and easily hurt. They put on a tough facade to protect themselves but appreciate a sensitive partner who is not fooled by their show of bravado and who can cheer them out of their occasional depressions. Male or female, they need companionship and a loving relationship is essential to their feeling content and secure, but there are some differences. Whereas both are attracted to members of the opposite sex who are stable and have good reputations and a gentle manner, "11-8" men are more apt to have double standards. They may, for instance, think nothing of having a harmless affair with someone they meet on a business trip (while their wife waits safe and unsuspecting at home). "11-8" women, on the other hand, are less likely to stray.

Romantics at heart, "11-8"s have high ideals and lofty dreams. Strong family ties are important to them and they have a storybook picture of the perfect mate who is understanding, supportive, loyal, practical and affectionate. Once they settle down, they really want it to be forever. Although they are willing to listen to the other side and do what they can to come up with a compromise on important issues, they are not willing to give up career goals to stay home and raise a family. Not satisfied with a life-style they consider mediocre or boring, they expect their mate to share their ideals and to encourage their dreams.

At work, "11-8"s have the talent and determination to put their visions into practical form, and once they have set their goals, they will labor tirelessly to obtain them, letting nothing stand in their way. Intuitive and perceptive, they have a good understanding of people and situations. They can always trust their first impressions as to the sincerity of a boss or client, and their instinctive sense of balance comes in handy for knowing when things are out of line. Because they expect so much from themselves and those they work with, they can seem demanding and even eccentric—especially to someone who is neither so dedicated nor so idealistic as they are. But appearances to the contrary, friendly camaraderie among coworkers is important to them, and any friction between themselves and anyone at work—be it boss, employee, or peer—will cause them tension and distress. They want a pleasant place to work, where they can develop and express their talents and make their dreams come true.

Also read the description for "2-8," which starts on page 180. "11" is such a high vibration that it is impossible to operate on it all the time. Children act like its lower octave—"2"—most of the time, and adults operate on the "2" at least part of the time.

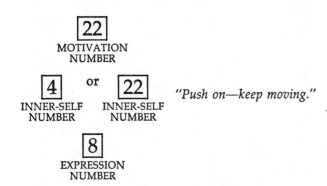

| 22 |
| MOTIVATION NUMBER |

| 4 | or | 22 |
| INNER-SELF NUMBER | | INNER-SELF NUMBER |

"Push on—keep moving."

—*Thomas Merton*

| 8 |
| EXPRESSION NUMBER |

You are most likely to meet "22-8"s someplace pertaining to work—a business trip, a meeting, a convention or the executive dining room, for example. They may at first seem difficult to approach, but they can be charming when it suits their purpose. They are attracted to people who are intelligent, sensual and sophisticated, but—especially if their inner-self number is a "22"—their lives are so wrapped up in the pursuit of prestige, acclaim and wealth, a prospective partner is unlikely to be included unless he/she fits in with "22-8"'s plans. They do have a need for companionship, but their expectations are so high they are frequently disappointed and may make do with one- or two-night stands, or a relationship that is intermittent or sporadic. They have little patience with anyone they consider petty or slow, and shy, sensitive types are apt to see them as overly aggressive and even crude.

"22-8" is a more difficult combination for a woman than for a man—especially when the inner-self number is "22" as well. First of all, there are less avenues open to them for fulfilling their tremendous potential. Even in our generation of equal opportunity, companies' corporate rosters include very few women who are presidents and chief executive officers. But even more frustrating is the fact that they are looking for a man who is at least as powerful and successful as they are—if not more so. Not only are such men very rare, but chances are that by the time "22-8" meets them, they are—ninety-nine times out of a hundred—already taken.

Once they have settled down, "22-8"'s may be so preoccupied with work and career aims that they neglect the needs of loved ones—seeming brusque, insensitive and unyielding. They can be demanding and critical but won't tolerate it the other way around. They expect their spouse to be practical, supportive and understanding, and a credit to their social standing as well. And if they feel they are not getting the emotional support and encouragement they need at home, they have a tendency to roam. Often compulsively neat, they have a fit if they find dishes in the sink, fingerprints on the wall, or children's toys on the living-room floor. They can be generous and endearing when they want to be, but when they're in a bad mood, watch out!

Born leaders, "22-8"'s excel at taking charge, at delegating responsibilities, and at pitching in and doing a great deal of the hard work themselves. They are real go-getters who can get things done and who have the vision and imagination to make things pay off. They have a talent for sizing up people and situations and for making important decisions. Responsible and practical but impatient with the tried-and-true, they seek change and innovation. They crave prestige and acclaim and need to be their own boss or to carry out their work their own way. They feel they know what's best and are not willing to be ordered around. "22-8"'s are interested in big business and may become greedy for power and gain to the point of being ruthless and manipulative in their pursuit of it.

Also read the description for "4-8," which starts on page 184. "22" is such a high vibration that it is impossible to operate on it all the time. Children act like its lower octave—"4"—most of the time and adults operate on the "4" at least part of the time.

XI
Compassion and Charisma: The Number 9

"9"s belong to the universe. They have a broad and open-minded outlook on life and need freedom to drift in and out of situations without too much commitment. Though they would like security and roots, the confines of a home are not for them. Travel and adventure beckon, and even when deeply in love, they cannot stand feeling restricted or having to account for every move. Ruled by their hearts and their emotions, they are sentimental idealists in love with love. They can love more than one person at a time and may have several secret affairs. Romance fades quickly when it doesn't live up to their ideals.

In spite of many friends, their lives are not always happy. Emotional interplay is very important to them and they need someone they can communicate with. Yet they cannot be bound too tightly and may find it hard to stay with any one person forever. Though they do not like to feel smothered, they themselves can be jealous and possessive. Quick-tempered and demanding, they are prone to emotional extremes and have a tendency to blame others when things go wrong. They may forgive, but they rarely forget, and priding themselves on their own integrity, they will turn against anyone they think is deceitful. Not easy to live with, their marriages frequently end in separation even though love may still remain. They are happiest with generous, thoughtful, tolerant mates who will allow them freedom of thought and action and who will take their outbursts of irritation in stride.

Easily moved, "9"s cannot bear to watch suffering of any kind. They want to help those in need, yet they may unwittingly be selfish and irresponsible with loved ones. Impractical and generous to a fault, they would, for example, give the shirt off their back to a less fortunate stranger. They are sympathetic and understanding of the needs of mankind, but may be neglectful of the needs of those close, arousing their resentment by being as generous and charitable with their time and possessions as they are with their own. They believe in a universal pool into which they are as willing to add as to take from.

Impulsive and sometimes lacking in good judgment, "9"s may give more of themselves than they should—ending up drained and depressed. Or, they may promise more than they can possibly hope to fulfill and earn themselves the reputation of "all talk, no action." Trusting to the point of being led astray, they are easily taken advantage of and may be prone to periods of self-pity, bitterness and melancholy.

Magnetic and charismatic, "9"s have tremendous audience appeal. Not too concerned with what others think of them, they tend to become involved in causes for which they are often self-appointed messiahs. They have a talent for arousing people's emotions and swaying the masses, and if they go off the deep end, it is not uncommon for them to take a number of devoted followers with them.

Interested in universal concepts and philosophies, "9"s want to make the world a better place according to their standards. They find happiness and fulfillment through humanitarian endeavors, such as the healing professions, the creative arts, politics or working for a church or philanthropic organization. Unless they become interested in some cause, however, they are prone to scatter their energies and dissipate their talents. Without a purpose, they may flounder and feel lost.

COMPATIBILITY GUIDE

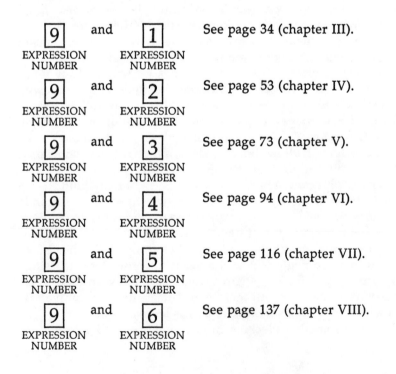

9	and	1	See page 34 (chapter III).
EXPRESSION NUMBER		EXPRESSION NUMBER	
9	and	2	See page 53 (chapter IV).
EXPRESSION NUMBER		EXPRESSION NUMBER	
9	and	3	See page 73 (chapter V).
EXPRESSION NUMBER		EXPRESSION NUMBER	
9	and	4	See page 94 (chapter VI).
EXPRESSION NUMBER		EXPRESSION NUMBER	
9	and	5	See page 116 (chapter VII).
EXPRESSION NUMBER		EXPRESSION NUMBER	
9	and	6	See page 137 (chapter VIII).
EXPRESSION NUMBER		EXPRESSION NUMBER	

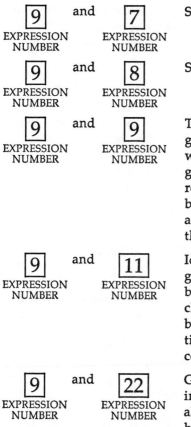

| 9 | and | 7 | See page 157 (chapter IX). |
| EXPRESSION NUMBER | | EXPRESSION NUMBER | |

| 9 | and | 8 | See page 178 (chapter X). |
| EXPRESSION NUMBER | | EXPRESSION NUMBER | |

9 and **9**
EXPRESSION NUMBER   EXPRESSION NUMBER

Talented, humanitarian combination—great for artistic achievement, but somewhat too scattered and impractical for good business results. Close personal relationships can be good as long as they both believe in the same causes. There is an emotional rapport between them, and they share common interests.

9 and **11**
EXPRESSION NUMBER   EXPRESSION NUMBER

Idealistic, humanitarian combination—good for spiritual or creative ventures, but may lack practicality or stability. In a close personal relationship, there could be some conflict between "11"'s domestic needs, and "9"'s aversion to feeling confined.

9 and **22**
EXPRESSION NUMBER   EXPRESSION NUMBER

Good business combination—"22" adding practicality to "9"'s talents and ideals. In a close personal relationship, however, "9" may find "22" unromantic and materialistic, while "22" may find "9" restless, fickle and extravagant.

Following are all possible combinations of a "9" expression number with the different motivation and inner-self numbers.

1
MOTIVATION NUMBER

8
INNER-SELF NUMBER

"His heart runs away with his head."

—Colman

9
EXPRESSION NUMBER

Always on the go, "1-9"s seem to have limitless energy. They enjoy being active and outdoors, and you are likely to meet them through friends or pursuing some sport such as skiing, tennis, or skating. Romantic and adventuresome, they are attracted to members of the opposite sex who are fun-loving, outgoing, sensual and open-minded and who share their need for excitement. Although they do expect loyalty and affection from a partner, they themselves are uninhibited and freedom-oriented, and resent having any limitations placed upon them. They are easily turned off by demands for constant togetherness or attempts to pin them down. It is possible for them to love more than one person at a time and their sweetheart can change from day to day. Even when they have settled down, they would see nothing wrong with having an occasional affair on the side. Free spirits, they may seem unconventional to someone who is used to following all the rules and who doesn't question established authority. A wise partner will accept them the way they are and will refrain from accusations or criticism when they are less than dependable.

There is nothing namby-pamby about "1-9"s. They may not always be steady or reliable, but they can be amorous and romantic and will put as much zest into making a special dinner for their new love interest as they do in to their new sales pitch for their job, and they expect some sign of appreciation. Confident and aggressive, they are go-getters who enjoy running the show. Without really meaning to be, they can be blunt and tactless at times and overlook the feelings of those close. Hotheaded and proud, they are unlikely to be the one who makes the first move to apologize after a fight or misunderstanding.

"1-9"s want to be leaders and to have at least some degree of independence in their work situation. If they are not involved in freelance work or they are not their own boss, they must at least feel free to carry out their jobs their own way, without someone constantly looking over their shoulder. Flexible hours are also a plus, as "1-9"s dislike feeling confined or restrained in any way.

"1-9"s are often attracted to the professional fields, such as law, medicine or the ministry. Having their own practice or congregation allows them to be independent and also gives them status and the opportunity to do something to benefit mankind. They are hard workers, who must be careful not to let themselves become drained. Their nervous energy is greater than their physical vitality and sometimes they just don't know when to stop.

"1-9" children want to please their parents and are hurt by any rejection, but in comparison to other children, they are relatively ambivalent about what other people think of them. Not easy to discipline, they don't understand *why* it's so important that their room be neat, *why* they should go to bed at a certain time, or *why* they sometimes have to act differently—being extra polite toward Grandma, for instance. Little spitfires, they like doing things *their* way and are not happy just following the crowd. Magnetic and pioneering, they have a way of getting others to do what they want, and are often leaders among their friends.

If "1-9"s like school, it's usually owing to the social life and extracurricular activities. Sports, band or debating club may inspire their enthusiasm and seem much more interesting than memorizing facts or learning how to spell. They don't have the patience to sit still for long (reading or studying, for example), but it's surprising how much they can accomplish in a short period of time when they put their minds to it.

| 2 |
| MOTIVATION NUMBER |

| 7 |
| INNER-SELF NUMBER |

| 9 |
| EXPRESSION NUMBER |

"She doeth little kindnesses
Which most leave undone . . ."

—*J. R. Lowell*

"2-9"s enjoy doing things in groups and often help organize social activities such as picnics, bridge parties, short trips to a county fair or amusement park or just plain gatherings in someone's living room. A member of the opposite sex who comes to one of these functions as a friend of a friend may be a likely candidate for their heart. Romantic, affectionate and giving, they are attracted to people who have similar qualities. Once they meet someone who appeals to them, they make little effort to conceal it, and objects of their affection who are the least bit reticent may interpret their intensity as "coming on too strong." "2-9"s often ruin potentially good relationships by being too impatient and trying to rush things instead of letting them follow a natural course. Both male and female need a partner to share their life with, but men seem to show the strains of being alone more than do women of this combination. Less self-sufficient, after a certain age they tend to develop an air of desperation and loneliness if left long without a mate.

Although their compassion and love extends to all humanity and they need something more than family interests to broaden their horizons, "2-9"s want a peaceful homelife and will make many sacrifices to please and care for loved ones. They may not always show it, but they are sensitive and emotional, and they feel everything deeply. Little things mean a lot to them and a personal touch makes their heart do flip-flops. A simple handmade gift, for instance, could be appreciated far more than an expensive fur coat. Their ideal way of celebrating a birthday or anniversary might be dinner and dancing with their mate and a favorite couple. When a busy evening is over, they cherish the tranquillity of their home and the security of their lover's arms. Although proud of their spouse and children, they are not the types who brag or who try to outdo the Joneses.

On the job, "2-9"s are better suited to some kind of service area than to the world of business. Money is not the most important issue when choosing a career. People-oriented, they care a great deal about liking and getting along with those they work with, and would be miserable in surroundings that were not pleasant. Sensitive and humanitarian, they want to feel they are helping some segment of mankind or nature—working with children or animals, for example. They do not seek publicity or a great deal of recognition for their toil; rather, their inner feeling of satisfaction is their reward and they are content to stay in the background.

"2-9"s are broad-minded and good at seeing the overall view of a project as well as the details. Valuable assets to any office (should they find themselves in one), they would be the person who knows where everything is and what "XYZ" client did twenty years ago. Responsible and easygoing, they are rarely paid what they are worth. They often have a job description that pays a certain amount and no more. Grossly underestimated and easily overlooked, management would as soon let them quit and hire someone half as qualified than give them a well-deserved hefty increase. Since they have a tendency to get lost in the corporate structure, "2-9"s are happier being employed by a small place where everyone pitches in and works together.

"2-9" children, like their adult counterparts, love to collect things, and items such as shells, baseball cards, butterflies or mementos of all the places they have been become their treasures. Great dreamers, they have an active fantasy life and are easily lost in reverie for long periods of time. They have a wide variety of interests and are as happy spending hours on the beach as they are reading a book or going to a cookout with the Scout troop.

Kindhearted and giving, "2-9" children are likely to befriend all the oddballs in school who are picked on by the other children. They do not like to see any suffering and are the combination most likely to ask, "If God is supposed to be good, why does He allow sickness and war to happen?" Adults may be astounded at the depth of the questions they ask, and even more perplexed as to how to answer them.

Compassionate and giving, "2-9"s love animals and may try to adopt all the strays in the neighborhood. Sensitive and easily hurt, their tears lie close to the surface, and they need constant reassurance that they are loved. Even at an early age they want someone to share their experiences—a special chum they can refer to as their best friend.

| 3 |
| MOTIVATION NUMBER |

| 6 |
| INNER-SELF NUMBER |

"Enthusiasm is the element of success in everything."

—*Unknown*

| 9 |
| EXPRESSION NUMBER |

Amiable "3-9"s want, and usually have, an active social life. Whether you meet them at a party, at a singles' event, through friends, or starring in a drama club production, you are likely to be impressed by their charm. Witty and sometimes flamboyant, they have a need to express themselves, to be appreciated, and to share their pleasure with others. When they are in love (which is usually most of the time), they are romantic, outspoken and uninhibited. Full of creative ideas, they expect their partner to be as enthusiastic as they are about trying new things. And if, for instance, they suggest going to the neighbor's Halloween party as Frankenstein and the Bride of Frankenstein, they will consider it a real letdown if their lover refuses to go at all if he or she has to wear a "silly" costume.

Looks are what first capture "3-9"'s attention, but they expect a partner to be verbal and affectionate, and a good listener as well. They may, for instance, meet someone interesting at a disco, convince them to go out for coffee (as the disco atmosphere is too loud for conversation), and talk his or her ear off. Friendly and outgoing, they love being the center of attention and may resent anyone's competing with them for an audience. Flattery and approval are the ways to their heart, and a person who acts interested in everything they say and who lets them have the limelight, will surely take a giant step toward fanning the sparks into a roaring flame.

Drawn to the beautiful people, "3-9"s have a tendency—often without realizing it—to place too much importance on physical beauty and status. As a result, they can be badly disappointed by love objects when it turns out there is no solid basis for the relationship. Unless they recognize their pattern, they may flit from one lovely flower to another wondering why they feel unfulfilled.

In spite of, or perhaps because of, their enthusiasm, "3-9"s have a tendency to scatter their energy. Just as they may tire of a lover, they may also become bored with a hobby or a project. Restless and impatient, they lack the discipline needed to see many of the things they start through. They may, for instance, become interested in philosophy, but after reading a couple of books on the subject not have the time or the inclination to pursue it further. Or, they may have a renewed interest in playing a musical instrument they learned as a child, but give it up again after a few weeks' practice. Not ones to concentrate on long-term goals, they need a push from a loved one to keep them going. "3-9"s are happiest with supportive, fun-loving, romantic mates who also have a practical down-to-earth side and can handle their emotionalism and occasional extravagance.

At work, "3-9"s want to do something creative and are often drawn to acting, painting, music or any of the performing or creative arts. Charismatic and imaginative, they have universal appeal, and give an individual touch to their work. Money is not their greatest incentive and they are happiest in a career that has some degree of prestige and glamour attached to it. And if they find themselves in a job that has little or no clout, they are good at using their imaginations to glamorize it. "3-9," for instance, is the janitor who calls him or herself a "mopologist."

"3-9"s do not fit in with the dog-eat-dog business world, and if they're not talented in any of the arts, they may have difficulty settling down to a job they like that has growth potential. They hate details and have a low tolerance for company politics or the petty goings-on that occur in most offices. To escape all these drawbacks, they may accept a job that doesn't require them to work in an office at all—such as one in construction, farming or sales.

"3-9" children crave attention and praise and will spend much energy figuring out ways to get it. Good little showmen, they put so much drama into situations, they can make asking for an ice-cream cone seem like a theatrical production. They have vivid imaginations and flamboyant personalities and they love to talk. Although their nonstop chatter may get annoying after a a while, it is important that their enthusiasm and creativity not be stifled.

"3-9" youngsters are usually talented in many areas, but their interests are scattered and they may have trouble settling down or concentrating on any one thing. Once their attention is centered, however, they can become quite accomplished in that area—whether it be dancing, singing, drawing, painting or playing a musical instrument, and they just love being star of the show at a school recital or talent night.

4
MOTIVATION
NUMBER

5
INNER-SELF
NUMBER

9
EXPRESSION
NUMBER

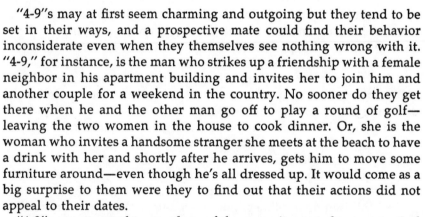

". . . A hive of contradictions—between his word and his deed, his will and his work, his life and his principles."

—Henrik Ibsen

"4-9"s may at first seem charming and outgoing but they tend to be set in their ways, and a prospective mate could find their behavior inconsiderate even when they themselves see nothing wrong with it. "4-9," for instance, is the man who strikes up a friendship with a female neighbor in his apartment building and invites her to join him and another couple for a weekend in the country. No sooner do they get there when he and the other man go off to play a round of golf—leaving the two women in the house to cook dinner. Or, she is the woman who invites a handsome stranger she meets at the beach to have a drink with her and shortly after he arrives, gets him to move some furniture around—even though he's all dressed up. It would come as a big surprise to them were they to find out that their actions did not appeal to their dates.

"4-9"s are attracted to members of the opposite sex who are practical but fun-loving, and who won't try to manipulate them or pin them down. They may go through many love affairs searching for an ideal mate, and it is even possible for them to see several people at the same time—enjoying the company of each. They are good at being noncommittal and rationalizing their playing the field, and a casual observer may sometimes wonder if it matters to "4-9"s whom they're with at all, as long as they have someone. But, appearances to the contrary, their needs *are* security-oriented and conservative. They have practical, down-to-earth desires, and may find change hard to handle or accept. A mass of contradictions, they can be stubborn and controlled at times, intense and dramatic at others; the life of the party on some occasions, a stick-in-the-mud on others; sometimes loyal and considerate, sometimes fickle and uncaring. All these conflicting aspects of their personality may lead to inner discontent and periods of depression.

Once they settle down, "4-9"s fit well into a suburban life-style, but they like to have access to the city as well so they can partake of its activities and opportunities for adventure. They also have a need for outside interests—whether these be playing golf on Saturdays or working in an amateur theater group one or two nights a week. Not always easy to live with, they can be jealous, possessive and prone to occasional outbursts of temper when things don't go their way. They are happiest with devoted, open-minded, understanding mates who don't question their every move and who are good at cheering them up when they get the blues. Material comfort and a loving atmosphere at home are important to their well-being and they may become bitter and even driven to drink without it. Although affectionate, open and uninhibited about expressing their love, they expect a lot in return and often take their spouse for granted.

On the job, "4-9"s like being employed in a place where there is a lot of activity and something is always going on. Yet they prefer a practical, down-to-earth occupation to one dealing with abstract theory. They enjoy working with people and are often found in service-oriented careers.

"4-9"s are the most structure-oriented of the "9"s and the least likely to object to routine. They are more apt to work for someone else than to have their own business unless it is a family business they happen to fall into. They like the security of a pension plan, a medical plan, life insurance, paid holidays, sick leave, and all the other benefits a big company has to offer. They also enjoy office activities such as luncheons, going-away parties, picnics and even coffee klatches. "4-9"s like to combine work and play, responsibility and fun.

"4-9" children do not like to feel cooped-up and can get very restless on rainy days when they can't go outdoors. They need physical activity to let off steam, and rough-and-tumble games such as Cowboys and Indians appeal to them. Their mothers may be tempted to enter their clothes in a contest to see which detergent works best on the dirtiest garments imaginable. Deprived of an outlet for their pent-up hostilities and frustrations, they can become quite stubborn and temperamental.

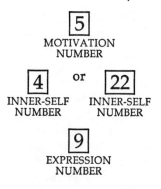

5
MOTIVATION
NUMBER

4   or   22
INNER-SELF   INNER-SELF
NUMBER   NUMBER

9
EXPRESSION
NUMBER

"The rolling stone covers a lot of ground."
—*Unknown*

Adventuresome, pleasure-loving, "5-9"s want to experience as much as possible in life. But in spite of their constant search for something new, they still tend to form relationships with people they meet in conventional ways—at work, on vacation, or through friends, for instance. They are attracted to members of the opposite sex who are fun-loving, open-minded and adaptable and who won't try to pressure them or pin them down. Fickle in their dating years, they may wonder if they'll ever really be in love. The unusual, the unexplored and the exotic beckon them constantly and they may seem unlikely to settle down. Yet they feel a conflict between needing security and wanting freedom . . . and this "wanting-their-cake-and-eating-it-too" syndrome causes many problems in their relationships. Sensual and romantic, they can be loyal, but they need the stimulation of new faces from time to time.

"5-9"s love hard, work hard and play hard. Fearless and daring, they are willing to try anything once, and they enjoy an occasional challenge. Restless and independent, they like to come and go as they please (especially if they have a "22" inner-self number) and will balk at attempts to restrain or confine them in any way. Free spirits at heart, they detest anyone asking them where they are going or what they have done, and prying into their personal affairs can quickly turn an affair sour. They tend to be possessive themselves, however, and to have double standards when it comes to their mates. Often reluctant to make compromises, they are not easy to live with and they tend to vent their frustrations on those closest to them—whether these be parents, spouses, children or coworkers. Prone to extremes of thought and action, they don't explode often, but when they do, watch out!

At work, "5-9"s thrive in an atmosphere of constant activity. Good at problem-solving, they pride themselves on finding ingenious solutions to things. Competition and pressure that would fluster most people, they take in stride. Even crisis situations don't disturb their air of self-confidence and ability to cope. But they do have a tendency to be impulsive once in a while and to fly off the handle, and they must be careful to think things through before they act.

"5-9"s are responsible and have a lot of drive, but being closely supervised dampens their spirit and makes them feel uneasy. People-contact appeals to them as well as a job that involves some travel. If they work at home, they may accomplish their tasks faster, but unless they get out a lot and maintain business contacts, they'll begin to feel cooped-up. Physical activity is important to them and they may be tempted to become professional athletes. Being on a sports team that travels around the world, or being a competitive skater or swimmer with an eye to Olympic gold are all possible "5-9" goals.

Like their adult counterparts, "5-9" children love sports and play to win. Their love of adventure is greater than their love for school and they'll probably tell people they think school is boring. Restless and impulsive, they can rationalize just about any kind of misbehaving, and they prefer learning through experience rather than by reading or being instructed. Even experience, however, may not prove to be an infallible teacher—"5-9" is the eight-year-old who, completely dressed, falls off the same dock into the same lake three times in one day.

MOTIVATION
NUMBER

INNER-SELF
NUMBER

EXPRESSION
NUMBER

"Full o' beans and benevolence."

—*Surtees*

Charming and outgoing, "6-9"s can meet someone just about any-where—at a dance, in a bar, at a lecture, on the beach, on a train, on vacation, at work or on the street. Their interest in the arts may even lead to romance with a fellow craftsman they meet at a sculpture exhibit, or someone who comes to hear them play the trumpet in their jazz band. They are attracted to members of the opposite sex who are stable, broad-minded, and domestically inclined. Food and flattery are ways to their heart, and they would enjoy being invited over for a home-cooked meal or even just some yummy hors d'oeuvres served with their favorite wine. They themselves are steady and reliable and like having someone special they can count on to go out to dinner or the theater or a concert with.

Married or single, home is "6-9"'s castle. They enjoy entertaining friends there and coming back to it every night. Although fussy about their personal appearance, they may tend to let the housework go—at least the parts no one can see (such as drawers, closets, basement or attic). More important things are on their minds, such as mailing a card to their sweetheart or composing a poem.

"6-9"s are romantic idealists—trustworthy to the point of being naive. They can become easily disillusioned when the realities of life seem harsh, and they are frequently disappointed when a partner fails to live up to their expectations. Nevertheless, they do have an instinctive understanding of others and can adjust to their behavior and attitudes without compromising their own beliefs. Once they settle down, they are devoted to their families, and although they can be flirtatious and playful at times, they don't mean to hurt anyone's feelings. Security is important to them and they will rarely initiate divorce or separation proceedings.

"6-9"s are creative and talented but they also relate to world problems and enjoy being philosophical and giving advice. Genial and outgoing, they are most often found in the arts or service fields. They enjoy working with people and do not want to be stuck in a corner in some office. They want to have responsibility. If they deal with clients, they care about what happens to them and will be conscientious about treating them well. "6-9," for instance, is the social worker who goes out of his way to find a special school for a handicapped child; or the musician who puts her heart into each performance.

"6-9"s' captivating and magnetic personalities enhance their professional talent, but if they haven't made a commitment to some goal, they may have difficulty applying themselves. They dislike routine, detail and restriction and can be miserable, for example, in the military services—unless perhaps it gives them an opportunity for travel and adventure which might not be available to them otherwise. Broadminded and curious, they enjoy learning about different life-styles and customs and are more than willing to talk about their own.

"6-9" children are close to their families and don't mind helping out at home and school. Although willing to run errands and do chores, however, they are not very good at being neat and orderly, and their mothers probably make sure their bedroom door is closed when company comes. It's not that they don't want to comply, it's just not in their natures to be regulated or structured. They need to express themselves in something creative, and often show a talent for playing a musical instrument. Rhythmic and sensitive to variations in tone, they may, however, have difficulty sticking to strict timing and pace, preferring to play as they feel—whether it's written that way or not. In drawing or painting the same sort of free expression may come out when they are reluctant to stay within a certain line or color scheme. Unsupervised they may not even want to stick to a drawing pad or canvas—they may decide their fingerpainting would look great on the refrigerator or livingroom wall.

Like their adult counterparts, "6-9" children like to give advice and may be nosy about everyone's business. Writing notes to friends in school may seem to be more fun than paying attention to the subject being taught, and they may be embarrassed when their teacher confiscates a note which reads "Don't you think Miss Wilson should go on a diet?"

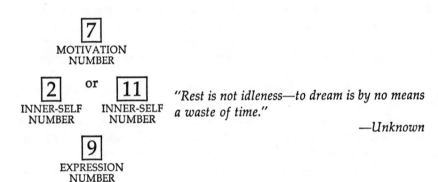

7
MOTIVATION NUMBER

2	or	11
INNER-SELF NUMBER		INNER-SELF NUMBER

"Rest is not idleness—to dream is by no means a waste of time."

—*Unknown*

9
EXPRESSION NUMBER

As a rule, "7-9"s are not domestically inclined, but are likely to end up with someone who is. "7-9," for instance, is the executive secretary who marries a teacher she meets through a girlfriend, who leaves his job at 3:30 P.M. every day, and has dinner ready for her when she comes home. Or, he is the stockbroker who settles down with a social worker who loves running the household and whom he met through one of his clients. More than one marriage, however, is common—especially for those with an "11" inner-self number—as they are very idealistic and tend to expect too much from a mate.

Once "7-9"s become interested in someone, they can be so congenial and eager to please that their sweetheart may be quite surprised at how insistent they can be about being left alone at times. While they may give in to someone else's preference for a restaurant or movie, go out of their way to pick up a partner's clothes from the cleaners, or prepare a special dinner to cheer up a friend, they will also demand privacy when they need it. Anyone who expects them to account for every minute of their time or who bombards them with a bunch of personal questions will surely turn them off. Even when in love, they may hesitate about making a commitment, especially if they feel it is being forced upon them. They don't like to do anything because they *have* to, but will do a lot when they *want* to.

"7-9"s are friendly toward everyone, but are very picky in their choice of close friends. It may take them a while to get to know someone well, and they become intimate with only a select few who have something special to offer. They have a humanitarian outlook on life and may, for instance, decide that since there are so many homeless babies in the world they will adopt one rather than have one of their own. Their home is rarely complete without a pet of some sort, and they may be the only person in the neighborhood who has a myna bird, a gerbil or an African wolfhound. "7-9"s appreciate the unique.

Perceptive and intuitive, "7-9"s are sensitive to their partners' moods, but they can also be critical and touchy when they feel slighted or hurt. They may have difficulty expressing exactly what bothers them and nag about little things instead. They feel much better when they get it off their chest, however, and then become their easygoing old selves again. A wise mate will realize the importance of keeping good channels of communication open between them. If they do settle down, "7-9"s are happiest with an affectionate, considerate, understanding spouse who knows when and how to draw them out of a blue mood and when to leave them alone, and who is more socially aggressive than they are.

"7-9"s would like to perfect themselves and become specialists in some area. It is important for them to have a goal they can work toward in order to gain self-satisfaction and peace of mind. Without a good education or a talent to develop, they may feel worthless, misguided and lost and try various methods of escape or decide that they don't want to work at all.

"7-9"s need to feel that what they are doing is worthwhile or helpful to some segment of humanity, but although fields such as sociology, religious service, or child care may attract them they do not necessarily wish to become closely associated with the people at work. Skeptical yet willing to explore other viewpoints, they may be drawn to philosophy or the occult sciences for answers to behavior and situations they feel are unexplained by science. Rarely, however, do they make any conclusions without first testing or evaluating them. They may be a great help to scientists or any of the so-called mind specialists, owing to their ability to weigh all the individual facts without losing track of the overall picture.

Like their adult counterparts, "7-9" children like to learn new things. Full of curiosity, they enjoy school and ask many questions—especially about the unknown and the intangible. "7-9," for instance, is the three-year-old who demands to know why the sky is blue, why there are oceans, or what form of life exists on other planets, and he or she can get quite irritated and upset if a parent does not give an acceptable answer. Although they may be obedient and seem to accept authority, they trust few adults with their private secrets. Pets, they think, are more understanding than many people, and they may feel more comfortable confiding in their dog.

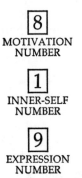

8
MOTIVATION
NUMBER

1
INNER-SELF
NUMBER

"Life is the greatest game; let us play it with honor, justice and courage."

—Unknown

9
EXPRESSION
NUMBER

The most likely way to meet "8-9"s is through work or through friends. Although they may seem carefree and hard to pin down, they want material and emotional security in their lives. Magnetic and sometimes flamboyant, they attract members of the opposite sex who are drawn by their air of independence and self-confidence rather than those who would like to settle down. A prospective mate may not take them seriously when they claim love and devotion because he or she feels they won't feel the same way the next morning—and they may not. Being career-oriented, "8-9"'s first goal is to secure a satisfying, well paying job. They may not plan on marriage at all. But usually, there eventually does come a time when they would like to make a commitment.

"8-9"s are attracted to people who are practical and understanding, who share their goals and who can be a credit to them. When they become interested in someone they tend to be dependable, attentive and giving. They can be so thoughtful about little things during courtship that a lover may be amazed, once they settle down, to see how much "8-9" has to learn on the domestic front. A mate, for instance, might scream in horror as they're about to water the plants with boiling water because they tuned out "Use the watering can next to . . ." and heard only "the pot of hot water." Their generosity, which was endearing before marriage, may now prove irritating at times—when they're saving to buy a house, for instance, and "8-9" still insists on going to the most expensive places.

Once they have settled down, "8-9"s are not always easy to live with, and good channels of communication are very important. Appearances to the contrary, they often suffer from feelings of insecurity or inadequacy, and the optimism and nonchalance they show to the outside world may disguise pessimism and depression. With loved ones they do not feel they have to impress, they can at times be obstinate and inconsiderate. Broad-minded and tolerant when speaking to others about community or world affairs, they nevertheless tend to dictate rather than compromise at home, and then wonder why those close accuse them of being demanding. Without thinking about the consequences, for instance, they may make an important decision—such as to go on a long business trip or to sell the house—without consulting their partner, and then defend themselves by saying, "I thought you'd go along with it." They are happiest with an intuitive, affectionate, appreciative mate who assures them that they are loved as they are, and who lets them be the boss at home.

At work, "8-9"s aspire to positions of power and influence in the world, and they enjoy things on a grand scale. Ambitious and strong-willed, they have good business heads and pioneering, determined spirits. Although they are able to see the overall view of plans and projects, they are not especially fond of taking care of the details themselves, and anything small or petty annoys them.

"8-9" 's magnetism and talent for organizing others often helps them get promoted to supervisory positions. Interested in getting results, they can be demanding bosses, but they have a way of making their staff think that their toil is for the common good of all and not just because "8-9" wants it that way. Though the bottom line is always on their minds, they are also concerned about improving conditions, benefits and morale.

"8-9"s are well suited to business, but other fields may attract them if the fringe benefits are good enough. Enticed by free travel and education, they often join some branch of military service and they like giving friends their APO address. Law and medicine may appeal to them because of their potential financial reward and also for the feeling of satisfaction they get from performing an important and useful service to humanity. Although they may not always express a materialistic attitude, money and status are major considerations when accepting any job.

"8-9" children, like their adult counterparts, have a competitive spirit and want to excel in whatever they do. When asked what they want to be when they grow up they are likely to reply, "the boss!" Even at an early age they can be most convincing when they announce, "I want you to do such and such." They expect conversations to be to the point—forget any baby talk—and will not repeat a statement if they think they made themselves clear the first time they said it. Bright and observant, they enjoy school and are efficient at getting their work done. Physical activity is important to them and without an outlet for their pent-up energy, they can be prone to temper tantrums and moodiness.

MOTIVATION
NUMBER

INNER-SELF
NUMBER

"Live and let live."

—*Schiller*

EXPRESSION
NUMBER

Broad-minded and freedom-oriented, "9-9"s have a live-and-let-live philosophy and may seem to exist for the moment only. Not ones to be pinned down, they may dodge the restrictions of a permanent relationship, but their constant quest for romance and adventure usually leads them into many varied and unusual affairs. Never at a loss as to how to approach someone who seems interesting, "9-9"s often meet prospective partners in unique ways. They may, for instance, follow a fellow cyclist in the park until they are side-by-side, strike up a conversation and suggest having a drink in a nearby outside café where they can keep an eye on their bikes. Or, they could go up to someone, pretend to be the social director at a singles' bar who is taking a survey to see what kinds of entertainment the patrons prefer, and then move in with an appropriate line.

Ruled by their heart and their emotions, "9-9"s don't like listening to practical advice and prefer following their own interests. In love with love, they crave attention and are easily led astray by flattery or swept off their feet by a new amour. Lively discussions keep them going, and they love to brag about their conquests—even in front of a new one. They enjoy having drama in their lives and seem to thrive on constant ups and downs that would drive most others to distraction. Friends may refer to their lives as better than a soap opera, but when they hear that "9-9" is breaking up with so-and-so for the tenth time and *this* time it's for good, they begin to get a little bored.

"9-9"s have a tendency to be unrealistic and absentminded. They dislike having to deal with mundane tasks, such as paying rent or balancing budgets, and they have a tendency to forget things like where they put the keys or why they circled a certain day on the calendar. Worse yet, they could forget to do something important, like feed and walk the neighbor's dog as they promised they would. They trust their intuition and do not like admitting to mistakes.

"9-9"s may seem to be promoters of brotherly love to some, drifters to others. Their frank, uninhibited personalities can seem totally giving, yet totally self-interested at the same time. Generous and compassionate, they will do anything for a friend, but likewise, they think nothing of asking for favors in return. Being selfish or possessive is not really their intention, however, and "9-9"s are free spirits with hearts of gold. They will loan money to near strangers, drive eighty miles to find a home for a stray cat, or break up a fight they see on the street. Nevertheless, their mate may not always appreciate their good intentions, when, for instance, they spend the rent money on a new coat for someone in need, or they invite unexpected guests home for dinner the same night he or she told them they had theater tickets.

Although capable of ascending to great artistic heights, "9-9"s may wander from one job to another unless they find something they feel dedicated to. Even when they do devote themselves to a career—music or acting, for example—they may still have difficulty making a good living. Impractical and lacking in good business sense, they are the combination most likely to benefit from a manager or agent they can trust.

Compassionate and humanitarian, "9-9"s are natural teachers and healers. Their charisma and enthusiasm when interested in something make them natural-born leaders, and whatever they do they do with a dramatic flair. "9-9," for instance, is the singer who moves an audience to tears; or the politician who can stir the public to become involved in human rights. Once they dedicate themselves to a cause, they have no difficulty spreading the word.

"9-9" children are versatile and imaginative. They have a wide range of interests, but without help in focusing and developing one or two, they may waste their potential. Often talented in music or drama, they would jump at the opportunity to learn more about the arts. They love animals and seem to have a special attunement with nature. When caring for a pet or garden, they are capable of foresight that may not be so evident on other occasions. "9-9," for instance, is the little farmgirl or boy who, concerned that his/her vegetables will perish during a drought, hitches a trough up to the horse and has him drag it over to the patch so it can be watered.

Like their adult counterparts, "9-9" youngsters do not like being confined—either mentally or physically. They may, for instance, stop going to religious school (telling the teachers they are moving), and then entice a friend to bring them to public school. Months later, when their parents find out they have switched schools, they'll explain that the first school was too strict, and besides, they would rather be with their friends.

MOTIVATION
NUMBER

INNER-SELF
NUMBER

EXPRESSION
NUMBER

"There is only one thing about which I am certain, This is that there is very little about which one can be certain."

—Unknown

You are more likely to meet "11-9" at a poetry reading or a photography exhibit, or even a concert in the park, than at a health club or on a tennis court. Idealistic and romantic, they are given to flights of fantasy and may sometimes have trouble separating their dreams from reality. It is easy for them to become infatuated with someone, but they're just as easily disillusioned when they find out that person isn't perfect. They respect intelligence as well as looks, and are attracted to members of the opposite sex who are clever, affectionate, practical and understanding and who share their ideals. Once someone has captured their attention, they can be charming and generous. Appearances to the contrary, however, they often feel insecure and may have to learn the hard way that honesty is the best policy. Wanting their affairs to be comparable to those in storybooks, they may refuse to discuss anything unpleasant. They may, for instance, avoid telling their mate that the house needs a new roof. Or, they may have a long-distance romance with someone they meet on a business trip, but neglect to tell him or her they are going through a divorce for fear he or she won't go out with them if they know they're still married. Such behavior usually backfires, for when the other party finds out the truth (and inevitably they do), they may never trust "11-9" again.

Sometimes "11-9"'s irrational behavior is an escape mechanism. Impressionable and emotionally vulnerable, they are easily hurt by rejection—real or imagined. They need constant assurance that they are loved and that everything will be alright. Having companionship is important to them, but sometimes the risk of failure scares them into claiming that they don't want to commit themselves to one person.

After a messy divorce, for instance, they may move to another city vowing they'll never marry again, only to tie the knot with another person six months later.

Spending time on their hobbies can be solace to "11-9"s. They often have a talent for sewing or crafts, and they also enjoy collecting something like stamps or antiques. Tired after a day's activities, they like to have some quiet moments to themselves in which to relax and unwind, read a book, or listen to music.

At work, "11-9"s are idealistic and humanitarian. They have great creative potential and may be dedicated to a cause and portray it through some artistic form, such as art, drama, poetry or photography. If they find themselves in the business world, they are loyal employees and conscientious workers and will make many sacrifices to accommodate their superiors. They will, however, draw the line if asked to do something they consider drastic, such as relocate to a city they don't like, or compromise their principles in any way.

Also read the description for "2-9," which starts on page 201. "11" is such a high vibration that it is impossible to operate on it all the time. Children act like its lower octave—"2"—most of the time and adults operate on the "2" at least part of the time.

| 22 |
| MOTIVATION NUMBER |

| 5 |
| INNER-SELF NUMBER |

| 9 |
| EXPRESSION NUMBER |

"Ah, but a man's reach should exceed his
   grasp,
Or what's a heaven for?"

—*Browning*

Restless and impatient, "22-9"s are so busy pursuing hobbies and outside interests in their spare time that they often don't put much energy into finding a mate. If however someone happens to come along who catches their eye and wins their heart, they will definitely make time in their busy schedule to pursue a relationship. Intelligence and talent are the qualities they find attractive in members of the opposite sex, and "22-9" may, for instance, be the man who starts dating the magician he meets at a workshop because he hopes she will show him how to do some of her tricks; or the woman who goes out with her French professor—initially because she likes the idea of getting in some extra practice in French conversation; or the person who falls in love with someone they meet at a party who just happens to own the same model guitar they do.

"22-9"s can be loyal, but they are difficult to pin down as far as making commitments goes. If they ever do settle down with one person, brains will rank higher than looks or domesticity. Although they prefer a combination of both, a mate with whom they can engage in an occasional battle of wits, a lively discussion, or a feigned dialogue is far more appealing to them than one whose main concern is keeping the house neat and spotless all the time. They do not appreciate being constantly told to pick up after themselves, clean this or straighten that, and in fact, nagging is their number-one pet peeve.

Far-sighted and imaginative, "22-9"s tend to view events from a broad, detached perspective—so long as they do not concern them personally. They can, however, be possessive and temperamental with those close. Once they settle down, they are happiest with an adventuresome, creative, fun-loving mate who is as bright as they are, and preferably has some of the same interests.

At work, "22-9"s will devote much energy into accomplishing their goals. They can control others through their emotions and be quite fanatical about something they believe in—even to the point of rabble-rousing. They are enthusiastic about broad problems, but shy away from pettiness of any kind. Brilliant, but not likely to stay chained to a desk, they are happiest in jobs that challenge their mental capacity while allowing them freedom to travel, take a vacation when they want to and meet new people. Always reaching for the stars, they don't, for instance, just want to be composers, they want to write for an entire orchestra; they don't want to just act, they want to produce and direct too; they don't want to be just teachers, they want to found a whole new school. "22-9"s have great potential, but without a good educational background it may be wasted, and since they have such high expectations, they can be easily disillusioned and frustrated when they see opportunities pass them by.

Also read the description for "4-9," which starts on page 205. "22" is such a high vibration that it is impossible to operate on it all the time. Children act like its lower octave—"4"—most of the time, and adults operate on the "4" at least part of the time.

XII
Visions and Dreams: The Number 11

Inspired and idealistic, "11"s are attracted to avant-garde ideas and concepts. Rarely satisfied with the way things are, they are visionaries who seek spiritual fulfillment. They want a better world and would like to inspire and reform humanity with their visions of truth and beauty. Their views, however, are not always conventional, and they may appear to defend strange causes. Dreamers pursuing rainbows, they may become wrapped up in ideals and theories and need a practical partner to help implement them. They often have trouble empathizing with people, and may have a hard time coming down to earth and actually relating to human needs on a practical level.

"11"s have difficulty making decisions and have a tendency to vacillate. Full of nervous tension, they may have trouble concentrating their energies on any one thing. They want to teach and inspire others, but do not always put their beliefs into practice themselves. They do not like to take sides, and find it hard to commit themselves. Once they do take a firm stand on something, however, they can become fanatical to the point of being willing to die for their convictions. Capable of achieving the heights of genius or the pits of degeneration, "11"s can gain fame through artistic or humanitarian endeavors, as well as through notoriety, crime or abuse of their mental powers.

"11"s gravitate toward people who share mutual interests. Quality-conscious and sensuous, they seek the finer things in life. They have trouble overlooking faults and usually find something wrong with everyone. Although homeloving as well as worldly, they may have a hard time finding a mate who can measure up to their high standards. They need someone patient, tolerant and loyal, who is their intellectual equal and who not only shares their ideals but lives up to them as well.

Extremely sensitive and emotional, "11"s dislike discord, strife or crudeness, and a harmonious atmosphere at home is essential to their well-being. However, they themselves are not easy to live with, having a tendency to be moody, high-strung, irritable and subject to emotional highs and lows. Although they feel deeply and may be extremely devoted, they are not always understanding of their partner's needs and may seem impersonal at times. Their tendency to avoid discussing unpleasant subjects may cause painful communication problems and misunderstandings, and loved ones may find it hard to feel close to them or understand them.

Easily discouraged and disappointed—especially when they feel unappreciated—"11"s can become depressed to the point of dissipating their talents and seeking escape through drugs or drink. Striking a balance between their dream world and reality may seem an impossible task, and they may prefer to be spaced-out and live in a world of fantasy and make-believe than face the harsh realities of life.

COMPATIBILITY GUIDE

| 11 | and | 1 | See page 34 (chapter III). |
EXPRESSION NUMBER — EXPRESSION NUMBER

| 11 | and | 2 | See page 54 (chapter IV). |
EXPRESSION NUMBER — EXPRESSION NUMBER

| 11 | and | 3 | See page 74 (chapter V). |
EXPRESSION NUMBER — EXPRESSION NUMBER

| 11 | and | 4 | See page 94 (chapter VI). |
EXPRESSION NUMBER — EXPRESSION NUMBER

| 11 | and | 5 | See page 116 (chapter VII). |
EXPRESSION NUMBER — EXPRESSION NUMBER

| 11 | and | 6 | See page 137 (chapter VIII). |
EXPRESSION NUMBER — EXPRESSION NUMBER

| 11 | and | 7 | See page 157 (chapter IX). |
EXPRESSION NUMBER — EXPRESSION NUMBER

| 11 | and | 8 | See page 178 (chapter X). |
EXPRESSION NUMBER — EXPRESSION NUMBER

| 11 | and | 9 | See page 199 (chapter XI). |
EXPRESSION NUMBER — EXPRESSION NUMBER

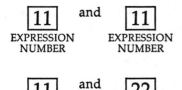

and

Good combination for business, marriage or friendship. Both are idealistic, intuitive, perceptive and able to yield to each others' needs.

11	and	22
EXPRESSION NUMBER		EXPRESSION NUMBER

Ideal combination for business, marriage or friendship—"22" lending practicality to "11"'s visions and ideas.

Following are all possible combinations of an "11" expression number with the different motivation and inner-self numbers.

1
MOTIVATION NUMBER

1
INNER-SELF NUMBER

"I would rather sit on a pumpkin and have it all to myself than be crowded on a velvet cushion."
                                    —*Thoreau*

11
EXPRESSION NUMBER

You can meet "1-11"s anywhere from a country-club pool to a bridge party, a fashion show or to an adult education class. They don't mind going places alone and, in fact, sometimes prefer it. They may, for instance, like shopping by themselves because it wastes too much time waiting around looking at stuff they're not interested in when they go with a friend. They would prefer to meet someone for lunch at a certain time, and then go off on their merry way again alone. Nevertheless, it is important to them to have a special person in their lives. Without a lover, they feel something is missing.

"1-11"s have two sides to their natures. Loners yet people-oriented at the same time, they are constantly striving for balance between these conflicting aspects of their personalities. Although they want to be independent, resourceful and self-sufficient, and expect their ideas to be respected even if they diverge from the group's in any way, they often act reserved and charming when they know they should really put their foot down and be forceful. At other times they may cause an argument by impulsively sticking their two-cents in when they know they should be quiet and listen.

To "1-11"s, brains rank higher than looks and they are attracted to members of the opposite sex who are their intellectual equals, share their ideals, and are independent enough to allow them a certain amount of freedom in the relationship. "1-11"s enjoy togetherness to a point, but they don't like to feel restricted or pinned down in any way. Knowing that they *could* come and go as they please (should they *want* to) is important to their well-being.

Though they seek comfort and security, "1-11"s are not always easy to live with, and good channels of communication are necessary for smooth sailing ahead. They can be loving and giving and have a heart of gold, but when they feel unappreciated, bitterness and resentment build up and are usually vented on those close. They can also be critical and somewhat dictatorial at home. Intelligent, versatile and idealistic but not always practical, they are happiest—once they settle down— with a loyal, down-to-earth mate who can give them moral support when they need it, as well as tolerate and understand their moods.

On the job, "1-11"s prefer working for a cause they believe in. Unless they feel appreciated or that their work is of benefit to others, they may lose interest in the task at hand. If they are in a subordinate position where they cannot do things the way they feel they should be done, or where they cannot voice their opinions, they may feel resentful. If it builds up, this inner tension can affect their health.

Full of inventive ideas, "1-11"s like to have the freedom to carry them out without someone looking over their shoulders. They can do well as departments of one, or working out of their homes, but people-contact of some kind during the day is important in order to satisfy their need for recognition and sociability.

Also read the description for "1-2," which starts on page 54. "11" is such a high vibration that it is impossible to operate on it all the time. Children act like its lower octave—"2"—most of the time and adults operate on the "2" at least part of the time.

| 2 |
MOTIVATION
NUMBER

| 9 |
INNER-SELF
NUMBER

| 11 |
EXPRESSION
NUMBER

"Some persons are very decisive when it comes to avoiding decisions."

—Brendan Francis

"2-11"s like to linger in places where they're likely to bump into people they know. Local gathering places such as bars, clubs or discos (or even the laundry room or neighborhood supermarket) are all places you can meet them. Comfortable with familiarity, however, they are not apt to make the first move. If, for instance, they were standing on line waiting to get the fat trimmed off their steak, and an intriguing stranger was next in line, they would be unlikely to strike up a conversation. But, if Harry the butcher introduced them first, they would gladly talk to him or her. That way they wouldn't feel like a pickup, and besides, any friend of Harry's must be okay.

Timid, but charming and giving, "2-11"s seek love, companionship and the security of a one-to-one relationship. They are attracted to members of the opposite sex who are romantic, dependable and considerate and who enjoy togetherness. But don't wait for them to make the first move. Appearances to the contrary, they tend to be cautious and fearful of rejection. If, for instance, you lust for your friend Cathy's brother (a gorgeous "2-11") from afar, but he doesn't seem to know you're alive, try baking his favorite cake for when the girls get together at Cathy's house. Make sure he gets a piece with the message that a little bird told you it was his favorite kind and you made it especially for him. He will surely be impressed by your thoughtfulness, and if he was too shy to ask you out before, he now has the perfect opportunity.

Little things are important to "2-11"s, and they are so readily nurturing themselves, that they are easily hurt if their partner does or says anything that is thoughtless or inconsiderate. They may appear calm, sympathetic and understanding, but underneath this placid exterior usually lies a great deal of emotional turmoil. Patient, cooperative and sensitive, they have a tendency to be overly selfless and to easily fall into the role of martyr. They often make compromises that lead to inner resentment and bitterness, such as going along with a partner's idea for a date when they really want to do something else; or dropping out of school in order to get a job that will help their spouse continue his or her education. They like to know where their lover is at all times, and if the other party detests nagging and having to constantly account for their whereabouts, it could lead to heated arguments. Since peace and tranquillity are so important to their well-being, such bickering— besides causing much misery—could result in real or imaginary physical ailments. Good open channels of communication plus a little extra patience and understanding on the part of a wise mate can help prevent problems later on. Once they have settled down, and even before, "2-11"s appreciate a strong shoulder to lean on and someone who can help them weather the emotional storms and periods of depression they are so prone to.

Though full of creative ideas, "2-11"s are not ones to push themselves at work. They have a great deal of patience, are content to take a background role, and willingly pursue detailed projects long after more restless associates would have thrown up their hands in despair. Beautiful objects such as handwoven tapestries or patched quilts can be the outcome of such dedication, no less than a well-kept set of books. However, without a practical partner to promote their talents, they have a tendency to settle for second best.

Friendly, congenial and easily satisfied, "2-11"s can fit into just about any office situation as long as they feel needed and appreciated. They enjoy working with others and being helpful and cooperative, but they must guard against becoming involved in petty quarrels or nasty gossip.

Also read the description for "2-2," which starts on page 56. "11" is such a high vibration that it is impossible to operate on it all the time. Children act like its lower octave—"2"—most of the time and adults operate on the "2" at least part of the time.

3
MOTIVATION
NUMBER

8
INNER-SELF
NUMBER

"Life is short; live it up."

—*Nikita Khrushchev*

11
EXPRESSION
NUMBER

You are more likely to meet "3-11"s at a party or through friends than working out in a gym or jogging. Flattery is the way to their hearts and they love being the center of attention. Colorful and cheerful, they are usually popular and very much sought after. In fact, attracting lovers seems so easy to them they may be bewildered by all the single people around who complain about their love lives and wish they were married. "If you want to get married, why *don't* you?" is likely to be "3-11"'s reaction. Yet they often marry impulsively, only to regret it later on when the realities of snoring, hair curlers, dirty ashtrays and money problems dull romantic bliss. Optimistic and carefree, they are too easily swept away by glamour and good looks.

Freedom of expression is essential to "3-11"s, whether it be through speaking, writing, music or physical touch. They often lack hangups that disturb others, and can, for instance, accept sex as merely one facet of a relationship—rarely suffering any guilt feelings over it. Should they decide to settle down and make a commitment, they are happiest with a patient, loving, practical partner who will forgive an occasional flirtation elsewhere, and who will help bring some of their ideas to fruition.

Artistic and creative, "3-11"s are drawn to careers that enable them to express themselves in some way. They also enjoy working with children, and their congenial, enthusiastic personalities make them welcome additions to any office. Although a good salary is important to them as well as status and aesthetic surroundings, job satisfaction is minimal unless teaching, inspiring, or healing others in some way is involved.

At work as in their private lives, "3-11"s love being the center of attention. Praise and recognition are music to their ears, but they would much prefer that it come from the parents of children they have helped in the pediatric ward, or from admirers of their photographs hanging in a museum than from the company accountant congratulating them for being underbudget last quarter.

Also read the description for "3-2," which starts on page 57. "11" is such a high vibration that it is impossible to operate on it all the time. Children act like its lower octave—"2"—most of the time and adults operate on the "2" at least part of the time.

| 4 |
MOTIVATION
NUMBER

| 7 |
INNER-SELF
NUMBER

| 11 |
EXPRESSION
NUMBER

"Life is full of misunderstandings and quiet sorrows."

—Unknown

"4-11"s are apt to comment, "So-and-so may not be good-looking but he's bright." Looks are nice but intelligence ranks higher in importance, and when forming close associations, they gravitate toward people who are their intellectual as well as economic equals, and who share similar goals. They seldom stray far from home, so to speak, and are more likely to form a tie with someone they either grew up with or are constantly being thrown together with at work. Basically conservative, they are attracted to members of the opposite sex who are as practical as they are and who can live up to their ideals. However, this may be a tall order to fill as they have definite opinions about everything and can be quite demanding. Though generous and dependable,

they are also prone to jealousy and possessiveness, and are often difficult to please. Their viewpoints may be limited, and they have a tendency to cling to first impressions. Of all the "11"s they are the most
likely to become bigoted or prejudiced, and they are fussy about the
company they keep.

Stubborn and proud, "4-11"s often have an air of haughtiness about
them, even though they may feel shy or inadequate inside. Maintaining
a routine in their daily lives is important, and they are unlikely to seek
change or long for far-away places. Feeling comfortable with their
familiar haunts, they seldom suggest trying a new restaurant, but are
willing to go to one (albeit reluctantly) to please a loved one. Nine times
out of ten, unless the waiter accidentally dumps their dinner on their
lap or scalds them with hot coffee, they will have a good time.

Appearances to the contrary, "4-11"s are very sensitive and emotional. They need love but have trouble expressing their true feelings. Even
when they want to be generous with their affections they may appear
somewhat aloof. They are hard to get to know well and even then
sometimes hard to understand. Not easy to live with, they are prone to
moodiness and unexpected "touchiness" when their ego feels threatened, and if they feel insecure, frustrated, unloved or unfulfilled, they
may seek escape through drugs or drinking. Once they have settled
down, "4-11"s are happiest with a warm, loyal, easygoing mate who can
lift their spirits and around whom they can always feel comfortable.

On the job, "4-11"s prefer working with the concrete rather than with
the abstract, and they expect their efforts to yield tangible results.
Although willing to start at the bottom of the ladder, they do not intend
to stay there. They may not care about making a million or running a
giant corporation, but they do want to be comfortable and free of
having to take orders from someone else. Clever in business as well as
technical skills, "4-11"s are the people who start out as floor sanders, for
example, and end up owning their own little floor company.

"4-11"s take pride in their work and will not tolerate anything
slipshod. Unless they can do a job well they do not want to do it at all.
Responsible and reliable they expect others to be so too. As bosses they
can be generous but demanding; as employees they can be devoted
workers, so long as they receive respect and financial reward for their
labor.

Also read the description for "4-2," which starts on page 59. "11" is
such a high vibration that it is impossible to operate on it all the time.
Children act like its lower octave—"2"—most of the time and adults
operate on the "2" at least part of the time.

MOTIVATION
NUMBER

INNER-SELF
NUMBER

$\boxed{11}$

EXPRESSION
NUMBER

*"The greatest pleasure in life is doing what people
say you cannot do."*

—*Walter Bagehot*

At first they may seem quiet and unpretentious, but "5-11"s are active, competitive souls that crave the sensual, different and unusual. They enjoy the speed of racing cars or horses, the adventure of traveling to new places, the pleasure of crawling into bed with a new partner, and they may meet people in many unusual ways. Cruise ships, racetracks, music festivals, county fairs, parades, record stores or gourmet shops all provide boy-meets-girl settings where one can just happen to find a reason to strike up a conversation. They are attracted to members of the opposite sex who are sensual and outgoing, but domestically oriented as well. They want to settle down to a home and family of their own someday, but freedom to do their own thing is also important to them and it takes a lot to pin them down. When they do meet someone who lives up to their ideals, they can be loyal and dependable. Age proves no barrier, and they are often drawn to people who are much older or much younger than they are.

"5-11"s like to make a flashy impression on a prospective partner and are apt to lead their intended into thinking they are richer or more successful than they really are. Consequently, they may be accused by some of being mostly talk and little action. One thing they do deliver, however, especially in the beginning, is romance . . . they'll wine-you and dine-you or take you dancing when you're together, and write mushy letters when you're apart. Generous and attentive, they'll buy little presents for no reason at all, and be sure to have a stock of your favorite delicacies at home for when they know you're coming over. Once they settle down, however, there seem to be two sides to "5-11"'s nature. They can be charming and thoughtful sometimes, obnoxious and inconsiderate at others. Creative but impulsive, there's a fine line between their childlike innocence on the one hand and their self-indulgence and irresponsibility on the other. Touchy and possessive they are prone to emotional extremes of highs and lows. Quick to anger, they are equally quick to beg forgiveness. They are happiest with a loyal, down-to-earth, practical mate who shares their love of adventure, can handle their moods, and can help give them some sense of direction.

Versatile and creative, "5-11" s' minds are always active, and at work as well as in their private lives they seek ingenious solutions to things. In need of constant mental stimulation, they thrive in competitive and challenging situations. Not ones to punch clocks or be chained to a desk, they prefer contact with people and a chance to express themselves and use their innovative ideas. Since they are so restless, they are usually happier in a job that affords some flexibility than in one that is rigid and structured.

"5-11"s may occasionally seem impractical and lacking in purpose. It is not unusual for them to change jobs several times before finding something they really enjoy. Or, they may have more than one at a time. For example, they could work for a liquor company selling wine to restaurants and bars, and on some of their days off be a tour guide for a local travel agency. A practical partner who has good business sense and who can implement their ideas can be of great benefit to "5-11."

Also read the description of "5-2," which starts on page 60. "11" is such a high vibration that it is impossible to operate on it all the time. Children act like its lower octave—"2"—most of the time and adults operate on the "2" at least part of the time.

6
MOTIVATION
NUMBER

5
INNER-SELF
NUMBER

"I am deeply concerned about our society's morality."

—*Unknown*

11
EXPRESSION
NUMBER

You could bump into "6-11"s just about anyplace during their busy day, but they are slow to form meaningful relationships. Great romantics at heart, they are attracted to members of the opposite sex who are compassionate and considerate, but they often play the field rather than risk the rejection or hurt that could accompany falling head-over-heels in love with one person. Although they come across easygoing and even carefree, they have high expectations and are easily hurt and disappointed when a partner fails to live up to them. Not so assertive as they might like to be, they tend to build up resentment rather than discuss what's bothering them, and they are not always realistic in their outlook.

"6-11"s love giving advice, and feel they know what's best for everyone. One of the surest ways to turn them off is to be critical of their ideas or to openly oppose them in any way. They are always looking for a cause, and a local political club, the PTA, their apartment building's Tenants' Association, a hospital volunteer group or the neighborhood Scout troop are all likely places to find them.

Once they have settled down, "6-11"s are not always easy to live with. Although they may appear charming, soft-spoken and tranquil, they can be temperamental and dictatorial at home. They are happiest with a loyal, domestically oriented mate who shares their values and encourages them to pursue their dreams. Those close are their most important concerns, and they willingly accept responsibility for taking care of the children. They do, however, expect them to live up to their expectations. If "6-11"s want their sons to be lawyers and their daughters to be doctors, for example, and the children in turn want to be auto mechanics or oceanographers, they would have a hard time accepting these choices.

On the job, "6-11"s prefer having a profession that benefits some segment of humanity. Although devoted and hard working, they like getting out and having contacts with people rather than being confined to a nine-to-five office job. Varied assignments, travel for business, and expense accounts all appeal to them and they enjoy being in positions of authority where others look to them for advice.

"6-11"s often combine their domestic talents with their work, and may, for example, manage a restaurant or health food store, own a deli or run a catering service. They are good at capitalizing on new ideas concerning food, such as selling ready-made picnic baskets, delivering breakfasts to be served in bed, or making special sandwiches shaped in hearts, diamonds, clubs and spades for bridge and poker clubs. No matter what they do, however, "6-11"s like to think they're providing a necessary service for someone less capable than themselves.

Also read the description for "6-2," which starts on page 62. "11" is such a high vibration that it is impossible to operate on it all the time. Children act like its lower octave—"2"—most of the time and adults operate on the "2" at least part of the time.

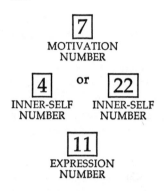

| 7 |
| MOTIVATION NUMBER |

| 4 | or | 22 |
| INNER-SELF NUMBER | | INNER-SELF NUMBER |

| 11 |
| EXPRESSION NUMBER |

"If a man does not keep pace with his companions perhaps it is because he hears a different drummer. Let him step to the music which he hears however measured or far away."
—*Thoreau*

You are most likely to meet "7-11"s in a class, at work, or while traveling. They may at first seem aloof and hard to approach, but if they warm up to you they may surprise you with their friendliness. Though they often appear sensitive, reserved or shy, they can be talkative and outgoing with people they like. Selective in their choice of friends, they gravitate toward those who share similar interests and who are stimulating, different, talented, and intellectually equal or superior to them. Some degree of snobbery, not to be confused with affectation, appeals to them and they admire exclusiveness and refinement. Even when they meet someone who fits their qualifications, however, they are difficult to pin down. On a scale from 1 to 10, they may consciously or subconsciously subtract one point for being too short, one point for being overweight, one point for smoking, one point for sweating too much, one point for capped teeth, one point for not having a sense of humor, one point for not knowing how to dance, one point for having obnoxious friends, and one point for not having a college degree (unless he or she is a self-made millionaire in spite of it). So no matter how impressed "7-11"s may have been at first, by the time they get through this list, they are likely to undergo a change of heart. Much as they crave the security of having someone special in their lives, the thought of making a commitment is apt to give them cold feet.

"7-11"s are perfectionists—demanding of themselves as well as others (especially if they have a "22" inner-self number). Quality is more important than quantity and they enjoy the finer things in life. Very easily disappointed, they soon conclude that no mate can satisfy all their needs or solve all their problems for them, so it is important for them to become self-sufficient. Being knowledgeable in some area is essential to their feeling of self-worth, and they are often found attending some workshop or other, or having a satisfying hobby.

Full of nervous tension and anxiety, "7-11"s may lack confidence in themselves and have a tendency to vacillate when having to make decisions. Homeloving and sentimental, they seek companionship and emotional support but they also need time alone for introspection and study. Should they decide to settle down, they are happiest with a loyal, romantic, intelligent, successful mate who respects their need for privacy, who shares their enjoyment of the good life and who lets them have more than half the closet space.

"7-11"s want to perfect themselves and become specialists in some area. Hard-working and good at details, they don't seek the limelight, but they do expect to earn a reputation for being good at whatever they do. Mental victories are important and they are often drawn to science, the occult or technical fields. If they don't find their niche in the working force, they can become extremely bitter and depressed. They may try several careers before finally settling down, or even have two jobs—one that pays well that they tolerate, and another lower paying one that they love. Intellectual stimulation and growth potential are of the utmost importance to them, and one of their greatest frustrations is to have a door closed to them because of lack of qualifications. For this reason alone, a good education is essential.

Also read the description for "7-2," which starts on page 63. "11" is such a high vibration that it is impossible to operate on it all the time. Children act like its lower octave—"2"—most of the time and adults operate on the "2" at least part of the time.

8
MOTIVATION
NUMBER

3
INNER-SELF
NUMBER

"The destiny of a man depends on the principles he holds."

—*Unknown*

11
EXPRESSION
NUMBER

"8-11"s are always striving for balance. Independent and stubborn one minute, soft and nurturing the next, they want some structure in their life-style and the security of a close relationship. But they also have a need for variety and an active social calendar. They are attracted to members of the opposite sex who are attractive and fun-loving and who can be a credit to them in some way. Romantic and dependable, they enjoy having a steady partner they can share things with. They can, however, be quickly turned off by attempts to manipulate them or pin them down. The grass may always seem greener on the other side of the fence, and it is not unusual for "8-11"s to set up housekeeping with a special someone, only to feel trapped and regret their loss of freedom. If the relationship breaks up, however, they will soon feel lonely again and long for a perfect mate to settle down with. They may resort to a series of one- or two-night stands—finding each encounter exciting and enjoyable for the moment—yet have a general feeling of emptiness when they have no one true love.

Material accomplishment is important—indeed, even essential—to "8-11" s' feelings of self-worth, but it would rarely be their only goal. Intuitive and idealistic, they are aware that there is more to life than money. They have strong principles and high expectations of both themselves and a mate and when they fail to assert themselves as they had intended to, or when they feel compromised in any way, a great deal of inner tension is likely to result.

Appearances to the contrary, "8-11"s can be quite sensitive and subject to periods of melancholy and they tend to brood over real or imagined imperfections. They don't always express what is bothering them, however, and a partner may not be aware of what is behind their bad mood. Good channels of communication are important, and once they settle down, "8-11"s are happiest with a warm and wise mate who makes them feel loved no matter what, and who senses when to delve for explanations and when to leave them alone.

At work, "8-11"s are idealists who aspire to positions of power and influence. They like the idea of helping humanity in some way, but they want to be appreciated and financially well rewarded for their efforts. Efficient and hard-working, they have the drive to put some of their creative ideas into practice—an advantage not all "11"s have. They actually enjoy organizing things around their work place, and will have their tools arranged so that they know just where to find everything.

In addition to the structured side of their personalities, "8-11"s have a good eye for proportion, color, style and rhythm, and often choose a career in the arts. They could, for instance, be photographers for ad agencies, choreographers who combine modern dance with ballet, or artists who design and paint sets for theater and television plays. "8-11"s pay attention to every detail and everything they do exudes quality.

Also read the description for "8-2," which starts on page 65. "11" is such a high vibration that it is impossible to operate on it all the time. Children act like its lower octave—"2"—most of the time and adults operate on the "2" at least part of the time.

9
MOTIVATION
NUMBER

2   or   11
INNER-SELF   INNER-SELF
NUMBER   NUMBER

"In love I find courage . . ."

—*Unknown*

11
EXPRESSION
NUMBER

You are most likely to meet "9-11"s someplace where people who share their interests congregate—a ski lounge, a beach hangout, a singles' bar, a theater group or a peace rally are all possibilities. And if the other party sounds interesting, they will not object to being fixed up with a friend of a friend either. They want to have someone special in their lives at all times, and are attracted to members of the opposite sex who are adventuresome and romantic. In love with love rather than with any one person forever, however, they are not always loyal. Yet they themselves can be jealous and possessive when the shoe is on the other foot. Magnetic and colorful, they attract many people and are hard to pin down.

Idealistic and imaginative (especially if they have an "11" inner-self number), "9-11"s live in a world of dreams, impressions, and often fantasy. Sometimes charming and uninhibited, at other times irrational and withdrawn, they are extremely emotional and prone to rapid mood swings. When they are dwelling on the negative they can become quite bitter and depressed. When they're elated and feeling up, their enthusiasm knows no bounds. They have hearts of gold but can also be selfish at times—so wrapped up in their own world that they fabricate stories with no basis in reality. "9-11"s are happiest when they have a humanitarian cause they can channel their energy into, and a loyal, practical mate who gives substance to their dreams.

At work, "9-11"s lack affinity for terms like assets and liabilities. They are better suited for a career in the arts or some humanitarian cause than in the cutthroat world of business. They can, however, adapt when necessary. "9-11"s, for instance, may dream of seeing their names in lights and support themselves by waiting tables in order to afford drama classes at night.

Not ones to be bound by conventions or fixed rules, "9-11"s have lofty ideals. However, they also tend to be impractical. Without guidance and encouragement to be realistic and to stick to a schedule, their dreams often remain dreams. Although they can achieve great heights if they put their minds to it, they may have trouble finding a goal. "9-11" can as easily be the professional baseball player who still doesn't know what he wants to do when he grows up, as the concert pianist whose inspiration and feeling can move an audience to tears.

Also read the description for "9-2," which starts on page 66. "11" is such a high vibration that it is impossible to operate on it all the time. Children act like its lower octave—"2"—most of the time and adults operate on the "2" at least part of the time.

MOTIVATION
NUMBER

INNER-SELF
NUMBER

"Don't part with your illusions. When they are gone, you may still exist, but you have ceased to live."
—Mark Twain

EXPRESSION
NUMBER

You are more likely to meet "11-11"s at a camera club, a poetry reading or an encounter group than on a tennis court or working out in a gym. Sensitive, impressionable, and emotionally vulnerable, they are easily influenced by their surroundings. A peaceful environment is essential to their well-being, and they are attracted to members of the opposite sex who are gentle, affectionate and considerate. Emotional compatibility is more important than are looks, and they are turned off by anyone critical or argumentative, or who tries to push them around. Sensual and romantic, they seek the security of a one-to-one relationship, but are unlikely to make the first move—even when they meet someone who captures their interest. Afraid of being rejected, they prefer to let the other person take the lead or they may get a third party to intervene.

Even though the first impression may be favorable, "11-11"s have a hard time meeting anyone who can live up to their ideals on a long-term basis. When they do, they can be loyal and dedicated, but if they feel their devotion is not appreciated or reciprocated, resentment builds up quickly. Bubbles have a tendency to pop, and sooner or later (usually sooner), they will find fault with everyone and then wonder why they just can't seem to find a special someone to share their lives with. Unhappiness in love makes them high-strung and often prone to a number of physical ailments or even hypochondria. In some cases, they may end up focusing their attention on career or spiritual matters and forego intimate personal relationships altogether. They often have trouble adjusting to the harsh realities of life, and a certain' amount of escapism—be it through daydreaming, reading or meditating—can be therapeutic.

Sometimes outgoing, sometimes shy and introspective, "11-11"s have vivid imaginations and may have difficulty differentiating fantasy from reality. They have a tendency to distort events in their own minds and may often interpret another person's attentions to mean more than they actually do. "11-11," for instance, is the woman who thinks her married chiropractor is interested in her because he's always friendly and flirts with her. When he asks for her opinion about a married man having an affair with another woman, she's sure he's about to proposition her. And when he confides in her that he's having a torrid romance with someone else and is even considering leaving his wife, she's convinced he's madly in love with her but wants to test her reaction before admitting it. Only when she meets the other woman and hears from her own lips that she and the chiropractor have set up housekeeping together will "11-11" 's delusion end.

Gifted with creative and visual minds, "11-11"s can contribute much to society. Thoughts come and go so quickly, however, it is important that they have specialized training in order to channel their talents and energies constructively. Otherwise their visions may remain dreams or their ideas may be stolen and used by someone else.

"11-11"s are not materialistic, but they enjoy the prestige of fame that comes from some intellectual or humanitarian achievement. Not ones to become involved in the political games that go on in most offices, they are often happier working in the arts or doing freelance work from their homes. Since they are versatile and good at details, it is not unusual for them to do more than one thing at a time, and "11-11" can, for instance, be the exclusive boutique owner who designs much of what he sells; or the teacher who writes a textbook in her spare time; or the antique dealer who enjoys traveling all over the world to find bargains for his or her store.

Also read the description for "2-2," which starts on page 56, for "11-2," which starts on page 68, and for "2-11," which starts on page 222. "11" is such a high vibration that it is impossible to operate on it all the time. Children act like its lower octave—"2"—most of the time and adults operate on the "2" at least part of the time.

22
MOTIVATION
NUMBER

7
INNER-SELF
NUMBER

"Good fame is better than good face."
                                    —*Anonymous*

11
EXPRESSION
NUMBER

Homeloving and earthy as well as worldly and career-oriented, "22-11"s would like to have a warm body to cuddle up to at night as well as a prominent position in a career and in an elite social circle. In their choice of friends, they gravitate toward those who are gifted in some way and who share their ideals. They are attracted to members of the opposite sex who are intelligent, well bred and sophisticated, and although sensuality is also a plus, brains rank higher than looks. No matter how sexy the other party may be, they are unlikely to pursue a relationship with someone who is not their intellectual equal.

"22-11"s demand a lot from a relationship. Their charm and wit make them delightful company, but their unpredictable moods and some-times irrational behavior make them hard to get close to and may turn people away. Easily disappointed when their partner fails to live up to their expectations, they can be prone to deep depression and negative thinking.

Idealistic and dedicated, "22-11"s have high expectations and would like to leave their mark on the world. They usually settle in big cities where they can find a greater number of the class of people they'd like to associate with, and cultural events or favorable in-places they can go to. If they don't have enough money to live the life-style they think they deserve, they feel a tremendous hardship. Women of this combi-nation who do not subscribe to the Women's Lib philosophy may hope to find a successful man to take them away from all this (just as in all the fairy tales the beautiful damsel in distress is rescued by the handsome prince). But even if they do marry happily, these women have a diffi-cult, if not impossible, time finding fulfillment as housewives, and the resulting frustration could well lead to pettiness, jealousy, boredom, self-pity, depression, and even psychosomatic illness.

"22-11"s can be miserable holding down insignificant jobs that do not utilize their talents or provide a challenge of some kind. A good education is of the utmost importance so that they can have the means to channel their potential toward good rather than evil. They work best with a practical partner who can help them make important decisions, whereas left to their own devices, they have a tendency to vacillate. Great visionaries, they are happiest having a cause to dedicate themselves to, and feeling they are doing something important that will benefit humanity.

(Also read "2" on page 51.)

Also read the description for "4-2," which starts on page 59, for "22-2," which starts on page 69, and for "4-11," which starts on page 225. "11" and "22" are such high vibrations that it is impossible to operate on them all the time. Children act like their lower octaves—"2" and "4"—most of the time and adults operate on the "2" and "4" at least part of the time.

XIII
Material Mastery and Practical Idealism: The Number 22

Far-sighted, resourceful, and promoters of big ideas, "22"s are gifted with unlimited potential. Able to turn their visions into reality, they are the practical idealists, the master builders who can improve material conditions for the good of all on a vast universal scale. They want to build for the future and reshape the world. So great is their desire to be powerful and organize money and/or people, that if thwarted or lacking in proper educational background and opportunities, they may use their potential destructively. "22"s have the capacity to uplift or destroy all that they touch, and can lead a life of enormous value or enormous waste. They can be a tremendous force for good or evil.

"22" 's minds are in constant whirls. Full of mental as well as physical energy, they are hard to keep up with and can be impatient and demanding. Appearances to the contrary, they are sensitive to criticism and even defensive at times. They seek to master every situation and find it as difficult to accept error in themselves as to tolerate it in others.

"22"s may experience frequent problems on the domestic scene. Their minds are often on their work, making them seem preoccupied, distant, even withdrawn, which can create misunderstandings and unnecessary bickering and tension with loved ones. Order and system are important to them and they like things to be well organized at home. They dislike chaos and will avoid a house that is messy, dirty or cluttered. Conservatives at heart, they like to dress stylishly but in good taste and expect their spouse and children to do likewise. Not easy to live with, they have a tendency to get bored, restless, and even drift away unless their partner is on the same wavelength as they are and can keep up with them. Once they decide to settle down and tie the knot, "22"s are happiest with a sensual, intelligent, active mate whose goals are worthy of their own and who respects, understands and encourages them.

Also read the description for "4" on page 92

COMPATIBILITY GUIDE

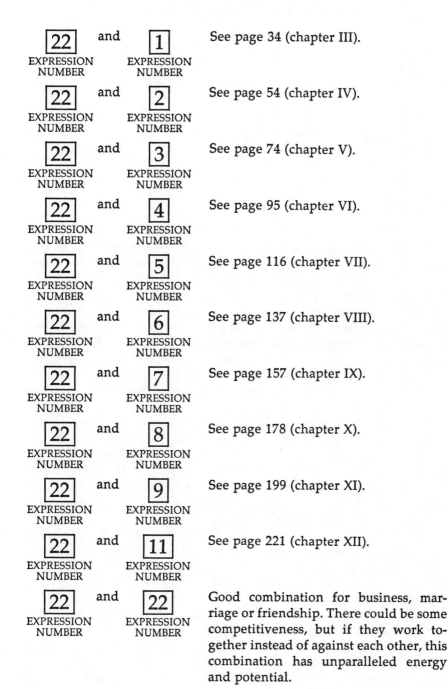

22 and 1
EXPRESSION NUMBER | EXPRESSION NUMBER
See page 34 (chapter III).

22 and 2
EXPRESSION NUMBER | EXPRESSION NUMBER
See page 54 (chapter IV).

22 and 3
EXPRESSION NUMBER | EXPRESSION NUMBER
See page 74 (chapter V).

22 and 4
EXPRESSION NUMBER | EXPRESSION NUMBER
See page 95 (chapter VI).

22 and 5
EXPRESSION NUMBER | EXPRESSION NUMBER
See page 116 (chapter VII).

22 and 6
EXPRESSION NUMBER | EXPRESSION NUMBER
See page 137 (chapter VIII).

22 and 7
EXPRESSION NUMBER | EXPRESSION NUMBER
See page 157 (chapter IX).

22 and 8
EXPRESSION NUMBER | EXPRESSION NUMBER
See page 178 (chapter X).

22 and 9
EXPRESSION NUMBER | EXPRESSION NUMBER
See page 199 (chapter XI).

22 and 11
EXPRESSION NUMBER | EXPRESSION NUMBER
See page 221 (chapter XII).

22 and 22
EXPRESSION NUMBER | EXPRESSION NUMBER
Good combination for business, marriage or friendship. There could be some competitiveness, but if they work together instead of against each other, this combination has unparalleled energy and potential.

Following are all possible combinations of a "22" expression number with the different motivation and inner-self numbers.

MOTIVATION
NUMBER

INNER-SELF
NUMBER

" . . . He can only find relaxation from one kind of labor by taking up another."

—Anatole France

EXPRESSION
NUMBER

The most likely place to meet "1-22"s is somewhere connected with their greatest love—their work. And though good looks and sophistication may catch their eye, the quickest way to attract their attention is to know something they would like to know. They enjoy being surrounded by wealth and beauty, but the prestige and recognition of an established career are often more important than marriage. They can be generous and attentive and sweep you off your feet, but don't expect undying loyalty! Once you have served your purpose they may suddenly disappear. Although it's small comfort, they most likely didn't disappoint you intentionally, but rather, got involved in something else, and are totally oblivious to your broken heart.

Headstrong and domineering, "1-22"s expect to get their way—especially at home, and woe to the partner who tries to compete for the position of boss. They have a great need to be independent and are quickly turned off by anyone who tries to manipulate them or pin them down. Patience is not their finest virtue—one reason being that they have so much talent and creativity themselves, they can't understand slowness or mediocrity in others. They detest stupidity of any kind, and become flustered and irritable if there is confusion or chaos in their surroundings. Should they decide to settle down, "1-22"s are happiest with an intelligent, practical, loyal mate who's ambitious but not competitive at home and who is as good a listener as he or she is a conversationalist.

Visionaries tuned-in to the future, "1-22"s are intuitive, perceptive and full of original ideas. Pioneering, innovative and idealistic, they can put their dreams into practical form and are willing to work hard toward their goals. Being cooperative does not come easily. They need to be their own boss or at least to be able to do things their way. As supervisors they tend to be demanding and can become impatient with slow learners or any sign of incompetence. Well suited for large-scale business, their charm and wit combined with their determination and organization make them naturals for convincing people at the top that their ideas are worth listening to.

Also read the description for "1-4," which starts on page 95. "22" is such a high vibration that it is impossible to operate on it all the time. Children act like its lower octave—"4"—most of the time and adults operate on the "4" at least part of the time.

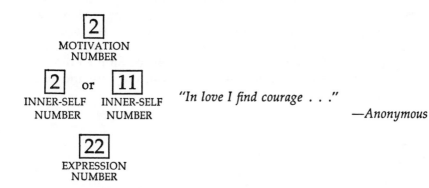

2
MOTIVATION NUMBER

2	or	11
INNER-SELF NUMBER		INNER-SELF NUMBER

"In love I find courage . . ."

—*Anonymous*

22
EXPRESSION NUMBER

You can bump into "2-22"s anywhere from a consciousness-raising workshop to a peace rally. They love being part of a group and when that group supports a good cause, so much the better. They are attracted to people who are reliable, thoughtful and intellectually stimulating, and if they have an "11" inner-self number, they may look for a special talent as well. Tolerant and compassionate, they will avoid anyone who is narrow-minded or critical or who tries to push them around. Considerateness ranks even above intelligence in importance when choosing a potential mate.

Sensitive and romantic, "2-22"s need affection and emotional support and a strong character they can respect. Once they have settled down, they are so eager for domestic tranquility, they are apt to pour more energy into running a household and helping their mate get ahead than into developing their own skills. They do not voice their needs, but are easily slighted or hurt when these are not met. Good channels of communication can go a long way toward preventing resentment and frustration from building up to unhealthful levels and being expressed inappropriately at unexpected times later on. Often unaware of how much power they have "2-22"s benefit from a warm, understanding, loyal mate who can encourage them to channel their energies toward the highest level possible.

The least ambitious of the "22"s, "2-22"s are content to work behind the scenes as long as they feel appreciated and like the people they deal with. Hard-working and good at details, they are also perceptive and imaginative—often coming up with innovative ideas that can improve conditions for all. They have great potential for financial success, but are apt to choose unostentatious ways of achieving it. They are more apt to make wise moves in real estate or the stock market, or to profit from collecting stamps, coins or art, for example, than to become corporate executive types who are always in the limelight. Having a partner in business is nearly as important to them as having one in their personal life, and they like to have someone they can bounce ideas off and who can pat them on the back when they have a good one. Money and success are nice to have, but an associate they can trust is priceless.

Also read the description for "2-4," which starts on page 96. "22" is such a high vibration that it is impossible to operate on it all the time. Children act like its lower octave—"4"—most of the time and adults operate on the "4" at least part of the time.

| 3 |
| MOTIVATION NUMBER |

| 1 |
| INNER-SELF NUMBER |

"Do I contradict myself? Very well, then I contradict myself. (I am large. I contain multitudes.)"
—Walt Whitman

| 22 |
| EXPRESSION NUMBER |

Congenial and outgoing, "3-22"s are often the life of the party. They are flirtatious and popular, but although they know many, many people, when it comes to being truly intimate and close to someone they have a hard time. Difficult to figure out or understand, they are apt (albeit unintentionally) to keep you guessing. You could, for instance, have several fun dates with them and still not be sure how they feel about you. At times they may act as though they'd like to have you around on a permanent basis, and then turn around and act as though they want no part of being tied down. "3-22"s may settle down eventually, but unless they have mental and physical stimulation they are not likely to remain in one relationship for a lifetime.

You are most apt to meet "3-22"s in connection with their work, but that by no means limits you to an office situation. They can, for instance, be the stage manager who adopts your pet goat for the day to star in a TV commercial; or the market researcher who stops you in the supermarket to ask you about a favorite product; or the camp director you meet when you drop off your little sister who tells you all about the international exchange program he or she has set up. Fascinated by the variety in human nature, they enjoy meeting people of different cultures and backgrounds and exchanging philosophies on everything from trade embargoes to the best recipes for brown rice. They are attracted to members of the opposite sex who are attractive and exciting. Flattery and admiration are ways to their heart, and an ideal partner will be an appreciative audience as well as lover and companion. Anyone who monopolizes conversations, is critical or a stick-in-the-mud will quickly turn them off. More than a little understanding and patience is needed to cope with their erratic mood swings and sometimes irrational behavior.

"3-22"s are happiest in creative jobs where they can express themselves freely. Their interest in communications and international affairs may lead them into the media in one way or another and they would enjoy being TV correspondents who get to cover stories all over the world, or journalists who get to meet interesting, talented, controversial people. Traveling with the jet set appeals to them, and they would have no trouble fitting in at all. They enjoy being where the action is.

Although they can be structured and hard-working, "3-22"s prefer positions that have some mobility—whether it be in the form of opportunities to travel, taking clients out to lunch, or just keeping irregular hours. Pleasant surroundings are important to them and creating beautiful environments may sometimes be part of their job—they may, for instance, design fountains or gardens, playgrounds or parks. They are also adept at handling children.

Also read the description for "3-4," which starts on page 98. "22" is such a high vibration that it is impossible to operate on it all the time. Children act like its lower octave—"4"—most of the time and adults operate on the "4" at least part of the time.

4
MOTIVATION
NUMBER

9
INNER-SELF
NUMBER

"Work hard. We are not here to play, to drift, to dream . . ."

—*Unknown*

22
EXPRESSION
NUMBER

You can meet "4-22"s anywhere from the Law library to a political campaign function to a picket line. They are attracted to members of the opposite sex who have good heads on their shoulders, who seem to know exactly what they want out of life, and who have goals similar to their own. They would not mind a partner being assertive about what movie to see, what color to paint the kitchen or where to go on vacation. And if he or she has intelligent ideas on inflation, Machiavellian philosophy or the Vietnam war, they may respect them for their debating ability. But be prepared for some heated discussions if your opinions oppose them on such important matters. They are unlikely to pursue a relationship with someone who does not share their major likes and dislikes or who fails to support issues that are of real importance to them.

"4-22"s may seem possessive and attentive sometimes, yet at other times they can be indifferent or aloof. Although they may give the impression of being erratic, however, they are earthy, practical and realistic, and seek stability and security in their relationships. In spite of their sense of obligation to those close, they know they cannot please everybody, and may worry that of the many who depend on them, someone is bound to be disappointed. They cannot be in more than one place at the same time, and quite often the demands of their career come first.

Once they have settled down, "4-22"s like domestic comforts and are handy to have around. They are good at taking care of things like broken toasters, faulty wiring or a cabinet door that doesn't shut right. Need more storage space? "4-22" will design and build a platform bed that can hide anything from suitcases to blankets, pillows to skiis. They enjoy puttering around the house and take their responsibilities seriously. However, they are not always easy to live with and can be stubborn and demanding. They are happiest with a patient, understanding, loving mate who is practical and efficient, and who can tolerate their occasional moodiness and temper.

Hard-working and resourceful "4-22"s are capable of achieving much in life. Firm in their convictions, they will not compromise their ideals and can be formidable opponents when challenged. Although determined to put their dreams into practice, they are not impulsive. They may take a calculated risk if it seems sensible, but will do a great deal of planning and deliberating before acting. Aware that one must learn to walk before one can run, they do not expect success overnight. Yet they often achieve more than they ever anticipated or desired. "4-22"s, for instance, may set out to own their own gas station, but soon find, through good contacts and an earned reputation of capability, that they own an entire chain. Though they may not plan it that way, their influence is usually felt throughout a wide territory.

Also read the description for "4-4," which starts on page 100. "22" is such a high vibration that it is impossible to operate on it all the time. Children act like its lower octave—"4"—most of the time and adults operate on the "4" at least part of the time.

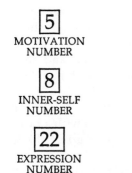

5
MOTIVATION
NUMBER

8
INNER-SELF
NUMBER

"Many would call me an adventurer . . ."
—*Chê Guevara*

22
EXPRESSION
NUMBER

Versatile, outgoing "5-22"s have many interests and are not ones to be tied down. Whether they be the troubleshooter your company hires to find out why sales are slipping, or the commodities broker your friend refers you to (just in case you want to gamble big on soybeans), or the politician running for senator who comes to your town to campaign, they are much easier to get to meet than to form a relationship with. Although they may seem charming and attentive, you would have to have what they consider some very special quality in order to capture a steady place in their busy schedule.

Restless and unpredictable, "5-22"s are easily bored with conventional one-to-one relationships. They may, for instance, suddenly disappear from a seemingly happy affair and then show up again a few weeks or months later to resume it as if nothing had happened. Of course it takes an understanding partner to put up with such an arrangement, but as long as commitment is no big issue, the good times had together can far outweigh or offset any emptiness felt when apart. "5-22"s enjoy sports, travel, adventure and the sensual things in life, and with them there is never a dull moment.

Although they may not appear to be the best candidates for marriage, once they finally settle down, "5-22"s can be devoted, family-oriented spouses. They may have an occasional discreet affair on the side, but they would want the security and appearance of a stable home life. Freedom-oriented themselves, they are the least possessive of the "22"s, and are happiest with a partner who has outside interests and is willing to be independent and do things on their own.

At work, "5-22"s need to have a sense of independence and a certain amount of freedom in their job. They can be successful in just about any business—the trick is to find something they like that doesn't bore them. There should be both frequent opportunity for learning something new, and unexpected situations that pop up often enough to make things interesting and keep them on their toes.

Masters of just about any situation, "5-22"s have a talent for saying the right thing at the right time and for coming up with ingenious solutions to problems. They make good spokesmen and are often chosen to be company representatives at meetings. Although they can be hard-working when necessary, they prefer being idea people and having others carry out the petty details. They can be loyal too, but if they start feeling unrewarded, unchallenged and unappreciated, a good pension plan or benefit program is not enough to keep them. "5-22," for instance, is the systems analyst who quits after twenty years with a firm, sells the house so they can live on a houseboat, and opens up a fishing tackle and bait business.

Also read the description for "5-4," which starts on page 101. "22" is such a high vibration that it is impossible to operate on it all the time. Children act like its lower octave—"4"—most of the time and adults operate on the "4" at least part of the time.

6
MOTIVATION
NUMBER

7
INNER-SELF
NUMBER

"I place the needs of our society above my own ambitions."

—*Ralph Nader*

22
EXPRESSION
NUMBER

"6-22"s are a mass of contradictions. Although domestic life does suit them and they feel much better having a loyal spouse behind them, they may be more enchanted with the idea of love than with maintaining a relationship. Charming and outgoing, they usually have many friends, yet at home they can be didactic and temperamental. Romantic and idealistic at heart, they mean well but the utopia they seem to expect is impossible to achieve. Unless there are good channels of communication open, many problems may be in store. Taking their responsibilities and commitments seriously, they may, for instance, continue to be friendly with and help out an ex-mate "for the sake of the children"—much to the chagrin of their current love. Socially oriented, they have great depth of understanding and can make valuable contributions to society, but they are not always so aware of the needs of those close as they are of those of the community, and may seem inconsiderate and frustrating at times. They can, however, be generous and appreciative of a warm, understanding spouse who supports their goals, who gives them moral as well as emotional support, and who does not constantly question their motives.

You are most likely to meet "6-22"s at work or through friends, but a tennis court, a social event or a community club are also possibilities. Although your first impression may be that they are totally self-sufficient and unlikely to be pinned down, the more time you spend together the more you are likely to become aware of just how important home and family ties are to them. If you were to ask them straight out if they'd like to get married someday, they may quickly deny it, but just watch what makes them happy. Did you ever meet anyone else who seems to have quite such a good time when you do laundry together? Or did you ever see a face light up so fast when you served him or her your special fish dish for dinner? Or, did you ever hear a more contented sigh than when you rub "6-22"s back after a hard day's work?

6-22"s want to feel involved in whatever work they do, and they are happiest in a service field where they can feel they are doing something to benefit others. Their dedication to a cause can often be felt over vast territory, for example, when they channel their energy into a world food distribution plan or into a program to get medical aid to underdeveloped nations. They often combine their love of giving advice with their strong sense of social obligation by going to an area where they are really needed and hence will be appreciated. "6-22," for instance, is the doctor who accepts a grant to practice in a small African village in the middle of nowhere. Or, the psychiatrist who writes a book about his or her insights on human behavior that can help people help themselves. Although difficult to understand and get along with at times, "6-22"s often seem like Rocks of Gibraltar and many a troubled soul may seek out their strong shoulder to lean on.

Also read the description for "6-4," which starts on page 103. "22" is such a high vibration that it is impossible to operate on it all the time. Children act like its lower octave—"4"—most of the time and adults operate on the "4" at least part of the time.

MOTIVATION
NUMBER

INNER-SELF
NUMBER

"He seems so near and yet so far."

—*Tennyson*

EXPRESSION
NUMBER

You are more likely to meet "7-22"s at work, through friends, in a library or at an auction than at a social event or in a bar. Although they may appear warm and friendly, they are reluctant to express their intimate feelings or to let anyone get too close. They are quick to put up barriers should they feel someone is getting too personal or seems to be prying into their private lives. They are attracted to members of the opposite sex who are mentally stimulating, with whom they can communicate, and who won't drain them emotionally. Intellectual maturity is important to them, and since they may have trouble finding it among their contemporaries who just don't seem to be on the same wavelength, they may tend to choose older friends and partners—especially in their earlier years. They often feel slightly alienated from the people in their environment, and when they find someone they have rapport with they value that friendship highly.

Paradoxical "7-22"s have two sides to their natures. They want a loving, special relationship, but they also want to be left alone to pursue their own interests or even just to think. This craving for solitude, however, may not even be apparent to someone they live with. Not ones to discuss what's on their minds, they may, for instance, lock themselves in the bathroom for an hour because that's the only place they can be alone. When questioned by a sensitive mate, they are more apt to complain of stomach pains than to admit that they just wanted to be by themselves for a while. When they do settle down, they are happiest with an independent partner who has a career and goals of his/her own. That way they can be free of guilt feelings when they decide to immerse themselves in their own private projects.

At work, "7-22"'s career opportunities are limited only by their imaginations. They have so much talent that they can succeed in just about anything they set their minds to. But finding the right career is difficult, and they often change their minds in midstream. For example, they could start out in college majoring in music, then switch to a premed program and finally quit that too to become a marketing rep for IBM.

"7-22"s want to be admired for their expertise and knowledge. Perceptive, logical and perfectionistic, they have inventive minds and are always striving for precision and accuracy. Although they prefer to work alone, they want interaction with people they respect and don't want to deal with someone just because they *have* to. They enjoy work that is challenging and expressive, and they would like their creativity to reach the masses.

Also read the description for "7-4," which starts on page 105. "22" is such a high vibration that it is impossible to operate on it all the time. Children act like its lower octave—"4"—most of the time and adults operate on the "4" at least part of the time.

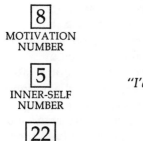

MOTIVATION
NUMBER

INNER-SELF
NUMBER

"I'd like to be rich and famous . . ."
—*John Lennon*

EXPRESSION
NUMBER

You are most likely to meet "8-22"s at work or through friends. Wealth, power and status are important to them, and they are attracted to people who can enhance their position in these crucial areas, who share the same values and who will help them further their goals. Ambitious and relentless, they won't accept second best in anything—mate included. Once they have met someone who captures their attention, they will pursue them relentlessly and can be most generous and attentive during courtship. They themselves, however, may sometimes seem detached from sentiment and emotion, and should you send them flowers, for example, they may respond with a "what did you do that for?" Even though such a reaction to a romantic gesture may seem perplexing, an intuitive partner will recognize their silent appreciation.

"8-22"s may at first give the impression of being calculating and independent and difficult to pin down, but actually companionship and emotional support are important to their well-being. Lively intellectual discussions, mutual interest, concern for their career, and a good earthy sex life are all the ingredients necessary for promoting a potential mate to a more permanent position in their lives. Forming acceptable relationships may be more difficult for women with this combination than for men. Because of the power behind these numbers, they may have trouble finding someone they feel is worthy of them, whom they can respect, and who is willing to accept their domineering attitude. Many therefore concentrate on getting ahead in a career and content themselves with having affairs instead.

Once they settle down with someone, "8-22"s can be loyal, responsible mates. However, they expect a spouse to take the back seat, so to speak. They may at times seem so wrapped up in their own needs and goals that they come across as inconsiderate and selfish. Or their minds may be on so many other things (such as that ten o'clock board meeting), that paying attention to little niceties seems unimportant to them and they may forget about them altogether. But they can be warm and appreciative of an understanding mate who supports them in whatever they choose to undertake, and who lets them be the boss at home.

At work, "8-22"s are master organizers who think big and can deliver. Logical, far-sighted and determined, they are good at promoting business ventures and money deals. They seem to have an uncanny knack for being in the right place at the right time, and their potential is so overwhelmingly obvious that they rarely have to start at the bottom. Indeed, their very first job is often that of a manager of some sort.

So great is "8-22"s' drive for power that they can be intolerant and even ruthless in their pursuit of it. Leadership comes so easily to them that they may be tempted to misuse their influence over others and use poor judgment. Their own greed can be their worst enemy. Channeling their energies positively, however, they can make important contributions to society and still have wealth and control as by-products of their success. "8-22" 's influence can be felt worldwide.

Also read the description for "8-4," which starts on page 107. "22" is such a high vibration that it is impossible to operate on it all the time. Children act like its lower octave—"4"—most of the time and adults operate on the "4" at least part of the time.

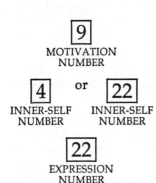

9
MOTIVATION
NUMBER

4   or   22   *"Climb high, climb far, your goal the sky, your*
INNER-SELF   INNER-SELF   *aim the star."*
NUMBER   NUMBER   —*Anonymous*

22
EXPRESSION
NUMBER

You are more likely to meet "9-22"s in a big urban environment than hidden away in some insignificant corner. Sophisticated in their tastes, they are attracted to people who have broad interests and are mentally as well as physically stimulating. They want someone with whom they can discuss Fellini, Sartre, traveling or French food, and may feel quite out of place in situations where local gossip or small talk are the norm.

Not easy to please, especially if their inner-self number is a "22," idealistic "9-22"s are looking for such contradictory qualities in potential mates, they are often disappointed in love. Not only do they expect him or her to share their interests, to be loyal, faithful and always there when needed, but they also expect them to be independent enough to allow them their freedom when they want it.

"9-22"s may have trouble deciding whether to follow their hearts or their minds. Dedicated and practical but also romantic and adventuresome, they find themselves drawn to the exotic and are the "22"s most likely to marry someone from a foreign background. Although home- and family-oriented, they have a yen to travel to far-away places. All those marvelous countries they've read about in history books, and cities they heard others rave about, beckon them, and should they have the opportunity to do so, they would pick up and go even if it meant leaving their valued comfort and security for months at a time.

Generous and giving themselves, "9-22"s can feel hurt or angry at what they interpret as someone else's selfishness or miserliness. They tend to overreact to situations and can be irritable and demanding when threatened. If they decide to settle down, a marriage where one or both partners are away a lot on business would probably have a better chance of survival than one that gave them too little freedom. "9-22"s do not like to feel hemmed-in in any way and may stray from home if their mate is possessive or nagging.

At work as in their private lives, "9-22"s are master humanitarians. Their charisma and dramatic flair often lead them into politics. However, although they enjoy being noticed and recognized, they are not driven for personal power as are many leaders. Broad-minded and dedicated, they are happiest devoting their energies to a cause they can put their whole heart and soul into.

Imaginative and quick, "9-22"s are good at coming up with more efficient ways of doing things. If anyone can find out how to eliminate the red tape and get the job done—whether it be passing a bill through Congress or sending a care package to India—it's "9-22." On first impression they may seem overbearing and impatient, but their many talents compensate for their idiosyncracies as does their heart of gold.

Also read the description for "9-4," which starts on page 109. "22" is such a high vibration that it is impossible to operate on it all the time. Children act like its lower octave—"4"—most of the time and adults operate on the "4" at least part of the time.

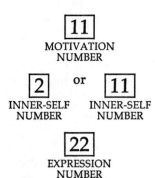

11	
MOTIVATION NUMBER	
2 or **11**	*"A sense of humor was given to man to console*
INNER-SELF INNER-SELF	*him for what he is—imagination to compensate*
NUMBER NUMBER	*him for what he is not."*
22	—*Unknown*
EXPRESSION NUMBER	

Since "11-22"s are never satisfied with anything so-called ordinary, you'll seldom find them in places such as bars, discos, or fast-food joints. They have a yearning to see the world and to set about making it a better place. Although they would prefer to have a partner behind them, they are so idealistic (especially if they have an "11" inner-self number) that they tend to have difficulty in real personal relationships. Prone to getting into emotional entanglements, they try to inspire each one with their own concept of perfect love and are easily disappointed when a partner fails to live up to their expectations. Friendship, compassion and intellectual rapport are valued much more than physical attractiveness and sex, in fact, may have very little importance in their relationships—especially when they are older.

Dating an "11-22" is likely to be an experience you'll never forget. They like to have friends from all different backgrounds, and a party at their house may look like a gathering from the United Nations. Imaginative and future-oriented, they have a tendency to fantasize (especially when they have an "11" inner-self number as well), and can sometimes give the impression of being spaced-out. "11-22," for instance, is the nutritionist who—while clearing the table—is so busy pondering what types of foods we are likely to be eating in the year 3000, that he absentmindedly puts the salt shaker in the refrigerator instead of the cupboard; or the science-fiction writer who is so involved in mentally describing a Martian City, she walks smack into a door.

Although "11-22"s need companionship, it is essential that their partner be supportive of their goals. If they find themselves stifled in any way, they feel miserable and tense. Sensitive and romantic, they appreciate small gestures and are easily hurt when an important occasion is overlooked or forgotten. They expect their lover to be as giving and cooperative as they are and build up resentment when he or she isn't.

Philosophizing and theorizing come much easier to "11-22"s than dealing with the actual realities of fixing broken dishwashers, handling in-laws or diapering a baby. When they do settle down, they should think twice about having children, especially if doing so would hamper their developing a creative talent or keep them from devoting time to their career. They are happiest with a talented, demonstrative, intelligent mate who showers them with affection, who understands their moods, and who shares common interests.

At work, "11-22"s need the satisfaction of doing something useful and would like to feel they are helping to make the world a better place. They have lofty ideals and avant-garde goals, such as becoming Secretary of Culture for the government, for example. Inspired and intellectual, they not only have vivid imaginations, but are also capable of putting their visions into practical form. "11-22" is the artist who sees a picture in a dream and then wakes up and paints it; or the engineer working for an automobile manufacturer who has an idea for a safer car and knows exactly how he or she can go about producing it; or the politician who thinks women should have equal pay for equal work and acts on this belief by supporting the right bills and groups which can begin changing things for the better.

So long as they have a cause, there can be no more dedicated workers than "11-22"s. But an "11-22" without a purpose is like a person without a country. Misery and depression are consequences, as well as the possibility that they might use their ingenuity for illegal or destructive purposes. "11-22" s' effects are far-reaching, and when they use their energies in a positive way, they can do much to acquaint the rest of the world with the principles of universal love and wisdom of the Aquarian age.

Also read the descriptions for "2-4" on page 96, for "11-4" on page 110, and for "2-22" on page 241. "11" and "22" are such high vibrations that it is impossible to operate on them all the time. Children act like their lower octave—"2" and "4"—most of the time and adults operate on the "2" and "4" at least part of the time.

MOTIVATION
NUMBER

INNER-SELF
NUMBER

EXPRESSION
NUMBER

"Impossible is a word only to be found in the diction-ary of fools."

—*Napoleon I*

You are more likely to meet "22-22" through work or an ecology club than in a neighborhood hangout or in a bar. Talented and inspired, they have difficulty adjusting to the limitations of others and have no patience with slowness or stupidity. They are attracted to people who have brains, humor and the ability to converse on a wide variety of subjects from politics to literature; foreign events to art. Once someone has captured their attention, they can be charming and attentive and sweep them off their feet, but once the novelty wears off, their ardor may cool as their busy minds turn to something else. Erratic behavior is usually the norm, and a wise partner will be understanding and adaptable. "22-22"s may, for instance, show up an hour early or late for a date, refuse to eat leftovers of any kind, expect to go out every night for a month, and then suddenly decide to hibernate for a week or two in order to work at rewiring their house or setting up a new stereo system.

Earthy, high-strung and energetic, "22-22"s are tuned-in to the future and are alert to anything unseen or untried. But although they enjoy travel and adventure, they also want the comforts of a home base and a family they can be proud of. They expect a great deal from their relationships, and once they settle down with someone they can be stubborn, bossy and demanding when things go wrong. It takes a great deal of patience and understanding as well as a strong ego to be able to take their outbursts in stride. "22-22"s are happiest with a practical, tolerant, intelligent mate who encourages their lofty aims, and who takes much of the responsibility of running the household so that they have enough free time to pursue their goals.

At work, "22-22"s can succeed in just about anything they put their mind to. They are visionaries who are not content with the ordinary, but will usually have far-reaching career goals that could affect the entire planet. They may, for instance, be a doctor determined to find a cure for cancer, an architect who plans cities under oceans or in outer space, an engineer who searches for efficient ways to use solar energy, or a scientist who is working on a robot that does housework.

Unless "22-22"s find direction early in life, and realize that the rewards of fame and fortune from work that benefits humanity is far more satisfying than that derived from selfish aims, they may use their power for evil. They may exploit others in order to aggrandize their own positions and could, for example, strive to control an entire industry, regulate banking policy, or even organize a crime ring. Whatever they do, be it good or evil, "22-22"s have unlimited potential and they literally have the power to change the world.

Also read the description for "4-4" on page 100, for "22-4" on page 112, and for "4-22" on page 243. "22" is such a high vibration it is impossible to operate on it all the time. Children act like its lower octave—"4"—most of the time and adults operate on the "4" at least part of the time.

XIV
An Additional Influence—Your Personal Year

Modern scientists have confirmed that everything in nature is regulated by rhythm and periodicity. Nothing is permanent but change. We cannot remain stationary however much we try. All living things alternate work with rest, active with inactive periods, and so it is with man also. Besides the obvious cycles of hours, days, weeks, months, seasons and years, we all have our own personal cycles based on our day of birth. Our lives operate on nine-year cycles which keep repeating themselves. Each of these years from one to nine has its own vibration which cannot be avoided. It has its own set of influences, opportunities and obstacles. It also has a color associated with it, and by wearing the color of your personal year or by having it around, even in a small item, you will attract vibrations harmonious to your special cycle.

Your personal year is the reduced sum of your birth month, the day of your birth, and the present calendar year. For example, if you were born on August 6, then 1980 will be a 5 personal year for you—$8 + 6 + 1980 = 1994 (1 + 9 + 9 + 4) = 23 (2 + 3) = 5$. Or if you were born on October 9, then 1980 will be a 1 year— $10 + 9 + 1980 = 1999 (1 + 9 + 9 + 9) = 28 (2 + 8) = 10 (1 + 0) = 1$. And so on . . .

This personal-year cycle repeats itself every nine years. Each year's influence begins gently in the October of the preceding year, and gradually increases until it is felt full force in January when the calendar year begins.

1

RED

This is the beginning of a new cycle that will last nine years. Now is the best time to start something new—change jobs, move, begin a romance, start a hobby. Whatever seeds are sown this year will influence the entire nine-year cycle.

During the 1 year, people are likely to feel more energetic, assertive and aggressive than usual. They may want to be independent and strike out on their own, and they will want to do things by themselves. Now is not the time to demand togetherness of them. Although they may appear selfish and opportunistic, take heart. By year's end, chances are

256

they will be feeling more sensitive to the moods of others and be more willing to share their time.

2

ORANGE

This is the year to exercise tact and diplomacy, to sit back a bit and wait for things to come one's way. It is a time to be receptive and listen to other points of view. Let the seeds planted last year germinate and mature.

During the 2 year, people are more sensitive and touchy than usual. Blue moods are not infrequent and tears may lie close to the surface. Friendships and associations will be very important to them and they will be very emotionally vulnerable.

3

YELLOW

This is the year to enjoy life and have a good time, to entertain and be entertained. It is a time to pamper oneself and to be seen and heard, to widen one's circle of friends—social contacts made now will be beneficial later on.

Self-expression is important in a 3 year, and creative outlets should be encouraged. People become more interested in their appearance and may be tempted to go on shopping sprees for new wardrobes. Be patient if your staid, solid partner suddenly seems restless, frivolous, extravagant and scattered—next year he or she will settle down again with the sobering influence of the 4.

4

GREEN, BROWN

This is the year to put one's nose to the grindstone and build a firm foundation for future security. System and structure are paramount. Now is the time to be hard-working, economical and practical. This is also a good year for marriage, since it deals so heavily with foundations.

People in a 4 year are likely to become more serious and reliable than they were last year, and more dependable than they will be next year. They may also seem more stubborn and intent on doing things their own way. Even the most scattered are apt to show some interest in structure and routine now; even the sloppiest are likely to want order at home. Often a person will feel burdened and weighed down by work and expenses—"3"s and "5"s especially may feel hemmed-in now. This could lead to depression, irritability and complaints of aches and pains and minor ailments. Encourage them to take heart—responsibilities won't seem so heavy next year.

5

LIGHT
BLUE

Expect the unexpected this year. Be adaptable!
Now is the time to promote oneself and one's
ideas. Indulge physical appetites and enjoy the
sensual pleasures of eating, drinking and sex—
without overdoing, of course!

Even the most stable person is apt to feel restless and bored in their 5
year, and may be tempted to do something impetuous, such as up and
quit a job on the spur of the moment. Even a stick-in-the-mud partner
may feel more adventuresome this year and more willing to take a
vacation or try something new. Anyone who has a weight or drinking
problem will have more trouble keeping it under control now since
self-discipline is often tossed to the wind. They will be more insistent
on freedom to do their own thing this year and may even seem inconsiderate. Now is not the time to nag or be possessive—affairs are not
unusual in a 5 year, but neither do they tend to be serious or of a
long-term nature. Chances are they'll be over by next year when the
settling 6 vibration is felt.

6

NAVY
BLUE

This year interests will center around family,
home and community. It is the time to be conscientious and aware of one's duties, to extend
love and services willingly. This is perhaps the
best year for getting married.

In the 6 year, spouses and lovers who have a tendency to stray may
become more responsible and family-oriented. They are more apt to
make adjustments and compromise. On the other hand, they may also
become meddlesome and prone to giving unwanted advice. This too
shall pass . . . (unless they have a "6" expression number).

7

VIOLET

This is a year to follow intellectual pursuits,
seek inner truths and analyze one's goals. It is a
time to withdraw from the rat race of superficial
social activities and to read, study and perfect
one's thinking. Rest is important and material
issues should not be forced.

People in their 7 year may not feel as energetic as usual—don't accuse
them of being lazy if they just want to stay home with a good book. It's a
good time for contemplation and they really do need more rest than
usual. Even the most outgoing will want some time alone now and will
want their privacy respected. This is not the year to nag a partner to ask
for a raise or to be more aggressive or social. Be patient and understanding—a more active, outgoing vibration is coming next year.

8

BLACK, GRAY, ROSE

This is the best year for making money, for pushing for the things one feels one deserves. Think big! Make things pay! Now is the time to take command, to ask for that raise or promotion. Remember the seeds that were planted in the 1 year? Their harvest is being reaped now.

Prone to being more egotistical and power hungry than usual, people in an 8 year may want to dictate—at home as well as at work. Their energy level will be higher than last year and they'll take more of an interest in organizing—whether it be kitchen cabinets or office files. Money is of prime concern now, and good judgment is needed to watch that it doesn't go out faster than it comes in. More than their bank account could expand this year—they could gain weight too.

9

ALL COLORS, BUT ESPE-CIALLY REDDISH GOLD AND AUTUMN TONES

The 9-year cycle has come to an end. Complete your projects. Now's the time to think about what seeds to plant next year, but don't start anything new yet. This is the year to get rid of anyone or anything that is no longer useful. It's an active fast-paced year and, among finishing things up, it's a good time to take a long trip.

In the 9 year, people's fancies may suddenly turn to sorting things out—cleaning attics or closets, giving away clothes that haven't been worn in five years. They may also feel nostalgic and even sad—it may not be easy to let some things go that must. This is an emotional time—toes are easily stepped on and tempers flare—beware!

11

See "2." An 11 year is much like a 2 year, but people may feel more creative, intuitive, idealistic and high-strung. They could also receive recognition for past efforts now.

22

See "4." A 22 year is much like a 4 year, but people are more likely to see results for their efforts and therefore to feel less limited than in the 4. Prone to extremes, they may also feel more nervous and tense.

XV
Choosing a Gift

At sometime during a relationship you will probably find yourself asking, "What sort of gift should I get for him?" What present would she like?" Numerology can offer some suggestions if you find yourself completely baffled.

Look at the entire chart—the motivation number (line 1), the inner-self number (line 3), the expression number (line 4). See which numerical value appears most frequently throughout the name, what the number value of the first letter is, what the number value of the first vowel is, what number the birthday reduces to. The more a number is repeated, the more relevant it becomes. Use the number that appears most frequently as your guide and look it up in the table below.

Another consideration for choosing a gift is one's personal year (see page 256). For example, in a 7 personal year a gift that can be enjoyed alone might be appreciated, whereas in a 3 year that same person might prefer being taken out. "3" and "5" get restless and bored; "4," "6," and "8" are happy with the conventional.

A tip for those of you who have narrowed down your gift but are in doubt as to what color to choose: people are often drawn to the color of their personal year. So if for example, you have decided on a sweater and the recipient is in a 5 personal year—a light blue would be a good bet. (See chapter XIV, page 256 to find out which color goes with which year.)

1   Give "1" something that is one of a kind, that no one else has anything like—even if it's as "far out" as a signed ostrich egg. Jewelry is a good choice as long as it's 18 karat (or at least 14) and the selection is unique. The design should be simple and in good taste. "1" tends to be a loner, and a gift that can be enjoyed alone is a wise choice—a calculator, book, fishing rod, crossword puzzles, electronic toy, anything "gimmicky."

2 "2"s like to feel cared for and will especially appreciate a gift that's sentimental and personal, one that clearly has much thought behind it. If you're gifted at writing poetry, your "2" would love a sonnet composed just for him or her. If not, a book of love poems or a copy of one of their favorites written inside a card would go over big. "2"s enjoy gifts that can be shared with others—jigsaw puzzles, games, cards, records, ballet or theater tickets, dinner out for just the two of you, and/or dancing. If your "2" is an "11-2", he or she would love a foreign "treasure"—a jewelry box from Poland, a silk scarf from France, a tapestry from Mexico, leather gloves from Italy, a scarab from Egypt, an antique ring from England, beads from Brazil, candlestick holders from Sweden.

3 "3"s like to be entertained and pampered. Take them out to a lovely restaurant and reserve a cozy, romantic table. If it's a special occasion such as a birthday or an anniversary, call ahead and order a birthday cake or something flambé to be brought out for dessert. Remember, "3"s love to be in the limelight and fussed over. If your "3" is on a boring diet, how about tickets to a show or concert? Jewelry or artwork are also good choices. "3"s love ornamentation, baubles, anything that makes them or the surroundings more beautiful—a necklace with robin's egg blue stones to match their eyes, or a painting for that bare spot in the hall.

4 Earthy and practical, "4"s appreciate gifts that are thoughtful and useful. They love nature and things from the earth—flowers or plants, gardening tools, real estate, or even some home-grown tomatoes would be ideal. If they shave twice a day and insist on using a new blade each time, they would surely appreciate a supply of razor blades. If you give them a coat, be sure it's well made, warm, and something they'll get a lot of wear out of. Gifts made out of wood, metal or earth products also appeal to "4"—a wooden chest or carving, copper utensils, a brass lamp, pottery. Stocks and bonds are also good "4" gifts, as is plain old cash. Add an international flavor if your "4" is a "22-4"—an assortment of spices from different nations, an electronic clock that gives the time for several different places in the world, an uncommon plant such as a coffee tree.

5 Appeal to "5" 's sense of adventure by giving a trip—to a South Sea Island or a nearby amusement park (depending, of course, on your budget). Or how about a night on the town to a place they have never been? Surprise your "5" by serving him or her wine in the bathtub—then joining them. "5"s always enjoy something "different." A sexy nightgown or underwear, special bath oils, a soft blanket or bedspread would all make good gifts, as would pillows for the couch or fluffy towels for the bathroom. Anything that is sensual and adds pleasure to everyday living would please a "5."

6 You can't go wrong buying something for the home or kitchen when you choose a gift for "6." Any gadget to make the chef's chores easier, from an egg slicer to a food processor, would be a good choice. If your "6" is on a health kick, try a book on health foods or membership to a health club he or she would enjoy. "6"s also appreciate thoughtfulness—something made with your own two hands—be it an ornament to hang in the window, an embroidered bureau cloth or a centerpiece for the table.

7 Books! Books! Books! "7"s crave knowledge and need to curl up with a good book at least once in a while. Find out what subject interests your "7." If they study astrology, a book on lunation cycles would be appreciated more than a murder mystery. If they're into fixing cars, a book on auto mechanics would go over far better than a book on art. If you know your "7" is extremely fussy and you want to be on the safe side, you can't go wrong with a gift certificate. And, remember, "7"s love quality no matter what the gift. It would be better to buy an expensive radio than a cheap stereo.

8 "8"s like things in little boxes. It's not just that they believe good things come in small packages, but *expensive* things come in small packages. (Not that "8" wouldn't appreciate fine furs, luxury cars, homes in the country and the like, but we want to cover a more realistic price range.) If you know their taste, fine jewelry, a quality watch, name-brand clothing, a good sweater are all safe bets. Like "4," "8" is an earthy number and "8"s love green—green grass and green cash! An outing in the country, or money to buy whatever they want would surely be appreciated.

9 Sentimental "9"s would prefer something romantic that they probably would not buy for themselves over something practical. Don't buy them a household gift unless you know for sure it's something they have their heart set on. A fine leather bag would go over better than a coffeepot, and some expensive after-shave would give more pleasure than an ordinary tie. Jewelry is risky unless you are sure of your "9"'s taste—you could be giving something that he or she would like but never wear. A bathrobe or fancy underwear might get more use. If your "9" is musically inclined, something in their special area would be appropriate—records, sheet music, guitar, synthesizer. Or if they like sports, a good gift would fall into the category of their activity—new skiis, tennis racket, golf equipment, jogging shoes, etc. A beautiful book on any subject that interests your "9" would certainly be appreciated. And if he or she loves to travel, how about a romantic weekend or cruise?

11 See "2."

22 See "4."

AFTERWORD
If the Shoe Doesn't Fit. . .

By now some of you may be wondering why the combinations of motivation and expression numbers seem to fit some people better than others, or why two people who share the same combination seem to be quite different from each other. This is because there are many other modifying factors that must be considered for an in-depth analysis. Using only the motivation, inner-self and expression numbers is a simplified way to become acquainted with the wonders of numerology.

Other numbers dealing with the life path, karma, challenges, cycles, turning points, and transits all have significance in determining compatibility, but their analysis is beyond the scope of this book. There is, however, one simple way to check out those people whose numbers may not seem to fit them. This is by quickly figuring out a name's intensification number, since this number may offset the three basic numbers. The intensification number is the one that appears most often in the name. For instance, someone who has a "4" expression but who has seven "5"s ("E's," "N's," and "W's") in her name may appear to be more like a "5" than a "4," like Ellen Newton below.

1. Vowels	5			5				5		6										**3**

Motivation Number

| 2. Name | E | L | L | E | N | | N | E | W | T | O | N | | | | | | |

| 3. Consonants | | 3 | 3 | | 5 | | 5 | | 5 | 2 | | 5 | | | | | | | **1** |

Inner-Self Number

| 4. Total | 5 | 3 | 3 | 5 | 5 | | 5 | 5 | 5 | 2 | 6 | 5 | | | | | | | **4** |

Expression Number

Readers who are interested in delving further are advised to consult with a professional numerologist and/or refer to the following basic texts:

Avery, Kevin Quinn, *The Numbers of Life,* Doubleday & Co., Inc., Garden City, New York, 1977.

Campbell, Florence, *Your Days Are Numbered,* The Gateway, Ferndale, Pennsylvania, 1976.

Johnson, Vera Scott and Thomas Wommack, *The Secrets of Numbers,* Dial Press, New York, New York, 1973.

Jordan, Dr. Juno, *Numerology: The Romance in Your Name,* DeVorss & Co., Inc., Marina del Rey, California, 1977.

Stein, Sandra Kovacs, *Instant Numerology,* Harper & Row, Inc. New York, New York, 1979.

Young, Ellin Dodge and Carol Ann Schuler, *The Vibes Book—A Game of Self-Analysis,* Samuel Weiser, Inc., New York, New York, 1979.